# Convergence Innovation in Asian Industries

T0351668

This book deals with both the understanding and explanation of knowledge about the causes, processes, and patterns of convergence innovation. It argues that the process of convergence innovation is a continuous disequilibrium between reference technology and its matching technology, adjusting the optimal balance between the functions of the two technologies. Contributors describe how convergence innovation is a learning process that requires both vertical and horizontal convergence, and case studies explore the different types of convergence innovation, such as outside-in and inside-out.

Convergence innovation has been taking place mainly by applying IT technologies to vast areas of conventional technologies, so that individuals or firms reap the benefits of the convergence between IT and conventional technologies. Such innovations are made possible by convergence, and they ultimately improve the welfare of human beings as companies solve diverse problems and increase employment. Examples in this book include biochemical companies in Indonesia, who were able to increase their market shares in bio-fertilizer and bio-pesticide products through bio-based technological convergence; and textile machinery firms in South Korea who have survived by achieving convergence innovation on their core competences.

This book was originally published as a special issue of the *Asian Journal of Technology Innovation*.

**Kong-rae Lee** is currently Chair Professor of the Management of Innovation Program at Daegu Institute of Science and Technology, South Korea. He has previously served as policy advisor to the Korean Minister of Science and Technology. His research areas are national, regional, and industrial innovation systems, as well as mega science policies. He has published many books and articles, including *The Source of Capital Goods Innovation* (1998).

# Convergence Innovation in Asian Industries

*Edited by*
**Kong-rae Lee**

Routledge
Taylor & Francis Group

LONDON AND NEW YORK

First published 2017 by Routledge

2 Park Square, Milton Park, Abingdon, Oxfordshire OX14 4RN
52 Vanderbilt Avenue, New York, NY 10017

*Routledge is an imprint of the Taylor & Francis Group, an informa business*

First issued in paperback 2018

*British Library Cataloguing in Publication Data*
A catalogue record for this book is available from the British Library

ISBN 13: 978-1-138-68120-0 (hbk)
ISBN 13: 978-0-367-02879-4 (pbk)

Typeset in Times New Roman
by RefineCatch Limited, Bungay, Suffolk

**Publisher's Note**
The publisher accepts responsibility for any inconsistencies that may have
arisen during the conversion of this book from journal articles to book chapters,
namely the possible inclusion of journal terminology.

**Disclaimer**
Every effort has been made to contact copyright holders for their permission to
reprint material in this book. The publishers would be grateful to hear from any
copyright holder who is not here acknowledged and will undertake to rectify
any errors or omissions in future editions of this book.

# Contents

# Citation Information

The chapters in this book were originally published in the *Asian Journal of Technology Innovation*, volume 23, issue S1 (April 2015). When citing this material, please use the original page numbering for each article, as follows:

**Chapter 1**

*Toward a new paradigm of technological innovation: convergence innovation*
Kong-rae Lee
*Asian Journal of Technology Innovation*, volume 23, issue S1 (April 2015), pp. 1–8

**Chapter 2**

*Technological convergence in Indonesian firms: cases of biobased chemical product innovation*
Erman Aminullah, Trina Fizzanty, Galuh S. Indraprahasta and Indri J. Asmara
*Asian Journal of Technology Innovation*, volume 23, issue S1 (April 2015), pp. 9–25

**Chapter 3**

*Convergence of service and technical skills: the case of ERP implementation in Israel*
Asaf Darr
*Asian Journal of Technology Innovation*, volume 23, issue S1 (April 2015), pp. 26–39

**Chapter 4**

*A semantic network analysis of technological innovation in dentistry: a case of CAD/CAM*
Jang Hyun Kim and Jinsuk Lee
*Asian Journal of Technology Innovation*, volume 23, issue S1 (April 2015), pp. 40–57

**Chapter 5**

*Convergence innovation of the textile machinery industry in Korea*
Kong-rae Lee, JinHyo Joseph Yun and Eui-Seob Jeong
*Asian Journal of Technology Innovation*, volume 23, issue S1 (April 2015), pp. 58–73

**Chapter 6**

*Innovation strategy and technological competence building to provide next generation network and services through convergence – the case of NTT in Japan*
Kumiko Miyazaki and Evelyn Giraldo
*Asian Journal of Technology Innovation*, volume 23, issue S1 (April 2015), pp. 74–92

**Chapter 7**

*Convergence innovation in railway technology: how ERL of Malaysia attained its co-evolution structure for systemic development*
Mazmiha Mohamed, Hon-Ngen Fung and Chan-Yuan Wong
*Asian Journal of Technology Innovation*, volume 23, issue S1 (April 2015), pp. 93–108

**Chapter 8**

*Is the technological capability gap between Hyundai and Mitsubishi converging or diverging? Findings from patent data analysis*
Chul Oh and Si Hyung Joo
*Asian Journal of Technology Innovation*, volume 23, issue S1 (April 2015), pp. 109–128

**Chapter 9**

*Do latecomer firms rely on 'recent' and 'scientific' knowledge more than incumbent firms do? Convergence or divergence in knowledge sourcing*
Jinhyuck Park and Keun Lee
*Asian Journal of Technology Innovation*, volume 23, issue S1 (April 2015), pp. 129–145

For any permission-related enquiries please visit:
http://www.tandfonline.com/page/help/permissions

# Toward a new paradigm of technological innovation: convergence innovation

Kong-rae Lee

*DGIST, Techno Jungang Daero, Hyeonpung-myeon, Dalseong-gun, Daegu, Korea*

This paper aims at creating knowledge value-added by exploring, and understanding knowledge about the causes, processes, and patterns of convergence innovation through a review of eight papers included in this issue. It argues that the process of convergence innovation is a continuous disequilibrium between reference technology and its matching technology, which adjusts optimal balance between the functions of the two technologies. The process of convergence innovation is also featured as a learning process that requires both vertical and horizontal convergence. Types of convergence innovation such as outside-in and inside-out, depending on market situation are discovered in some case explorations. Convergence innovation has been taking place mainly by applying IT technologies to vast areas of conventional technologies. This is because individuals or firms get benefit from the convergence between IT and conventional technologies. Such innovations made possible by convergence ultimately improve the welfare of human beings as companies can solve diverse problems or increase employment. Many examples are found in Asian industries, for instance, biochemical companies of Indonesia were able to increase their market shares in biofertilizer and biopesticide products through bio-based technological convergence. Textile machinery firms of Korea have survived by achieving convergence innovation on their core competences.

## 1. Introduction

Ten years have passed since the first ASIALICS Conference was held in 2004. There is a proverb in Korea that 'even the shapes of rivers and mountains can change in ten years'. It implies 10 years is a period of time long enough to make changes possible that are unlikely. We deserve to be proud, but need to thoroughly think back on the achievements of ASIALICS over the last 10 years. Following the 10th Conference held in Tokyo in 2013, the 11th ASIALICS Conference was held at DGIST Campus in Daegu, Korea on 24–27 September 2014 under the theme of convergence, innovation, and creative economy. About 239 professionals from 24 countries participated in the conference and 129 papers were presented including 8 presentations of invited speakers in the conference. It was the second time for Korea to host the conference after the country's first hosting of the 2nd ASIALICS Conference in Jeju Island on 17–20 April 2005, which was jointly organised by the Science and Technology Policy Institute (STEPI) and the Korea Society of Innovation Management and Economics (KOSIME) on the agenda of 'Innovation

1

Policy and Management in Changing Asia'. About 120 professionals participated and 60 papers were presented in the conference.

Asia has been a serious player not only in science, technology, and innovation but also in linking different cultures of the world. This is in line with the ongoing Asia-wide cooperation schemes that emphasise knowledge and experience sharing and joint efforts to promote knowledge-based and learning economies. To achieve this aspiration, a group of Asian scholars from Asian countries with strong support from GLOBELICS held the first international conference on the agenda of 'Asian Innovation Systems' in Bangkok in April 2004. About 150 professionals who participated in the conference agreed to organise the ASIALICS Conference annually, publish a journal and books on Asian innovation system and clusters, and explore possibilities of joint research and training in this field.

ASIALICS aims to explore and develop the concept of learning, innovation, competence building, and coevolution studies as an analytical framework. The objective of ASIALICS is to stimulate the establishment of knowledge-based strategies for economic development in Asia. This idea is basically to bring together interesting issues about what is going on in Asian countries and companies and to share their experiences regarding methodology, analytical results, and policies.

The key theme of the 11th ASIALICS Conference held in Daegu, Korea was 'Convergence, Innovation and Creative Economy'. The contemporary economies of many countries have tendencies for slow growth, and this gives rise to fears of a global economic slump. Consecutive periods of low economic growth, as well as economic growth without job creation, have inevitably generated a lot of social problems such as the rise of unemployment, greater polarisation between the rich and the poor, the widening of the income gap, decrease in quality of life, and more. Governments around the world have sought solutions to shift their economies towards more sustainable growth. It has been frequently stated in Korea that the promotion of a creative economy might be a solution to cure the current problems of slow growth in the economy.[1] It is believed that convergence innovation can be vital in achieving this creative economy so as to increase the economic growth and employment level. This belief has led to adopting 'Convergence, Innovation and Creative Economy' as the agenda of the 11th ASIALICS Conference.

This paper deals with the key issues of convergence innovation as it attempts to explore and understand knowledge about the causes, processes, and patterns of and strategies for convergence innovation based on eight papers included in this issue. Among Asian industries that these eight papers examined are the automobile industry of Korea and Japan, the chemical industry of Indonesia, the medical service industry and textile machinery industry of Korea, the railway industry of Malaysia, the telecommunication industry of Japan, and the enterprise resource management (ERP) of Israel. They were presented at the general sessions of the 11th ASIALICS Conference held in Daegu on 25–27 September 2014.

## 2. Why convergence innovation as an agenda of a special issue?

Modern innovations have had a strong tendency of technological convergence in which information and telecommunication (IT) technology plays a central role as it has been applied to vast areas of industries, generating variety of new products and services. Not only IT technologies but also other technologies are converging or being converged at varying degrees of integration routinely creating intellectual property rights. The phenomenon of convergence innovation is likely to even deepen and widen in the future due to intense competition among firms in global markets. Particularly, manufacturing firms in Asian countries have been quite active in technological convergence leading industrial innovation of the world.

Looking back on the history of technological innovation as Rosenberg (1963, 1982) found, the phenomenon of convergence innovation emerged at the end of the nineteenth century as closely related technological problems were solved and shared among manufacturers of different types of machines. Machines confronted a similar collection of technological problems dealing with such matters as power transmission, control devices, feed mechanisms, friction reduction, and a broad array of problems connected with the properties of metals. These problems became common to the production of a wide range of commodities. These were apparently unrelated from the point of view of the nature of the final product. The uses, however, of the final product were very closely related on a technological basis. Rosenberg called this phenomenon as 'technological convergence' and argued that the intensive degree of specialisation which developed in the second half of the nineteenth century owed its existence to a combination of this technological convergence.

The similar terminology, 'technological fusion' was used in Kodama's paper (1986) and a paper written by Kong-rae Lee (2007). He argued that there are two fundamental types of innovation: one is the technological breakthrough and the other is technology fusion. According to Kodama, breakthrough innovations are associated with strong leadership in a particular technology, and technology fusion can be possible through concerted efforts by several different industries. He put particular emphasis on the latter because it contributes not only to the rapid growth of companies that make technology fusion possible, but also to the gradual growth of all the companies in many industries. He empirically observed a phenomenon of technology fusion that occurred first between machinery industries and electronic industries in 1970, and later among variety of industries including chemicals, foods, and pharmaceutical industries in 1974 and 1975 (Lee and Hwang 2005).

Kodama's paper mainly featured new trends in Japanese innovations aside from the phenomenon of technological convergence. However, he did not clearly define technological convergence. What he mentioned was that technology fusion can be made possible through concerted efforts by several different industries. A concrete definition on convergence innovation has to be made before identifying its patterns and processes. Technological convergence is defined here as a horizontal integration of diverse technologies. Horizontal integration means an absorption of diverse fields of technologies for the purpose of creating new functions and products, which often broadens the scope of their technological specialisation that can interact with partner companies.

The reasons why convergence innovation is chosen as agenda of this special issue are as follows. First, the phenomenon of convergence innovation is prevailed in contemporary innovation, which has mainly centred on information and telecommunication technology. Technological convergence may nowadays have evolved up to the point that different technologies are deeply integrated and even chemically mixed, resulting in completely new types of technologies and products. Firms and R&D organisations are desperately pursuing innovations through convergence in order to obtain their competitive advantage. New products developed through this convergence increasingly appear in the modern innovation. There may be no ways for firms to pursue innovations for the convergence innovation. For instance, a newly developed music receiver called an MP3 is a product of convergence innovation of many different technologies associated with records, digital music, compact disc players, the internet, and etc.

Secondly, not much research work on convergence innovation has been carried out in the past. Innovation scholars have not paid much attention to the convergence innovation although it is prevailing in the real world. Nevertheless, some scholars have investigated convergence innovation at the micro- or the meso-level, which little discovered and proposed new theories and hypotheses. Part of them will be introduced in this issue. We ensure that making a special issue on convergence innovation motivates innovation scholars and students to do more research on the issue afterwards.

Finally, there is a high demand for policy implications and tools to promote convergence innovation in both developed and developing countries. A substantial portion of government R&D projects and programmes has a characteristic of technological convergence. Therefore, government officials in charge of R&D planning want to obtain fundamental knowledge on convergence innovation. Needless to say, firms that pursue innovations also require policy tools and implications on how to achieve technological convergence at the organisational level. This special issue on convergence innovation in Asian industries may, to a great degree, contribute to the satisfaction of their demand.

## 3. Causes and processes of convergence innovation

Why do firms pursue convergence innovation? Technical problems arising in machining and processing metals were main causes of technological convergence at the beginning of the twentieth century as Rosenberg discovered. However, convergence innovations in modern times are mostly taking place in order to exploit technological opportunities created by the emergence of information and telecommunication technology. There have been innovations in conventional technologies, but in a limited scope with less opportunities than convergence innovation integrated with IT technology. In the twenty-first century, IT technology becomes an infrastructural technology due to its application to vast industrial areas. As the results of convergence of IT technology, innovation opportunities have greatly increased.

According to a study on the innovation of textile machinery (Lee, Yun, and Jeong 2015), convergence innovation takes place mainly when a firm enters into new industrial areas based on their core competence in textile machinery technologies. Firms having a core competence in some technology areas tend to endeavour to make outside-in or inside-out type convergence innovation depending on market situation. When a firm loses a market in its core competence areas, the firm tries to apply them to make new products and processes, which can help the firm enter into new markets. This is called inside-out type of convergence innovation. Conversely, a firm that gains competitive advantage in core competence areas tends to actively apply other technologies to make new innovations in its own areas and this is called outside-in type of convergence innovation.

On the process of convergence innovation, there has been growing trends of innovation studies, particularly at the micro-level. As introduced in Kong-rae Lee's paper of this issue, the convergence innovation is the process of continuous disequilibrium between converging technologies which are divided into two types: reference technology and its matching technology (Kim 2014). Two types of converging technologies tend to innovate at differing degrees of speed in such a manner that when one technology is innovated generating disequilibrium, the other technology called as matching technology necessarily innovates to adjust optimal balance between the functions of the two technologies. Euiseok Kim stated that the process of mutual matching and minute adjustment across disparate technologies to achieve a target performance is one of the most critical attributes in convergence innovation.

The process of convergence innovation is featured in terms of a learning process that requires both vertical and horizontal convergence. Based on a case study of railway technology in Malaysia (Mohamed, Fung, and Wong 2015), Mohamed argued that the horizontal convergence relates to the assimilation of advanced foreign technology with the existing railway technology available, while the vertical convergence relates to the step-by-step accumulation of technology in-depth in operating and maintaining a high-speed railway system. Both types of convergence in technological learning of an organisation contribute to substantial gain of its technological capability within a short time frame.

The processes of convergence innovation can be also explained from the viewpoint of social communication. The paper by Jang Hyun Kim and Jinsuk Lee (2015) in this issue based on the case of dentistry implies that an innovation can be diffused bringing forth a convergence through social networks. The stronger the link between individual nodes or organisations in a network, the greater their reciprocal influence will become so that a socially or economically desirable technological innovation can be rapidly converged. It is because communication among a group of people homogenises their thought and leads them to easily adopt an innovation once they think it is desirable. Innovations of various medical technologies and services such as the application of CAD/CAM to dentistry have been diffused among dentists revealing a social convergence of an innovated medical technology. Such convergence processes can be universally applied in all technological fields and industrial areas.

## 4. Patterns of and strategies for convergence innovation

Convergence innovation takes place to meet the needs of different sources as well as the divergent market demands. Sources such as customers, ideas and knowledge of users and suppliers, knowledge-intensive services, scientific and technological knowledge, and networks can be triggers or drivers of convergence innovation. The ability to utilise such diverse sources strategically enables a firm to make convergence innovation and gain a unique advantage which becomes a core competence of the firm.

Based on the investigation into the case of ERP implementation in Israel, Darr (2015) argued that service and technical skills that are important elements of ERP implementation are increasingly converging due to the growing digitalisation of production. According to his paper, the growing convergence of service and technical skills is rooted in a shift in advanced economies from sales of a product to sales of a process. This shift has created the flow of technical experts from R&D labs into service or sales functions, where they customise innovative products to clients' needs. It has led to the growing convergence of technical skill and service, causing the blurring of boundaries between technical skills and service.

Aminullah, Fizzanty, Indraprahasta, and Asmara (2015) argued that the innovation of chemical products has converged to bio-based products in Indonesia. The triggers of the convergence are the accumulation of deeper knowledge from the developmental work and public concerns over pollution problems from plastic wastes as well as the growing demand for environmentally friendly industries. The convergence has been achieved through academic and experimental research by cross-disciplinary teams or research collaborations in chemical and biological sciences. The collaborative R&D work on bio-based chemical technology has created many bio-plastic, biofertilizer, and biopesticide products. It is argued that the main drivers of the technological convergence in the Indonesian bio-based chemical industry are the changes in raw materials and the shift of market demand from oil-based to bio-based chemicals.

In a paper on the case of dentistry, Jang-Hyun Kim and Jinsuk Lee (2015) discovered an interesting phenomenon of convergence innovation in dentistry. They found that innovations in dental medicine have been a result of complex evolution of clinical techniques, materials development, appliance/device development, software enhancement, information technology, and better understanding of human body. The application of computer aided design (CAD)/computer aided manufacturing (CAM) technology in this innovation represents an exemplary case of continual convergence innovation in dental medicine. It is postulated that communication between people in a certain group homogenises thought of dentists on the application of CAD/CAM. According to their analysis, the mutuality and centrality of CAD/CAM word have increased over time indicating that the importance of CAD/CAM and its application is increasing and so is its convergence along with the innovation of zirconia, 3D CT and 3D printers and emergence of diverse techniques of dental implants.

On the other hand, there is an interesting study on the research question, 'do the late-comer firms rely more on "recent" and "scientific" knowledge than the incumbent firms: convergence or divergence?'. Park and Lee (2015) found a significant difference in the short cycle-technology-based sectors, such that the late-comer firms tend to rely more on recent and scientific knowledge than the incumbents. The findings suggest that whether there is convergence or divergence in knowledge sourcing depends on the knowledge regime of the sectors, more specifically the cycle time of the technologies of sectors. They argued that the late-comer firms afford to rely only on recent technologies in short cycle sectors where technologies tend to change or become obsolete quickly, and that they are also keen, in their knowledge sourcing, to search broadly not only into technological knowledge (patents), but also scientific knowledge (articles) in short cycle sectors with rapid change of technologies.

At the organisational level, Chul Oh and Si Hyung Joo (2015) compared convergence of technological capability between two automobile companies, Mitsubishi Motor in Japan and Hyundai Motor in Korea. They argued that Hyundai has narrowed down the technological capability gap with Mitsubishi using incremental innovation based on sustaining technology. According to their findings, Hyundai, as a late-comer, has accumulated technological capabilities as a stepping stone for catch-up in the market. It has also taken an innovation strategy to create new technologies and take different technological paths from Mitsubishi. The analysis of Oh and Joo (2015) using citation data showed that Hyundai's self-citation ratio has an increasing trend, eventually approaching Mitsubishi's. It implies that Hyundai has become as self-reliant as Mitsubishi by increasingly developing technologies that are different from those of other firms. They concluded that Hyundai is becoming less dependent on Mitsubishi. They argued that technology alone cannot lead to the success of Hyundai although accumulated technological capabilities can be the main factor for the converging. In addition to building up technological capability, various components such as entrepreneurship, marketing strategy, or globalisation strategy led Hyundai to successful convergence in technological capability to Mitsubishi over the last two decades.

Similarly at an organisational level, Miyazaki and Giraldo (2015) carried out an investigation into the case of NTT in Japan and argued that the company pursued strategies to become a more integrated operator by shifting its focus towards the upper layer of technological applications and services for providing next generation network and services. In the search for the right combination of competences, a firm may explore different innovation paths in diverse technological fields to improve their knowledge base since technological trajectory or paths of the firm can be the base to obtain their core competences (Pavitt 1992). Miyazaki and Giraldo (2015) observed that NTT has been shifting emphasis towards more sophisticated applications such as speech recognition and video analysis to create highly competitive next generation network and services. For the development of a killer-application such as IPTV, NTT has shown a convergence in their accumulation of speech and video technologies, which has been achieved through active R&D work as well as participation in international standardisation of speech, video, and image compression technologies.

## 5. Concluding remarks

We went through the causes, processes, and patterns of convergence innovation and strategies for convergence innovation based on the review of eight papers included in this issue. From this review of eight papers, we can see that convergence innovation can be analysed at various levels. Some papers investigated convergence innovation at the sector level (textile machinery, chemical products, ERP, and railway technology), while other papers analysed it at the organisational level (NTT, Hyundai Motor, and Mitsubishi Motor). Convergence phenomenon can also be analysed at social dimension such as a diffusion process of CAD/CAM in dentistry. Each analysis produces interesting results providing different insights into strategy formulation at the organisational level and policy implications at the national level for convergence innovation.

The process of convergence innovation is featured as a continuous disequilibrium between reference technology and its matching technology. These converging technologies tend to innovate at differing degrees of speed in such a manner that when one technology is innovated generating disequilibrium, matching technology necessarily innovates to adjust optimal balance between the functions of the two technologies. This explanation reveals a possibility to formulate various theoretical models on convergence innovation as creatively described in terms of a learning process that requires both vertical and horizontal convergence in the case of railway technology in Malaysia. Also, such types of convergence innovation as outside-in and inside-out, depending on market situation are discovered in the case exploration of textile machinery industry in Korea.

As argued previously, convergence innovation has been taking place mainly by applying IT technologies to vast areas of conventional technologies. This is because people or firms get benefits from converging IT technologies and conventional technologies. Convergence innovation might be pursued for the purpose of solving both technical and economic problems which societies and organisations face in the process of building up their unique competences. Solving technological problems requires not the innovation of conventional technologies, but also the convergence innovations of more than one technology. Therefore, the degree of convergence out of entire innovations may increasingly appear in advanced firms and industrialised countries as time goes by.

It is as well believed that such innovations made by convergence ultimately improve the welfare of human beings as firms solve diverse problems or increase employment by convergence innovation. A railway company (E-MAS) in Malaysia acquired high-speed railway system through both horizontal and vertical convergence of technological learning and, as a result, can provide engineering services and export innovative operating solutions to other firms abroad. In Indonesia, biochemical companies were able to increase their market shares in bio-fertilizer and biopesticide products by bio-based technological convergence. Textile machinery firms in Korea have survived by making convergence innovation on their core competence. NTT in Japan acquired a killer-application such as IPTV through a convergence strategy in their accumulation of speech and video technologies. Other papers also imply that late-comer firms can be successful in catching up with incumbent firms by adopting a convergence strategy.

However, it is not clear to confirm desirable effects of convergence innovation at the macro-level. New innovations may increase employment or replace the existing employment with new employment opportunities, which can positively or negatively affect people's welfare at the national level. That is, impacts of convergence innovation deserve to receive more attention and require further studies. The reason why the jargon 'creative economy' was adopted as an agenda of the ASIALICS Conference 2014 is that it has a close association with convergence innovation because it plays an important role in solving economic problems that many countries are facing. This special issue limits the scope of studies on convergence innovation to the pre-impact level of convergence innovation.

## Note

1.  A creative economy is defined by the convergence of science and technology with industry, the fusion of culture with industry, and the blossoming of creativity in the border regions that were once permeated by barriers.

## References

Aminullah, E., Fizzanty, T., Indraprahasta, G.S., and Asmara, I. (2015), 'Technological convergence in Indonesian firms: case of bio-based chemical product innovation', *Asian Journal of Technology Innovation*, 23(S1), 9–25.

Darr, A. (2015), 'Convergence of service and technical skills: the case of ERP implementation in Israel', *Asian Journal of Technology Innovation*, 23(S1), 26–39.

Kim, Euiseok. (2014), 'Evolutionary patterns and dynamics of technological convergence: the case of printed electronics', Ph.D. dissertation, KAIST, Daejeon.

Kim, Jang-Hyun and Lee, Jinsuk. (2015), 'A semantic network analysis of technological innovation in dentistry: a case of CAD/CAM', *Asian Journal of Technology Innovation*, 23(S1), 40–57.

Kodama, F. (1986), 'Inter-disciplinary research: Japanese innovation in mechatronics technology', *Science and Public Policy*, 13(1), 44–51.

Lee, Kong-rae. (2007), 'Patterns and processes of contemporary technology fusion: the case of intelligent robots', *Asian Journal of Technology Innovation*, 15(2), 45–65.

Lee, Kong-rae, and Hwang, Jung-tae. (2005), *A Study on Innovation System with Multi-technology Fusion (in Korean)*, Seoul: STEPI Policy Study 2005–17.

Lee, Kong-rae, Yun, Jin-hyo Joseph, and Jeong, Eui-Seob. (2015), 'Convergence innovation of the textile machinery industry in Korea', *Asian Journal of Technology Innovation*, 23(S1), 58–73.

Miyazaki, K., and Giraldo, E. (2015), 'Innovation strategy and technological competence building to provide next generation network and services through convergence: the case of NTT in Japan', *Asian Journal of Technology Innovation*, 23(S1), 74–92.

Mohamed, M., Fung, Hon-Ngen, and Wong, Chan-Yuan. (2015), 'Convergence innovation in railway technology: how ERL of Malaysia attained its co-evolution structure for systemic development', *Asian Journal of Technology Innovation*, 23(S1), 93–108.

Oh, Chul, and Joo, Si Hyung. (2015), 'Is technological capability gap between Hyundai Motor and Mitsubishi Motor converging or diverging?' *Asian Journal of Technology Innovation*, 23(S1), 109–128.

Park, Jinhyuck, and Lee, Keun. (2015), 'Do the latecomer firms rely more on 'recent' and 'scientific' knowledge than the incumbent firms? convergence or divergence in knowledge sourcing', *Asian Journal of Technology Innovation*, 23(S1), 129–145.

Pavitt, K. (1992), 'Paths: exploiting technological trajectories', in *Managing Innovation*, eds. J. Tidd, J. Bessant and K. Pavitt, London: Wiley, pp. 111–135.

Rosenberg, N. (1963), 'Technological change in the machine tool industry, 1840-1910', *Journal of Economic History*, 23(4), 414–446.

Rosenberg, N. (1982), *Inside the Black Box-Technology and Economics*, Cambridge: Cambridge University Press.

# Technological convergence in Indonesian firms: cases of biobased chemical product innovation

Erman Aminullah, Trina Fizzanty, Galuh S. Indraprahasta and Indri J. Asmara

*The Indonesian Institute of Sciences (LIPI), Jakarta, Indonesia*

This paper attempts to explain how technological convergence has occurred in Indonesian chemical firms. Viewed from the sectoral innovation system, the enabling factors of biobased chemical products innovation are the availability of scientist and researcher at university and research collaboration in company. The ways forward to promote technological convergence in Indonesian biobased chemical firms are to enhance its internal and external R&D capacity by supporting chemical firms to interact with public R&D and university. To enable the biobased chemical sector to take the opportunities to grow through technological convergence, the Indonesian government policy should (i) provide strong support for research, development, and commercialisation of innovative biobased products, and incentives for pioneering the commercial production and (ii) facilitate the biobased chemical value chains to develop by supporting biobased chemical investment, the advocation of using biobased chemical products in society, and limiting of using petroleum-based chemical products in the market.

## 1. Introduction

Biobased chemical products are gradually gaining public interest as the alternative products to petroleum based chemicals. Biobased chemicals from renewable resources supplied by plant materials have been substituting some petroleum-based chemicals. Currently, raw materials such as starches, cellulose, and oil have been extracted from plants for the production of some biomaterials, chemicals, and fuel products. The emergence of biobased chemical products is more than the phenomenon of products substitution; it is the *convergence* of green chemistry with industrial biotechnology. Biobased chemicals products are produced through a biomass origin and/or a bioprocessing route that makes use of biotechnology in the production of chemicals (Philp, Ritchie, and Allan 2013).

The phenomenon of convergence is the combination of certain knowledge and technology with an existing industry to create new product, process, solution, and even a new industrial firm or sector. For example, the product of camera phone was created by combining the camera technology with the telecom industry, the solution for packaging was emerged by combining the information technology with the pulp and paper industry, and the functional food product has come out by combining the life science with the food industry. Hacklin identified the phenomenon of convergence as the process along an evolutionary trajectory, representing a foundation for determining the dynamics of innovation (Hacklin 2008).

The reality of convergence phenomena has been found in genomics, robotics, bioinformatics, and artificial intelligence applications. It is more than ordinary growth of multidisciplinary or interdisciplinary fields with the greatest possible implications for the economy, society, and culture (Bainbridge and Roco 2006). It requires new organisations and business models, as well as solutions for preparing the economy, such as multifunctional research facilities and integrative technology platforms (Roco 2006). The phenomena of convergences can be identified through technological interactions in government spending, university programmes, inter-firm strategic alliances, intra-firm expansion, and patent citations (Michelson 2006).

Most recent research on technological convergence revealed the relationship between technological convergence and open innovation, as the external environment is constantly changing, particularly in digital convergence and standards networks, it leads to the increasingly widespread trend of companies to engage in external capabilities and knowledge sources as a way to extend their knowledge boundaries (Lee, Ji-Hoon, Yong-Il, and Hi-Jung 2008). Furthermore, Jang's research found that that the 'entrepreneurship' of technological convergence formed through industrial research collaboration, more diverse industrial research collaborations under an autonomous environment might result in more strategic and entrepreneurial technological convergences (Jang 2009).

The phenomena of technological convergence also take place in some Indonesian industrial sectors, such as pharmaceuticals and the chemical industry. This paper attempts to explain how the technological convergence has occurred and the ways forward to promote technological convergence in Indonesian biobased chemical firms, more specifically what innovation policy should be addressed by policy-makers to enable the biobased chemical firms to take the opportunities to grow through technological convergence.

## 2. Research methodology

The object of the study was inspired by the application of technological convergence in Indonesian pharmaceutical and chemical firms. The firms were the winner of Indonesian Institute of Sciences' (LIPI) R&D-based industrial innovation award 2013. We chose to study the chemical industry that produced biobased chemical commodities, such as bioplastic, biofertiliser, and biopesticide products to explore and understand technological convergence. The reasons of choosing biobased chemical products were based on its important functions to substitute the use of petroleum-based chemical products. The study was done as follows.

The *First aim* was to portray the technological capacity of the Indonesian chemical industry. The data of indicators described the current status and challenges that would be faced by the chemical industry in applying the principles of technological convergence in the future. The data source was reprocessed from the ERIA survey 2013.

The *Second* was to collect relevant information on the existing structure of the chemical sector and mapping its upstream, midstream, and downstream industrial linkages to the biobased chemical products. The existing structure of the chemical sector was used to identify the enabling factors of developing a biobased chemical industry viewed from the sectoral innovation system (SIS) perspective.

The *Third* was to interview three firms for case studies those which practise the different types of technological convergences, including understanding the drivers, triggers, and enabling factors of technological convergence for the company to grow in the future.

The *Fourth* was to analyse the ways forward to promote technological convergence in the Indonesian biobased chemical industry, by using a cross cases analysis of three case studies.

The focus of the analysis was to find the stages and determinants (drivers, triggers, and enabling factors) of technological convergence as a continuum process of creating a new industry.

The *Fifth* was to provide recommendations of how firms and policy-makers should support technological convergence for the growth of the industrial sector in the future. The findings could also contribute to enhancing innovation policies on technological convergence in Indonesia.

## 3. Changes in technological capacity of Indonesian chemical firms

### 3.1. *Technological capacity of Indonesian chemical firms*

The technological capacity of Indonesian chemical firms has the potency of shifting to bio-based chemicals as reflected by indicators: capital investment, R&D activities, intellectual property rights (IPR), product innovation and design, and source of innovation. Based on the survey results in 2013 (see the Appendix), Indonesian chemical firms invested in capital to increase its innovative capacity. The investment was largely allocated to increase the degree of automation in the production process as well as to modify existing capital goods. The firms invested partly for logistics purposes to reach consumers in a more efficient way. Although, their investment to introduce a new capital goods and R&D facility was very limited, the firms mostly engaged in R&D activities. There were two-thirds of chemical firms engaged in R&D activities, one third of them expended on R&D more than 1% of sales. Engaging in R&D activities had opened the opportunities for chemical firms to innovate and explore the possibilities of combining the existing technologies to develop new products.

The chemical firms predominantly engaged in creating new products and the majority of the firms held IPR. The new products were primarily dedicated for the existing markets and new markets, but the limited number of the products innovation resulted from existing and new technologies. In designing new products, the chemical firms generally innovated to respond to market requirements in implementing the user innovation. The sources of innovation ideas were mostly the final consumers, its competitors, and local customers, but public research institute and university were less utilised.

Furthermore, the innovation activities of plastic firms are similar to the general description of chemical firms. The plastic firms also engaged in R&D activities with the majority of them expending less than 0.5% of sales or below the average of chemical firms in general. The product development was also primarily undertaken by the firm itself, and only a few firms were supported by their parent firms. The firms typically developed the design of new products as a result of more interactions with the customers, but fewer interactions with suppliers. The source of innovation ideas was also dominated by interacting with users and the interactions between business and academia in Indonesian plastic firms were relatively weak.

Other chemicals non-plastic commodities (including fertiliser, pharmaceutical, health-care products) also invested in modifying the existing capital and increasing the degree of automation in production, but none of them invested in introducing new technology. The chemical non-plastic firms had more intensive R&D activities than that of plastic firms. Interestingly, all chemicals non-plastic firms engaged in R&D, and majority of them expended on R&D more than 1% of sales. The large proportion of firms engaged in R&D had resulted in most of the chemicals non-plastic firms holding IPR. Innovation ideas mainly came from final consumers, followed by competitors and local customers. The role of public research institutes and universities as the sources of innovation was larger in chemical non-plastic than plastic firms.

### 3.2. *Transition to the biobased chemical industry*

A shift from petroleum-based chemical towards the biobased chemical industry is more likely to happen in the near future due to (i) pollution problem from plastic waste continuing to grow; (ii) excessive use of synthetic pesticides has caused environmental problems and rendered the agricultural production system uneconomical; (iii) new regulations are emerging for managing and treating waste; (iv) new products, biodegradable, or recyclable materials, are coming into market; and (v) manufacturing businesses will develop more environmental-friendly products.

The petroleum-based chemical industry can be grouped vertically into: (i) upstream industries such as olefins, aromatic, and ammonia, (ii) midstream industries derived from upstream petrochemicals such as polymers and urea, and (iii) downstream industries, those produce products utilised by the end-user industries, such as industrial plastics, fertilisers, and pesticides (see Figure 1).

The Indonesian biobased chemical products that have already been in market are bioplastic, biopesticide, and biofertiliser. Bioplastics are plastic materials which are biobased, biodegradable, or feature both properties. The 'biobased' plastic means that the material or product is (partly) derived from biomass (plants). The biomass used for bioplastics stems from, for example, starch. Biofertiliser contains inoculants with an active ingredient or living organism that serves to improve certain nutrients or facilitates the availability of nutrients in the soil for the plants. Biopesticide is a pesticide containing an organism as the active agent that can be used to suppress losses due to pests and diseases in all agricultural activities, both on- and off-farms.

The initial step of establishing a biobased chemical industry that has been applied by Indonesian firms starts from developing 'niche products'. The products are novel products and materials, yielding significant environmental benefits and of relatively smaller scale. This is a common step in research, development, and commercialisation of biobased industrial products that are typically

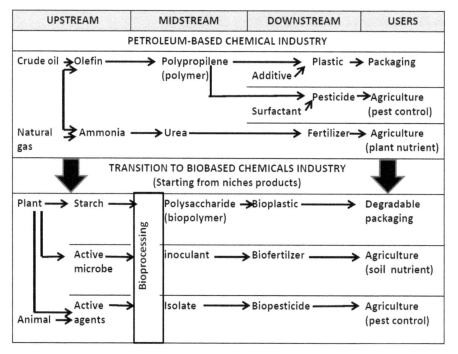

**Figure 1:** Transition to biobased chemicals industry.
Source: Various references and interview with key persons of case studies.

developed by small businesses led by innovative entrepreneurs, where the speed in commercialisation is crucial, and support consequently must be available without excessive delays. Once the process technology, favourable economics, and product characteristics are established, market penetration can begin rapidly (NRC 2000, pp. 211–212).

## 4. Theoretical perspectives on stages and determinants of technological convergence

### 4.1. *Stages of technological convergence*

The emergence of technological convergence can be anticipated from the stages of technological convergence: science, technology, market, and industrial convergences (Curran, Bröring, and Leker 2010). *Science convergence* of the different disciplines can be initiated by cross-disciplinary citations leading to research collaboration of separate disciplines, that is, research on biomaterials from collaboration of materials science and biology disciplines. *Technology convergence* of the different areas of technologies can be identified from convergence of nanomaterials, biotechnology, and chemical technologies, that is, the invention of nanobioplastic technology. *Market convergence* of the different set of demands can be anticipated from, the convergence of demands for plastic and bioplastic products with the demand for the high-quality nanobioplastic products. *Industrial convergence* of the different companies/business will only take place when technologies and markets converge, that is, a nanobioplastic company is a result of the integration of companies producing starch (upstream), biopolymer (midstream), and nanobioplastic (downstream) converging with the business of nanobioplastic products (demand). In order to succeed in the new market, a company has to customise its products, processes, services, and competences to meet the needs of new customers (Hacklin 2008).

### 4.2. *Determinants of technological convergence*

#### 4.2.1. *Drivers and triggers*

The causes of convergence are commonly referred to as drivers and triggers. Driver is a factor that brings about or sustains the phenomenon of convergence. 'Trigger' is an event or situation that makes convergence happen. Therefore, the triggers of convergence may not necessarily drive its further development. On a general level, the drivers of convergence are categorised based on: technological drivers (scientists/researchers), managerial drivers (business models of managers), industrial drivers (market structure of companies), political drivers (regulation and legal issues from governments), and societal drivers (developments of societies/consumers) (Curran 2013).

The drivers of convergence that alter the structure of the chemical industry include the alteration of raw materials base for shifting from oil-based chemicals towards biobased chemicals. The convergence was triggered by the fact that the world's oil reserves are definitely limited and an increasing environmental awareness. The increasing interest in products derived from biomaterials (such as bioplastic) serves to substitute the oil-derived synthetic chemical products (i.e. plastic). This could lead to the industrial convergence between the parts of the chemical industry and the parts of the agricultural industry (Curran 2013).

#### 4.2.2. *Enabling factors*

As described in Section 3, the potentials of technological convergence in Indonesian chemical firms need to enhance its internal and external R&D capacity. Supporting chemical firms to interact with public R&D and university becomes the important strategy of promoting technological innovation. In terms of capital investment, a majority of firms invested in the production system, and only a few invested on R&D. In realising the potentials of technological convergence, which is viewed from the SIS, developing biobased chemical products innovation depends on three enabling factors: (i) knowledge and technology; (ii) actors and networks; and (iii) market demand and institutional support on biobased chemical product innovation (see Figure 2).

4.2.2.1. *Knowledge and technology*. Acquiring, developing, and accumulating the knowledge and technology in biobased chemical firms here are seen as *an interactive learning system by various actors that carry out interactions through networks, which are determined by the institution* (Malerba 2004; Malerba and Sunil 2009). The process of innovation in biobased chemicals depends on interactive learning among R&D, production, marketing units inside the biobased firms and its interaction with external sources of knowledge (universities, research institution, suppliers, and users). The modes of learning to acquire knowledge basically are gained through STI (Science, Technology, and Innovation) modes (R&D activities, scientific advancement, and technology spillover), but for the small firms it can be gained through learning by DUI (doing, using, and interacting) inside their small laboratory.

The biobased chemical technology developed by firms is to solve the negative environmental impact, to find effective pest control and to improve soil fertility as well as to meet the standard of safety and security of biobased chemical products. Innovation in the biobased chemical product is achieved by the demand: (i) to solve the environmental problems induced by petroleum-based products; (ii) to find innovative raw material supply; and (iii) to develop processing technology to meet the standard of safety and security of biobased chemical products. The challenge to push innovation in biobased chemical products is generally to increase the existing low demand and economies of scale as well.

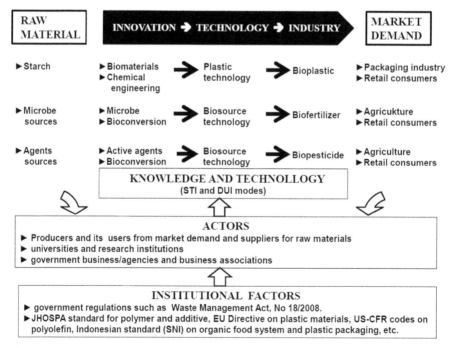

**Figure 2:** The enabling factors of innovation in biobased chemicals.
Source: Created by authors from various references and interview with key persons of case studies.

4.2.2.2. *Actors and networks*. The actors of biobased chemical firms are categorised by individual and organisation. Individual actor includes consumers, businessmen, and scientists. The actor of organisation comprises firms with their internal units (i.e. R&D, production, and marketing) and various external organs, such as: (i) *universities and research institutions* such as Bogor Agricultural Institute (IPB), Center for Bioindustry Technology (PTB) of the Agency for Assessment and Application of Technology (BPPT), Indonesian Institute of Sciences (LIPI), National Atomic Agency (BATAN), and Plastic, Rubber, and Leather Research Unit (BKKP) of the Ministry of Industry; (ii) *government business/agencies and business associations* such as Agency of Food and Drugs Control (BPOM), petrochemical state-owned companies (PG and PUSRI), Indonesian Association of Plastic and Olefin Industry (INAPLAS), and producer association of organic fertiliser and biofertiliser (APPOHI), organic food certification institution (BIOCERT), and Seloliman organic food certification institution (LESOS); (iii) *the users of* biobased chemical products such as the packaging industry, food industry, agricultural businesses; and (iv) *the suppliers* of raw material for biobased chemical products such as starch and chemical substance suppliers. The *networks* are described in various ways in which the *actors* are connected in the system. The networks provide various paths to access knowledge and technology in the system. The variations of accesses are characterised by market and non-market relationships such as domestic/global competition and society, industry, academia, and government relationships.

4.2.2.3. *Demand and institution*. Demand refers to a group of actors that interact with the producers. The actors of demand for biobased chemical products are represented by the consumers of the packaging industry, food industry, agricultural businesses, the government cooperative businesses and so on. There are three key drivers affecting the global biobased chemicals market: (i) moving away from petroleum dependency; (ii) increased consumers' responsibility on environmental protection; and (iii) movement towards sustainability manufacturers. The key markets are solvents, surfactants, adhesives and sealants, plastics for packaging, food services, consumer goods, and agriculture (Deschamps 2013).

The interaction of actors in the system is determined by those *institutions* that arise through binding norms and non-binding agreements. The binding norms for bioplastic-based products are Waste management act No. 18/2008 on producers which is required to manage plastic packaging and/or goods, Japan hygienic olefin and styrene plastics association (JHOSPA) standard for polymer and additive, and EU directive on: (i) tolerable daily intake, (ii) limited set of heavy metals, and (iii) testing migration of additive and constituent of plastic. Other regulations are US Code of Federal Regulations (CFR) on maximum extractable of polyolefin, Indonesian national standards (SNI) on organic food system and plastic packaging. Besides them, there are market institutions such as competition in the market of biobased chemicals and also non-market institutions, that is, government programmes on green economy and its implementation by local government agencies.

## 5.   Case investigations into biobased chemical products innovation

This section will reveal the findings of case studies in three companies those have practised the different types of technological convergence. The discussion will focus on the enabling factors of biobased chemical products innovation which are categorised as follows: (i) knowledge and technology; (ii) actors and networks; (iii) market demand and institutional support in biobased chemical product innovation; and (iv) the challenge to commercialise the innovative product for the company to grow in the future.

## 5.1. *Case 1: Company A*

Company A is one of Indonesian companies in the chemical industry located in Tangerang, Indonesia. The founder is a chemist who obtained rich experiences on chemical aspects from his family business and working in a multinational company. Before the company was established in 1985, he had run a chemical trading company since 1983. The company was initially the producer of waterproofing coating, then grew to produce diverse chemical products for building and construction. The company consistently operated in chemical business since its establishment and was known as the market leader for several chemical products, such as waterproofing coating and plastic products. The market position was achieved through continually launching innovative products. The Indonesian Ministry of Industry (Kemenperin) and Indonesian Institute of Sciences (LIPI) awarded the company as the most innovative company in chemical products. The company was certified by ISO 9001 in 2000, OHSAS 18,001 in 2007, and ISO 14,001 in 2012 showing strong management capability. In 2006, the company's founder was awarded by Ernst & Young as Entrepreneur of the Year.

The company continues innovating to sustain its market position by producing new product, which is new to the local market, new to the company (to replace imported product), and new to the chemical industry. Its first innovative product was a specific coating material for protecting building from water leakage in 1985, which was also new to the local market. The success in commercialising the innovative product is followed by creating other building and construction chemical products, and the company started producing plastic masterbatch and polymer compound in 1990. The local product has succeeded in replacing the imported masterbatch. In 2006, the company launched a new product of biobased chemical. It gained the Industrial Technology Pioneer Award from the Indonesian Ministry of Industry. The product development was driven by company's vision to become a leader in chemically renewable sources, in response to the facts that: *First*, an increasing awareness on environmental issues such as pollution, particularly by world environmental activists. *Second*, the world stock of fossil base resources for petrochemical has become limited that would increase the energy price significantly in the future.

### 5.1.1. *Knowledge and technology*

The company registered the bioplastic as a specific brand. The company is a pioneer in Indonesia for biodegradable plastic bags. The bioplastic was resulted from knowledge accumulation and technological capabilities in the chemical industry. The company's competency in bioplastic accumulated from long experiences in chemical business, experimental testing, and R&D activities. The bioplastic degraded in nature after six months, so this product is friendlier to environment. The bioplastic is made of starch and vegetable oil derivatives.

The product is considered be more 'green chemistry' than other bioplastics products as its production process is very much different from the generic one. Some advantages of the product are that it dissolves instantly in hot water, softens in cold water, almost disappears in soil within three to six months depending on soil conditions and leaves only a small amount of ash when burnt. Some challenges still remain such as meeting international standard (certification of EN13432) for export market and the limited types of bioplastic products because of the water-sensitive issue due to its hydrophilic characteristics.

### 5.1.2. *Actors and networks*

The main actor behind the bioplastic product is the founding father who is also a president director of the company. His vision and competence had influenced him to enter business in green product before others could think about this issue. The internal R&D team involved in the bioplastic project consisted of one Ph.D. in chemistry (graduated from a France university) and seven chemical engineers as laboratory staff. Since this new business needs to modify current production system, including raw material, formulation, and production machine, staff from different disciplines such as chemical engineering, mechanical engineering, and industrial engineering have to work collaboratively.

To modify its production line, the company had developed its own design in mechanical production. The company worked with small business (a workshop) to implement its design into the production line. The scale up of bioplastic resulted from the R&D process and interactive learning among internal and external teams. R&D on bioplastic was conducted for nearly six years. The research was conducted in the company and other countries by an international consortium particularly of Asian scientists. The company developed collaborative work with a foreign university intensively but less interaction with local universities and public R&D. One of reputable university in Indonesia, for example, has assisted them in chemical testing. And, they also built collaboration with Indonesian public R&D on pulp and paper in the recycling test.

The company has wide business networks since its establishment. The networks consist of business partners and customers from local markets and local investors. In order to promote its new product, the company has actively involved in several exhibitions in domestic and abroad. For example, Eco-Products International Fair in Taipei, Tokyo, Singapore, and Hong Kong. Through participating in the international exhibitions, the company found that its bioplastic is unique compared to similar products. Since this business is new for the local market, there is no association yet that could assist the company in communicating with many stakeholders, especially government sectors.

### 5.1.3. *Demand and institution*

The institutional issues including standard and government policy support are found to be critical in creating the demand for green product. Currently, the company has to deal with the problems of testing procedures and meeting international standards of bioplastic, such as suitable biodegradation media/parameters. The low domestic demand is due to a lack of government concern to limit the use of non-compostable plastic. However, the world's growing awareness of environmental issues in using plastic had contributed to the increasing demand of bioplastic. In the last two years, the bioplastic market grew significantly, particularly in developed countries, due to the use of conventional plastic being banned.

The imposing of local regulation had opened opportunity for the bioplastic to be a promising business in the future, but this is not the case in Indonesia. For example, the local government of Jakarta has regulated the use environmental-friendly plastic as plastic bags in shopping malls. However, the implementation of this regulation is still far behind. Consequently, the market for bioplastic in Indonesia has not grown yet. Currently, none of the shopping malls or the state companies placed order to the company, except only several small stores, restaurants, or hotels. Besides, the higher price of bioplastic than that of the conventional one may hinder customers' attraction to buy this product.

The company keeps its position as the market leader (pioneer), in producing something new that others have not produced yet. The challenge for a pioneer firm like company A is obtaining market trust. Since bioplastic is still new for the local market, the company has to educate the customers and keep evaluating this new product compared to the conventional one. Hence, the firm should educate its potential market intensively before the market grows. When the market grows, the company will be the frontrunner in bioplastic business. Currently, the main challenge for the bioplastic company is the lack of economies of scale.

### 5.2. *Case 2: Company B*

Company B is a local company in biopesticide business located in Bandung, West Java, Indonesia. The founder of the company is an environmental expert from a reputable university in Indonesia. The company has entered the biopesticide business since 2005 for particular reasons; as a response to the minister's demand and dealing with environmental problems resulting from current agricultural practices. In seeking the effective formula for his biopesticide products, he had conducted various experimental research and development for years.

#### 5.2.1. *Knowledge and technology*

Although Company B is not the pioneer in biopesticide products, the company represented one of a small number of pesticide producers which are dominated by chemical-based pesticides products. This company has produced two brands of biopesticide product, X and Y. The brand X is used to disinfect caterpillar pest, while the brand Y is used to resolve fungal pest. The company and its products were built upon knowledge accumulation resulting from the R&D activities, mainly conducted by the founder himself. An intensive R&D activity was conducted before the establishment of the company.

The source of the idea to create a biopesticide product was rooted in the founder's knowledge in assessing contaminated water from the chemicals used in the project of agricultural protection in 1999. He tried to combine his knowledge in environmental technology with agricultural sciences. Initially, several colleagues questioned his effort in doing biopesticide R&D and regarded this as a useless activity. Yet, he had continued to conduct research and to learn new things through experimental research for years. He had to spent five years in R&D to find the right formula for his products. His biopesticide products have proved to increase the plants productivity and functioned effectively as a disinfectant.

In producing the biopesticide, the company does not use sophisticated machines, but applied special treatment to maintain the equipments. Several equipments could be easily found in the market and several others were designed and made by the founder's colleagues from the University.

#### 5.2.2. *Actors and networks*

The main actors of product development are the founder and his wife. The company's networks have been built since the establishment of their consulting company. The experience of building networks in consulting company is one of critical modalities to create its further networks. The company's network consists of business partners and government sectors, both national and regional governments. Its national government network, particularly the Minister of Environmental Affairs had driven the founder to create a biopesticide product and establish the company.

Initially, the R&D activity was solely based on his passion to reduce the extensive use of chemical pesticide, later the R&D results were developed by the company into a commercial product. The main funding source for developing a biopesticide product was their consulting company. To conduct field trials, company B collaborated with several local governments and other companies, in particular with the state-owned enterprise having core business in agricultural seed. These partners provided demonstration plot to test the level of productivity and effectiveness to disinfect pests. The cooperation with the state-owned company lasted for one year in 2006. Several local governments had also provided demonstration plots for the field trials of company's biopesticide products.

### 5.2.3. *Demand and institution*

Company B obtained permit as a pesticide producer after four years through a complicated bureaucratic process. The products of company had to pass several standard tests, such as toxicity and smell test, in several appointed laboratories belonging to the designated University and Ministry of Agriculture. The Ministry of Agriculture had launched the so-called green agriculture movement, opening up an opportunity for biopesticide development as non-chemical inputs for agricultural uses. The government imposed the same standard and registration procedure for biopesticide products as those of chemical products due to the market for biopesticide products was still very limited.

Lack of standard has become the constraint of biopesticide development. Since there is no institution that provides the biopesticide standard in Indonesia, the company tried to find standard information abroad, such as that imposed in the USA, but did not follow it due to the high cost of standard testing abroad. Another institutional barrier faced by the company is the time uncertainty in the bureaucratic permit process. Consequently, after getting the permit in 2009 that has been valid for five years, the company does not have an intention to renew it in 2014. The company views that it is more important to support farmers using the product than getting the permit.

The market of biopesticide in Indonesia has not well grown yet. The use of biopesticide is more encouraged by individual awareness than institutional support. The company has actually produced several products for different commodities, such as paddy, palm oil, and tea. The company focuses on marketing the products for paddy. For other two products, the company has been facing difficulties entering the market. The internal policy of palm oil plantation enterprise still prioritises the use of self-produced biofertiliser. In the case of tea plantation, the use of chemical pesticide has become enterprise policy, which is not easy to influence the policy level.

The market competition tends to stand for chemical products which are dominated by the large and well-established enterprises. New and/or small-scale enterprises face barrier to enter new markets. After the company successfully introduced biopesticide to farmers, the large chemical enterprise made the efforts not to lose its farmers by establishing an agricultural clinic located near the farmers. As a result, the farmers in that area used the chemical pesticide again. Company B realises that it has no good marketing team to interact routinely with its users (farmers). The company emphasises to increase the market share of biopesticide products by educating the farmers regularly. The continuous demand for their products depends on its loyal customers and company's distributors.

## 5.3. *Case 3: Company C*

Company C is a local start-up company located in Bogor City, West Java, established in 2010. The business is the spin-off business unit from a university in Bogor, and owned by the university lecturers and its alumni. All products originally resulted from intensive research in the fields of plant protection in the university. The research activities seek the effective formula of biofertiliser and biopesticide.

The risk avoiding character of local entrepreneurs has driven the lecturers to take a risk of establishing the start-up company in biofertiliser and biopesticide. Although the new product has proved scientifically, only one local investor showed interest but has low motivation to take risks investing in this new business. Most of them require a technology package including the secret formula, a factory design, and a marketing strategy. These requirements could not be easily met by the university researchers. This situation had driven the university lecturers to collaborate and establish their own company to accelerate the commercialisation of product innovation. To manage the start-up business, the company hired an executive manager with five permanent staff in research, production and marketing activities, finance, and administration jobs.

The company produced biofertiliser, with a specific brand, which is also effective as a biopesticide. The product contains specific microbes and has been applied typically for seed treatment to help plants grow faster as well as to protect them from particular diseases. The product type is unique in a powder form compared to other biofertilisers which are formed in granules. Their research found that the powder type is more effective and efficient than the granules.

The product has been registered with the Indonesian Ministry of Agriculture and distributed in the local market. The production capacity was only 500 kilograms per month, but its capacity increased slowly as the market expanded. Since the product is new to the local market, the company should educate the customers in ways to apply it.

### 5.3.1. *Knowledge and technology*

The company produces biofertiliser and biopesticide based on research on microbes for seven years. The research was conducted by the lecturers in the discipline of plant protection. Based on intensive experiments on various organic products, the lecturers finally found the effective biofertiliser product.

The product was originally commercialised for a particular commodity, chilli plant, but then it was also found to be effective for other horticulture commodities and crops. The biofertiliser can be used for several purposes. Among them are for plant protection, growth regulator in horticulture commodities such as fruits and vegetables, to increase productivity of food crops, and to shorten the nursery period of palm oil. The research also proved the effectiveness of biofertiliser in reducing pest and plant diseases, that is, the effectiveness was 55% for papaya and 90% for onions.

It took years to introduce the innovation into market. Several steps were applied, from laboratory to screening test in green house, and experiments in multiple locations. The multiple location tests were conducted in 2008 or five years after the experiments. The research confirmed the biopesticide effectiveness for certain commodities compared to the chemical pesticide. The challenge in developing mass production is to increase the lifetime of microbes, from one year to a minimum of two years. Some experiments are still in progress to solve the problem.

### 5.3.2. *Actors and networks*

Major actors in this company are the owners, manager, staff, and other external actors. The owners are university lecturers and Ph.D. holders from a university abroad. The manager and staff were professional staff, acting out daily business activities. In doing the business, competition with imported biofertiliser from China and Japan is the most challenging issue. The importers were more advanced in the marketing strategy and able to provide more intensive supervision to the consumers.

Both business and government networks have contributed to the company's business innovation capacity. To expand its market, the company built partnerships with the distributors and an agricultural seed company, which have extensive business networks. Through these networks, the company obtained continuous feedback from customers and information on potential of new markets. The company also built the networks with the government for supporting their business and involved in business associations, such as The National Union of Pesticide Association. Then, being a resource person the minister's support was useful for the company's owner to advocate the government policy, especially to reduce the bureaucracy process.

### 5.3.3. *Demand and institution*

In the local market, the local biopesticide has faced increasing competition from imported biopesticide and chemical pesticide products. The local market was likely threatened by imported products, although the imported products contain microbes which may not be effective for local crops at all seasons. Therefore, the most challenging issue is to educate local farmers to consider the importance of local microorganism for their crops. The more farmers are getting aware of this knowledge, the bigger market opportunity would be open for the local biopesticide. Demand for local biopesticide is also affected by the chemical pesticide. Biopesticide demand is likely to increase, when the chemical pesticide is no longer effective.

The main customers of the company were small farmers, but the company seeks to meet the standard of demand from industrial customers such as plantation companies. Currently, there was only one plantation company as its customer. Two major issues should be addressed, such as educating the small farmers and increasing the quality to meet the standard of large company's demand. To expand its future market, the following issues still remain: continuous exploration on local microorganism and its functions to the plants protection, performance improvement in biopesticide formula, and promoting mass production, and developing market management and its roadmap of expansion.

Despite the growing awareness of government on sustainable agriculture and plantation, institutional issues such as bureaucracy still remain. This problem has some consequences. *First*, the bureaucracy and long registration process resulted in high uncertainty and cost for business. For instance, the company took two years for the registration of its new product. The *second*, some small-scale producers have not registered yet but they have operated in the market, which contributes to a lack of consumers' trust on biopesticide. The *third*, a similar treatment on product testing for biopesticide and chemical pesticide was applied, which would discourage the biopesticide producers. Both products have to pass three types of testing: quality test, application test, and toxicity test. The *fourth*, the registration process for biofertiliser was simpler than that of biopesticide. Hence, this issue motivated the business to register their biopesticide products as biofertiliser, while both products have different safety standard on using micro-organisms.

### 5.4. *Summary of three case studies*

Viewed from the stages of convergence: science, technology, market, corporate/industrial convergences, the technological convergence is more than combining the well-developed knowledge in biological sciences and the existing chemical industries to create new innovation in biochemicals. It is transforming the biochemical innovation into biochemical technology products that drives new industrial growth. Subsequently, it is a continuous process of converging in *scientific disciplines, technologies, markets,* and *industry.* Starting with a scientific convergence will be initiated by cross-disciplinary research and eventually develop further into research collaborations. The applied science and technology development leads to technology convergence. Then, new product–market combinations will emerge leading to market convergence and, once firms have begun to merge with each other, the process will be finalised by industrial convergence.

The complete stages of convergence are creating new products and service combinations, which bring the industry deal with new actors (customers, employees, suppliers, competitors, and business partners), new regulators/institutions, and new organisations which have different behaviours and expectations. Table 1 explains the cross analysis of three case studies in terms of stages and determinants of technological convergence.

In the case of bioplastic, some challenges are the meeting of international standard (certification of EN13432) for export market and the limited types of bioplastic products due to the strengthness issue. In developing technological capability, the company developed collaboration with a foreign university intensively but less interaction with local universities and public R&D. The bioplastic business is new for the local market and the company lacks a medium (i.e. business

**Table 1:** The stages and determinants of technological convergence.

| Determinants | Stages of convergence | | | |
| --- | --- | --- | --- | --- |
| | Science convergence | Technology convergence | Market convergence | Industrial convergence |
| Drivers | Changing the chemical industry structure by shifting the raw materials base from oil-based chemical towards biobased chemicals | | | |
| Triggers | • Public concerns on inorganic waste from plastic  • Growing demand on environmental-friendly industry | | | |
| *Enabling factors* — Company A | International collaborative research | Founder vision and academic background | Information on global market | Having industrial structure/linkage |
| Knowledge and technology | Having experimental research culture | Managerial creativity to change business line | Business background and networks in chemicals | Applied supply chain management |
| Actors and networks | Needs interaction with universities and R&D institution | Obtained granted patent | Enterpreneurship and marketing effort | |
| Demand and institutions | | High intensity of Internet use | Abundant supply of local raw material | |
| | | Product quality and standard | Needs to influence customer habits and knowledge | |
| | | Product diversification | Needs regulatory regime and government support | |
| | | | Needs to reduce production cost and product price | |
| Company B | Doing experimental research | Ever-present biopesticide technology | Founder business networks | |
| | University research cooperation | High intensity of Internet use | Enterpreneurship creativity of founder | |
| | Institutional push/ministry request | Needs special government regulatory on standard | Needs to influence customer habits and knowledge | |
| | Needs more long lifetime of microbes | | | |
| Company C | Doing academic research | Ever-present biopesticide and biofertiliser technology | Enterpreneurship creativity of founder | |
| | University scientists support | Needs special government regulatory on standard | Needs to influence customer habits and knowledge | |
| | Needs longer lifetime of microbes | | | |

*Source:* The data were processed from three case studies.

association) to communicate with stakeholders, especially government sectors. Since bioplastic is still new for the local market, the company have to educate customers in the beginning to obtain trust from the market.

For biopesticide and biofertiliser, there are some challenges to be addressed by companies, such as educating small farmers and reaching quality standard, which are becoming two major factors of success for the large company. The company needs to organise a good marketing team which will interact routinely with its users (farmers). The company needs to increase the market share of biofertilizer and biopesticide products by providing continuous education to farmers. In terms of technology convergence, the challenges are the increase in the lifetime for microbes by continuous exploration on local micro-organisms and its functions, improving technology performance on formula and mass production, besides technological governance including market roadmap for biofertiliser and biopesticide.

In short, the biobased technological convergences are generally still in the stages of science and technology convergence, in the forms of doing academic and experimental research by a cross-disciplinary team or research collaborations. The application of chemical and biological sciences in developing industrial technology led to the creation of bioplastic, biofertiliser, and biopesticide products. The biochemical convergence was mostly driven by scientists and researchers at the university and through research collaboration in the company. Shifting the stages of technological convergence towards market and industrial convergence will become the future challenges for Indonesian biobased chemical firms, such as: (i) government regulation and product standard; (ii) market structure and supply chains; (iii) managerial creativity and enterpreneurship; and (iv) social awareness and consumer habits.

## 6. Conclusions and policy implications

The stages of technological convergence in Indonesian biobased chemical firms are generally still in the stages of science and technology convergence. The convergence focusses on doing academic and experimental research by a cross-disciplinary team or research collaborations in chemical and biological sciences. The developmental research in biobased industrial technology has created bioplastic, biofertiliser, and biopesticide products.

The triggers of innovation in biobased chemicals are a deeper knowledge and public concern on pollution problems from plastic waste as well as growing demand on environmental-friendly industry. The drivers of technological convergence in the biobased chemical industry are changing the raw materials base and shifting from oil-based chemical towards biobased chemicals. More specifically viewed from the SIS, the enabling factors of biobased chemical products innovation are the availability of actors and networks, especially scientists and researchers at university as well as research collaboration in company. These findings can be seen as enrichment of Curran's (2013) work on the stages of convergence, its drivers, and triggers. By applying the SIS perspective, the drivers and the triggers are necessary but not sufficient, the enabling factors should be considered in promoting the growth of biobased chemical firms through technological convergence.

The ways forward to promote technological convergence in Indonesian biobased chemical firms are to enhance their internal and external R&D capacity by supporting chemical firms to interact with public R&D and university. The sectoral innovation policy should be addressed by policy-makers to enable the biobased chemical firms to take the opportunities to grow through technological convergence. The Indonesian government policy should: (i) provide strong support for research, development, and commercialisation of innovative biobased products, and incentives for pioneering the commercial production and (ii) facilitate the biobased chemical value chains to develop by supporting biobased chemical investment, the advocation of using biobased chemical products in society, and limiting of using petroleum-based chemical products in the market.

## Acknowledgements

The authors are indebted to Professor Kong Rae Lee for his final touch and suggestions to make this paper become eligible for publication. We are grateful to Dr Yasushi Ueki for his comments to improve the draft of this paper. We also thank ERIA that allowed us to utilise the selected data of ERIA's survey report on *Entrepreneurship and Local Technological Capacity in the East Asian Natural Resource-Based Production Network*, ERIA/IDE-JETRO Study Project in Indonesia, 2013. The views expressed and argument used in this paper are those of the authors and do not necessarily reflect the views of the institutions stated in this paper.

## References

Bainbridge, W.S., and Roco, M.C. (2006), 'Progressive convergence', in *Managing Nano-Bio-Info-Cognoinnovations, Nonverging Technologies in Society*, eds. W.S. Bainbridge and M.C. Roco, Dordrecht: Springer, pp. 2–3.

Curran, C.S. (2013), *The Anticipation of Converging Industries: A Concept Applied to Nutraceuticals and Functional Foods*, London: Springer-Verlag, pp. 14, 29–30, 47.

Curran, C.S., Bröring, S., and Leker, J. (2010), 'Anticipating converging industries using publicly available data', *Technological Forecasting & Social Change*, 77, 387–390.

Deschamps, N. (2013), *The Market for Bio-Based Chemicals*, presentation, http://www.albertacanada.com/files/albertacanada/AIS_BRC-Presentation-May-23–2013.pdf (accessed March 23, 2014).

Hacklin, F. (2008), *Management of Convergence in Innovation*, Heidelberg: Physica-Verlag, pp. 200, 390.

Jang, Y. (2009), 'Technological convergence through industrial research collaboration: a comparative analysis between the U.S. and Korea', *Asian Journal of Technology Innovation*, 17(1), 101–120.

Lee, Y.-G., Ji-Hoon, L., Yong-Il, S., and Hi-Jung, K. (2008), 'Technological convergence and open innovation in the mobile telecommunication industry', *Asian Journal of Technology Innovation*, 16(1), 45–62.

Malerba, F. (ed.) (2004), *Sectoral System of Innovation: Concepts, Issues and Analysis of Six Major Sectors Europe*, Cambridge: Cambridge University Press, pp. 9–35.

Malerba, F., and Sunil, M. (eds.) (2009), *Sectoral System of Innovation and Production in Developing Countries: Actors, Structure and Evolution*, Cheltenham: Edward Elgar, pp. 3–22.

Michelson, E.S. (2006), 'Measuring the merger: examining the onset of converging technologies', in *Managing Nano-Bio-Info-Cognoinnovations, Converging Technologies in Society*, eds. W.S. Bainbridge and M.C. Roco, Dordrecht: Springer, pp. 47–48.

National Research Council (NRC) (2000), *Biobased Industrial Products: Priorities for Research and Commercialization*, Washington, DC: National Academy Press, pp. 211–212.

Philp, J.C., Ritchie, R.J., and Allan, J.E.M. (2013), 'Biobased chemicals: the convergence of green chemistry with industrial biotechnology', *Trends in Biotechnology*, 31(4), 220–221.

Roco, M.C. (2006), 'The emergence and policy implications of converging new technologies', in *Managing Nano-Bio-Info-Cognoinnovations, Converging Technologies in Society*, eds. W.S. Bainbridge and M.C. Roco, Dordrecht: Springer, pp. 9–10.

## Appendix. Technological capacity of Indonesian chemical firms (2013)

| No. | Indicator | Frequency (%) | | |
|---|---|---|---|---|
| | | Plastic | Chemical non-plastic | Chemical total |
| | | $N = 23$ | $N = 6$ | $N = 29$ |
| 1 | *Capital investment* | | | |
| | Modified existing capital goods in the last two years | 39.1 | 50.0 | 41.38 |
| | Introduced new capital goods in the last two years | 21.7 | 0.0 | 17.24 |
| | Increased degree of automation in the production process | 47.8 | 50.0 | 48.28 |
| | Equipment or system for monitoring production lines | 13.0 | 16.7 | 13.79 |
| | R&D facilities | 8.7 | 16.7 | 10.34 |
| | Testing facilities/laboratories | 13.0 | 16.7 | 13.79 |
| | Logistics | 30.4 | 0.0 | 24.14 |
| 2 | *R&D activities* | | | |
| | Engage in R&D activities | 56.5 | 100.0 | 65.5 |
| | R&D expenditure/sales, less than 0.5% | 53.8 ($n = 13$) | 16.7 ($n = 6$) | 42.1 ($n = 19$) |
| | R&D expenditure/sales, 0.5–1% | 23.1 ($n = 13$) | 33.3 ($n = 6$) | 26.3 ($n = 19$) |
| | R&D expenditure/sales, more than 1% | 23.1 ($n = 13$) | 50.0 ($n = 6$) | 31.6 ($n = 19$) |
| 3 | *IPR* | | | |
| | Hold an IPR | 30.4 | 66.7 | 37.9 |
| | Obtain an IPR in the last two years | 13.0 | 16.7 | 13.8 |
| 4 | *Product development* | | | |
| | Engage in product development in the last two years | 100.0 | 100.0 | 100.0 |
| | Undertaken by the firm itself | 73.9 | 66.7 | 72.4 |
| | Undertaken by theparent firm | 26.1 | 33.3 | 27.6 |
| 5 | *New product development* | | | |
| | Introduce a new product in the last two years | 65.2 | 50.0 | 62.1 |
| | New product for new markets | 60.0 ($n = 15$) | 100.0 ($n = 3$) | 66.7 ($n = 18$) |
| | New product for existing markets | 86.7 ($n = 15$) | 100.0 ($n = 3$) | 88.9 ($n = 18$) |
| | New product based on new technologies | 40.0 ($n = 15$) | 100.0 ($n = 3$) | 50.0 ($n = 18$) |
| | New product based on existing technologies | 46.7 ($n = 15$) | 100.0 ($n = 3$) | 55.6 ($n = 18$) |
| 6 | *Design new product interact with* | | | |
| | The customer | 30.4 | 0.0 | 24.1 |
| | The supplier | 8.7 | 0.0 | 6.9 |
| 7 | *Most important source of innovation* | | | |
| | Final consumer | 52.2 | 50.0 | 51.7 |
| | Competitor | 34.8 | 33.3 | 34.5 |
| | Buyer or trading company | 13.0 | 16.7 | 13.8 |
| | Consultant | 4.3 | 16.7 | 6.9 |
| | Local customer (100% local capital) | 30.4 | 33.3 | 31.0 |
| | Local supplier | 21.7 | 16.7 | 20.7 |
| | Domestic MNC/joint venture (JV) customer | 30.4 | 16.7 | 27.6 |
| | Domestic MNC/JV supplier | 13.0 | 16.7 | 13.8 |
| | MNC/JV customer located in a foreign country | 30.4 | 16.7 | 27.6 |
| | MNC/JV supplier located in a foreign country | 26.1 | 16.7 | 24.1 |
| | Public organisation | 17.4 | 16.7 | 17.2 |
| | Local business organisation | 17.4 | 16.7 | 17.2 |
| | University or public research institute | 4.3 | 16.7 | 6.9 |

Source: The figures above are based on the reprocessing of selected data from the research project '*Entrepreneurship and Local Technological Capacity in the East Asian Natural Resource-Based Production Network*', ERIA/IDE-JETRO Study Project, 2013.

# Convergence of service and technical skills: the case of ERP implementation in Israel

Asaf Darr

*Department of Sociology and Anthropology, University of Haifa, Haifa, Israel*

This empirical study points to the rise of the techno-service sector of the economy, and questions the analytical distinction between technical and social skills, a distinction which underpins governments' and economic institutions' attempts to measure and quantify types of skills and the complexity of different lines of work. By focusing on Enterprise Resource Planning (ERP) implementers, this study points to the growing interdependency and to the convergence of service and technical skills in the techno-service sector. The paper also provides empirical indication of the growing penetration of professional work into the heart of the industrial enterprise.

## 1. Introduction

Creating a so-called 'knowledge economy' has become a major goal of many advanced industrial societies such as the USA and the UK (see Reich, 1993; Blair, 1998). In some of these societies this sector of the economy seems to be growing rapidly. Reich (1993), a former US secretary of labour, who sees the American knowledge sector as a key to sustained growth, claims that the number of symbolic analysts in the US workforce rose from around 8% in the 1950s to around 20% by 1990. Analysing occupational trend data between 1950 and 1990, Castells and Aoyama (1994, p. 23) confirm that white-collar work has expanded in the advanced economies, mostly among managers, professionals and technicians, whose occupations they term 'informational'. Barley and Orr (1997, p. 3) further claim that 'The number of professional and technical jobs in the United States has grown by more than 300 percent since 1950' and that 'no other occupational sector has experienced nearly as great a growth rate'. More recently, Hecker (2005, p. 71) in his analysis of the Bureau of Labor Statistics (BLS) occupational employment projections for 2004–2014 states: ' ... professional occupations are projected to grow the fastest, chiefly because they are concentrated in some fast-growing sectors, such as health care and social assistance as well as *professional, scientific, and technical services* ... ' (italics added). While the growth and growing importance of the knowledge sector is well documented, other changes are taking place in contemporary world of work, the single most important one in the rapid growth in the service sector.

The growth on the knowledge sector on the one hand and the service sector on the other seem to be opposing trends, each shaping the current landscape of the workforce in distinct ways. On the one hand, ample data point to the rapid growth of the service sector, typically described as producing low-skilled and low-paid jobs. On the other hand, the literature is replete with studies heralding the birth and rapid growth of the knowledge sector, composed of highly skilled individuals who hold college degrees and enjoy wide occupational autonomy and a high salary. These opposing trends seem to contribute to the polarisation of the US labour force, that is, to the dwindling of semi-skilled jobs and of the middle class as a whole (for a review and critique of the polarisation thesis, see Autor, Katz, and Kearney 2006).

While both trends seem to be well grounded in empirical research, sociologists as well as economists tend to treat them as vectors pointing in opposing directions. But they fail to identify what scholars who study innovation management long argue: that a growing interdependency of service and knowledge work exists within some areas of service work, particularly the Knowledge-Intensive Business Services (KIBS) (see Lee 2004; Miles 2005; Miozzo and Grimshaw 2005). Economists and sociologists of work fail to identify the growing interdependency of service and knowledge work since they use ready-made occupational classifications and do not attempt to critically examine the changing nature of work within occupations. I claim that the robust interface between service and techno-scientific work (which here I equate with knowledge work) creates new skill compositions and blurs traditional divisions of labour. The growing interdependency of service and technical skill is rooted in a shift in advanced economies from sales of a product to sales of a process in high-tech markets, and carries important implications for educational programmes.

In emergent technology markets, for example, the substitution of a process for a product is grounded in the lack of a clear agreement between sellers and buyers about the future use of products (see Darr 2006). For example, in the software industry sellers often sell a concept, a goal which must be negotiated and customised through a lengthy process. Likewise, software implementation (e.g. ERP systems) and various consulting jobs involve exchange of a process rather than a traditional product. More generally and in other industries, a few scholars (see Pine 1993) have claimed that 'mass customisation' is substituting mass production as the main production paradigm. Computers and computer-integrated machinery, according to these writers, allow service and manufacturing firms to shift from mass production to mass batch production or mass customisation. This flexibility in production also accelerates the shift from selling a product to selling a customisation process. Selling a process causes technical experts to stream to front-line positions where they interact directly with the clients' representatives.

Knowledge has always been utilised in work practice. My position is that what is new about knowledge workers is the increasing integration of service and technical skills. The polarisation thesis is based on income distribution of aggregate occupational data, which do not provide indicators of the different ways in which work is carried out within existing occupational titles. While I do not dispute polarisation, I am opposed to the assumption that polarisation occurs along the traditional service-knowledge dichotomy. Instead, I maintain in line with KIBS research (Lee 2004; Miles 2005) that a closer look at the changing nature of work will highlight the need to rearrange our aggregate occupational data so as to include special categories for a hybrid form: the techno-service sector.

The growth of techno-service jobs has already made an impact on the US labour force. For example, Hecker (2005, p. 71), in his analysis of the BLS occupational employment projections for 2004–2014, points out that network systems and data communications analysts, computer software engineers: application, and computer software engineer: system software are 3 out of the 10 fastest-growing occupations in the US labour force. These three occupations, I claim, combine sophisticated knowledge and skill with strong service elements. Others such as dental hygienists and medical assistants can also be seen as members of the techno-service sector. The growth of a techno-service sector poses a substantial challenge to our educational institutions, which tend to view knowledge workers as the ideal type of industrial research and development (R&D) engineers or scientists. I suggest that simply offering students more of the same (e.g. enhancing science and maths classes in K12 and undergraduate programmes) will not create a better fit between many of the graduates and future labour market demands. Instead, new types of skills such as interactive social skills and the ability to create a technological dialogue with the clients' technical experts (Pacey 1992) should be integrated into engineering and scientific training.

Figure 1 represents my attempt to move away from portraying service and knowledge work as opposite trends or opposite ends on the status and income ladder and instead to create a typology based on the degree to which knowledge and service elements are intertwined in a specific line of work.

As Figure 1 indicates, traditional manufacturing jobs are low on both service and knowledge elements. Burger flippers and waiters are high on service but low on knowledge elements. Scientists and R&D engineers, who are typically buffered from market exigencies, are low on service elements but high on knowledge elements. However, I believe that at the core of the so-called 'knowledge economy' is the rise of a group of occupations that had been neglected by the sociological research literature. These occupations, which according to my claim compose the techno-service sector, combine service and techno-scientific elements in their daily work. These occupations include, but are not limited to, software application engineers; technical support; engineering and scientific consultants; software implementers; some qualified call centre workers and detailers. Two ideal types of these occupations are sales engineering and software implementers.

A small but growing body of literature in sociology of work practice has recently suggested that sales departments in industries leading the current transformation of the socio-economic infrastructure are undergoing a technisation process (Darr 2002). For example, in US leading-edge industries the percentage of engineers holding formal academic degrees in the sales force almost doubled during the 1980s, from 12% to 22% (US Department of Labor 1985, 1988, 1991). The BLS figures project a growth of 14% in the number of sales engineers in the years 2004–2014. Similarly, sales support in the software industry increasingly involves technical

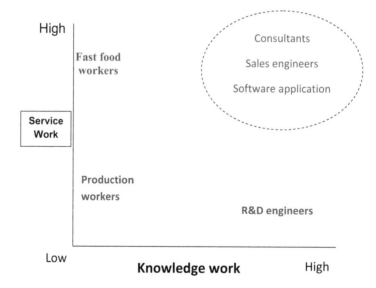

**Figure 1:** Occupational typology based on service and knowledge elements.

experts (Pentland 1997). This is a clear, yet limited, indication that knowledge and service work are intertwined. Increasingly, firms are oriented to their clients and must enhance their workers' social skills to provide quality service, in addition to exhibiting technical competence in producing high-quality goods. In this paper I focus on ERP implementers as a key example of an emerging cluster of occupations where social and technical skills are interdependent.

ERP implementers fall well within the core definition of knowledge work. This group comprises software engineers and programmers as well as 'content experts' such as former human resource (HR) managers or economists, who have a deep understanding of a specific area in which the ERP software is implemented such as the finance or the HR department. Yet, this paper will go beyond a description of the type of knowledge and skills these workers perform. It will also question the analytical distinction between knowledge and service work, which underpins most accepted classifications of work. Service and knowledge work are often perceived as standing at opposite ends of the occupational status ladder. In contrast to this perception, this paper will point to the growing interdependency of technical and service work, and more importantly, to the rise of a techno-service sector. The workers in this sector combine in their daily work, scientific, technical, and service knowledge, and the content of their work poses a serious challenge not only to existing classifications but also to training programmes in science and engineering, as well as in the service sector.

## 2. Research design and methods

This study is an exploratory one designed to capture the work process and types of knowledge employed in the process of ERP implementation. It is based on a snowball sampling technique with seven separate starting points. Given the sample size and sampling technique no generalisability of the results is claimed. Instead, the study is meant to expose the main dynamics and types of knowledge and skills being employed within the occupational community of ERP implementers. This research can help design a quantitative study which used well-grounded categories to depict techno-service work. At the heart of this study are data derived from 50 in-depth interviews with key players in the Israeli ERP market. Table 1 provides a breakdown of interviewees by their occupation.

The sample was created by a snowball technique, which began with leads provided by several different people working in implementing business software or members of client organisations. These people suggested other potential interviewees. When one snowball stopped rolling I began another. Since the snowball sampling started from different actors which were not previously

**Table 1:** Interviewees by occupation.

| Occupation | Number of interviewees |
| --- | --- |
| Project managers | 6 |
| Sales and marketing | 5 |
| Freelancers | 6 |
| Implementers working for implementing organisation | 9 |
| Representatives working for client organisation | 12 |
| Programmers | 3 |
| Training and education | 3 |
| Consultants | 2 |
| Entrepreneurs | 2 |
| QA | 1 |
| VC manager | 1 |

linked, I was able to avoid the danger associated with this research method of getting caught up within a single clique.

The study also included a newspaper archival research aimed at providing the history of the Israeli ERP market. Observations were conducted at a day long sales promotion carried out in a Tel-Aviv Hotel, where DAL (an alias name for a global company developing and selling ERP programmes) representatives presented the software and a line of satisfied clients to prospective buyers, all high ranking managers from very large corporations.

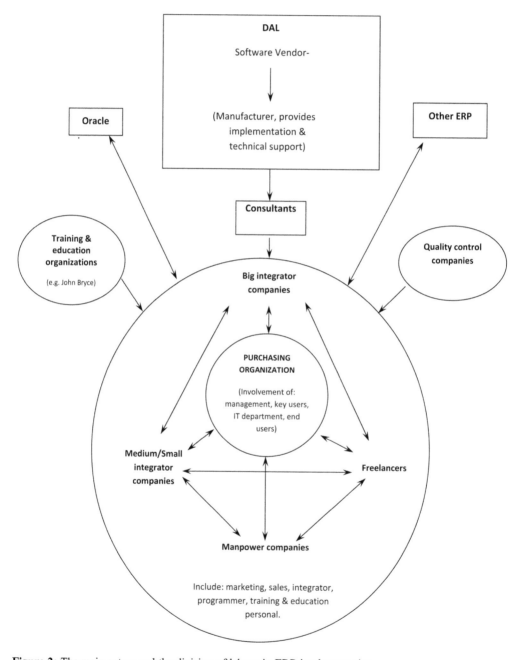

**Figure 2:** The main actors and the division of labour in ERP implementation.

The initial objective of this study was to identify the different players in the ERP market and to locate each of them within the broader and, as we shall see, the global division of labour. The market for IT services in Israel is estimated at $3.5 billion US dollars (Hatoni 2013), and there are no reliable figures of the portion of ERP implementation out of this figure. Figure 2 provides a graphic presentation of these issues.

## 3.   Main players and work process in the ERP implementation sector

DAL is a global company manufacturing ERP software. DAL is a giant company, with an annual income of about 4.6 billion US dollars, which represent 40% of the total revenues in this market (*The Marker*, Sep. 15, 2008, p. 34). The DAL ERP software creates an online organisation, with workflows, documents, forms, and authority structures all being boxed within the software, which is made up of a large number of modules. These are designed to cater to the needs of various organisational functions: finance, logistics, and HR management, among others. DAL claims that its software is standard yet very flexible, mainly due to its built in customised menus, thus requiring little if any adaptation to specific client's needs. Yet, as we shall see, implementing ERP software is lengthy and complex, and there is a flourishing sector of ERP implementers who thrive on software localisation.

Up to about 10 years ago DAL had only one vendor, GOL in Israel, which was authorised to sell the software licenses. DAL provides technical support for organisations that have purchased their software mainly through GOL but also directly via the Internet. In addition to being, up until recently, the only licensing company for DAL products, GOL provides ERP implementation services and acts as intermediary for DAL and the Israeli clients. Given its wide array of functions, the company employs marketing, implementation, programming, and training personnel.

While GOL until very recently held a monopoly over licensing, it has to compete today with global and local firms in the ERP implementation market. Other global implementers include global firms, with branches all over the world. A number of local Israeli firms also offer ERP implementation services. These small and local companies employ a range of consulting, implementation, and programming personnel. They typically do not win significant implementation contracts, but are instead sub-contracted by larger and often global consulting firms. The smaller local firms provide expert workers when there is a need, and constantly train their workforce both formally and by work experience. A few HR and head hunters also specialise in providing personnel with ERP implementation skills, both locally and globally. Unlike the small implementers, the HR companies do not engage in any technical work or sub-contracting.

## 4.   Large and often global implementation companies

The large global companies typically employ project managers and a small number of key programmers. Once they sign a contract with a client, they construct a project team led by their own employees, but composed largely of programmers and content experts who are sub-contracted from the smaller local firms. At times the global firms also hire local freelance workers who specialise in one or two software modules. I will elaborate on the unique sub-contracting system in this field when describing the ERP implementation division of labour.

## 5.   Small/medium implementation companies

*Consultants.* Usually with a computer system background, and who have formerly worked in large organisations, these are people who help client organisations during the implementation process.

*QA companies*. These small consulting organisations provide quality assurance for ERP software implementation. They are hired by client organisations and supervise the work of the implementers.

*Implementers*. These are people who specialise in one DAL module or more, usually working for an implementing organisation (unless they are freelancers). When their job in one project ends, they move on to another client organisation.

*DAL programmers*. These specialise in ABAP, the DAL programming language. They usually join a project after initial characterisation of the project has been completed.

*Training and education personal*. These are experts in documentation and in training others to work with DAL. They are usually the last to join a project. At present John Bryce is the biggest company providing such services in Israel. Implementation companies may have their own training and education departments.

*Client organisations*. These are the organisations interested in purchasing ERP software, as well as the services of an implementing organisation.

## 6.   Findings

### 6.1. The global division of labour and the composition of project teams

The implementation of ERP systems in Israeli organisations is nested within a global division of labour. The vast majority of client organisations in Israel contract with global implementation companies, which run national branches all over the world, while employing mainly project managers and a few top programmers in each branch. The project managers take an active role in contract negotiation with prospective clients and, after a contract has been signed, start to compose an implementation team. A top manager at the Israeli branch of 'ERP International', a leading global implementation company, described the kind of people employed by his branch:

> Our people at ERP Israel have the relevant education. They are accountants, economists, engineering management graduates. These are not typical IT people, but rather people who understand business [the term said in English – A.D.]. [We employ – A.D.] purchasers, operation people who can talk to someone on an equal footing. It is very important in managing the implementation process.

This excerpt points to a primary emic distinction, the separation of business and technical knowledge and skills. The global implementation firms employed only older more experienced people with a strong managerial background. After all, these employees will spend most of their time negotiating contract details with the clients' top managers. Following contract signing, the project managers try to put together an implementation team which will operate for a year or longer until ERP implementation in the client's plant is complete.

Given the high level of required expertise associated with ERP implementation, composing a project team is not an easy task. The team managers, who are typically employees of a global implementation firm, start to sub-contract with smaller and local firms employing ERP implementers and programmers. In addition, the project manager needs to hire freelance consultants, and, mainly in the early years of ERP implementation, global experts. A top manager working for a global ERP implementation company described the sub-contracting system as follows:

> No company has all the people it will need at all times … so if I need more people I start to look around for them. As a result, you go to someone [a different implementation company] who did not take part in the tender or someone who lost the tender to you and you sign a contract with them about their implementers.

One can wonder why such a sub-contracting system takes place. Why did the global firm employ mainly project managers and not their own implementers? This study can offer two possible answers. The first has to do with the cyclical nature of the ERP market. Transactions in this market are very large in monetary terms, but spread out unevenly along the year. Thus, the global firms, exploiting their ability to sign the most lucrative contracts, transfer the risk associated with long-term employment of experts in a highly volatile market to the smaller and local companies. This economic explanation is expressed in the following excerpt from an interview with an experienced implementer:

> This is a sector ... with seasons, it all depends on the number of projects we get. You can hire a whole team and fire them when you no longer need them. But I employ only a certain core of people. When necessary I take sub-contractors. A company like 'Local ERP' [a small local implementation company – A.D.] doesn't do projects, they sell heads. ... That is what they do and it is good business, they make a profit from people. I also sell people on rare occasions.

This excerpt exemplifies the central role of sub-contracting in the ERP sector, and how risk is forced down the business hierarchy. Also, note the use of the verb 'sell' when talking about the sub-contracting of experts in this field. It is almost as if it is the expertise which is sold rather than the people who move around the market.

The second explanation for the sub-contracting system is related to the contextual nature of much of the knowledge employed by the implementers. Each and every project requires people who know the specific way in which a client organisation conducts its work and structures their workflows. In addition, the implementers are required to intimately know the local business system in which the client organisation operates. Thus, it is more cost effective to choose the right people for each of the implementation teams by sub-contracting with them rather than offering year-long full employment to a very wide range of implementers, to cover all possible implementation projects. Given the combination of local yet highly specialised knowledge and skills required for good implementation work, putting together the right implementation team for a specific job, with all its diversity, is the single most important task of the project manager.

Interestingly, composing a project team is often done with the active agency of the clients. The failure rate of ERP exceeds 50%, and client organisations are well aware of the high risk associated with the implementation project. Partly as a result, some client organisations hire their own experts to guide them through the long and risky process of choosing the right ERP system, and to supervise the lengthy implementation process. Based on the professional advice of the experts they hire, it is not uncommon for client organisations to request that specific experts be hired by the global implementation firm to become part of the project team. For example, in the case of a leading university in Israel, the client presented the global implementation company with a list of local experts, which they wanted to include in the implementation team. A few of the experts required by the client had experience with previous ERP implementation in a different Israeli university. This is but one indication of how specialised skill and knowledge are within the ERP field, and how they are attached to specific people. Another example of the active role of clients in putting together an implementation team is from an interview with an experienced project manager:

> There is also horse trading. The teams which are offered by the implementation firms are screened very carefully by the clients. The client conducts detailed inquiries, holds interviews [with suggested project team members –A.D.]. They call previous clients, ask, a really careful screening. Clients also reject certain candidates. They ask: 'change this one, and, this one I'm ready to accept.' At the end the composition [of the project team – A.D.] presented to the client is meaningful, and the choice of the project manager is critical.

The elaborate screening mechanisms employed by the clients are surprising, but can be understood when both the high price of ERP implementation as well as the great impact of the software on central organisational processes are considered. Yet, this excerpt also demonstrates the existence of what Freidson (1970) calls 'imputed expertise', namely the ability of members of an occupational community (ERP implementers in this case) to ascribe varying levels of skills to various co-members.

ERP project teams are often global in terms of their human composition, and this was true particularly in the early days of ERP implementation in Israel. In the second half of the 1990s, integrator teams were composed of experts from all over the world. As one veteran implementer, who in time became a project manager, describes:

> Then, when it all [ERP] started it was a buzzword [said in English – A.D.]. No one knew how it was done. For example, when we did our first project in the Dead Sea, there were no people with experience so they weaved together in the project team an English-Irish expert [sic], and another English person with some experience, and a support person from South Africa, and a German to teach me. Everything was new in 1997. Today, ... we only bring in people according to a specific need, when we don't know a certain new module ... The core already exists, there is a lot of knowledge here [in Israel – A.D.], so we bring fewer people from outside.

Based on this excerpt and other interviews, it emerges that in the early years of ERP the implementation teams were global. The basic technical skills and knowledge, such as knowing the different menus and adjustments required for implementation work were located outside of Israel. But within a few years this has changed, and the teams have become more local. In fact, from the early twenty-first century, Israel has started to export ERP specialists for projects in Europe and the USA. One of the implementers interviewed, described his own career around the year 2000, with the fear of Bug 2000 looming large:

> I took part in the first DAL ERP implementation in Israel, and then I left Israel and started traveling around, since there were so few people in the world with the knowledge of DAL. It was worthwhile and good to sell your knowledge. I first went to Taiwan. From there I was sent to Manila in the Philippines, then to Singapore. I worked in Paris, then back to Israel and England, and them Finland.

This impressive global market where implementation experts frequently move is an indication of the important role of contextual elements in implementation work. The knowledge and skills of the menus and workflows which are required for a successful implementation of DAL ERP is transferred not only by reading formal software documentation, but rather through the shared practice between global experts and local novices. Shared engagement in work practice, as the literature tells us (see Barley and Bechky 1994), is particularly conducive to the transfer of contextual knowledge. It is interesting to note that even in the case of standard software which is very well documented, some elements of knowledge resist codification and require social engagement and shared practice in order to be transferred. While the terms formal and contextual knowledge provide initial tools to understand ERP work, we need to better understand the emic perceptions of skills and knowledge in ERP implementation. In the following section, I describe how project managers, programmers, and implementers classify the types of skills and knowledge utilised as part of ERP implementation.

### 6.2. Implementers view of knowledge and skills in ERP work

The separation between managerial and technical skills presented in the previous section does not capture the complexity of implementation work. In fact, when we focus only on the work practice of implementers, the most significant distinction employed by the implementers to make sense of their daily work is between three types of knowledge and skills.

The first type is technical knowledge and skill, which denotes here not actual programming, but an intimate knowledge of the different menus offered by the software and the different work-flows which are boxed in it. These computerised workflows are defined by DAL as 'best practice' in the various subject fields which the software covers.

The second type of knowledge and skills is called by my informants simply 'content', which comprises: (A) Extensive knowledge of and experience in a specific subject area such as account-ing or human resource management; (B) An intimate knowledge of and experience in the local Israeli business system; and (C) Work experience in the similar sector to the one of the client organisation, which provides a better understanding of the existing work practices and the inner politics in the client organisation.

The third type is interactive social skills, which, more generally, are most characteristic of the emerging techno-service sector. As the data presented below demonstrate, the interactive social skills required in ERP implementation work are divided by the implementers into three sub-sets: (A) The ability to extract technical information from the client through social engagement; (B) Persuasion skills and (C) The ability to construct professional trust with the client's key users. Below I demonstrate how this categorisation of knowledge and skills is reflected in the interviews with my informants.

One of my informants, a veteran implementer, who is now a top manager at a global implementation firm, described the set of required skills in implementation work, and how the skill composition in Israeli project teams has changed over the years:

> In the first wave [of DAL ERP implementation] which started in 1995–6, there were content people and they learned all the computer stuff. They hired accountants, engineers etc., and they trained us abroad, in a school near Brussels, Belgium. The course lasted about a month or a month and a half. Then we returned and worked in the field with people who came from abroad. In the second wave people came with a background of information systems and it was harder to train them.

This interview excerpt points to an emic separation between 'content' and 'computer stuff' in the work practice of implementers. Content denotes here a subject matter to which a specific software module belongs. For example, the HR module represents an attempt by DAL to standardise and then box knowledge and skills from the field of HR Management, and to present a large number of workflows as 'best practice'. 'Computer stuff' here denotes not programming, which is hardly performed within implementation teams, but instead an intimate knowledge of the large variety of menus and computerised workflows offered by the software. Note that in the excerpt the speaker describes two periods in the development of implementation teams. During the first phase, content experts were hired and trained abroad in working with the software. These were people with rich experience in the various content fields and probably with strong social skills developed through their work experience. After their training in Belgium, they engaged in shared practice with experts outside of Israel. In the second stage of the development of project teams, formal education in information technologies took precedence over content, and the speaker sees that as a problem. The reason is that both the subject matter and the social skills required for a successful implementation are much harder to acquire when compared to IT education. The head of a medium-sized and local implementation company expressed a similar view when commenting on the composition of project teams:

> The people I would hire, the ones I would like to have as implementers, are not those with a computer background, but with a background of processes. I prefer an accountant with a leaning towards com-puters than the other way around.

An experienced ERP implementer, who came from an information systems background, described the two types of knowledge and skills she had to master in order to become what she perceived as a good implementer: 'At the beginning, I was a type of "top user", I knew less about the way the organization itself worked, and more about the software. But slowly I learned how things work within the [client – A.D.] organization.' Learning to understand how specific client organisations constructed their workflows proved vital to the success of the implementation process as a whole. The ability to understand how the client works depends on the application of interactive social skills. The head of the implementation department in a small local company describes the type of a person he would like to hire as an implementer by saying 'I want someone who knows how to extract the information. This is a quality that some people come with, but it can also be taught.'

While ERP implementers were not required to know how to write code, they were required to master both the subject matter and the different menus representing 'best practice' which were offered by the software. This is reflected in the following quote from an interview with an experienced implementer:

> With regular systems [the previous generations of organizational software – A.D.], one needs to read a normal workflow, and capture it within the computer system. This is done by programmers, system analysts etc. . . . ERP is totally different. It is like medicine, you have a basket of solutions designed by the software producer, and it applies to a collection of workflows which were defined as best practice. There are 100 types of purchasing processes, for example, designed with some built in flexibility. The implementer needs to understand the problem of the client . . . and to choose out of the collections of workflows something which will fit the client. The type of people needed for this task . . . are people who know more than computing, who know the system's capabilities and how to tailor a solution to a specific problem. You need knowledge and experience in workflows.

This excerpt is more focussed on the work of implementers, and the speaker once again makes a distinction between computing (relating here to in-depth knowledge of the different menus and not to active programming and practical experience in the relevant field, such as accounting or HR). But, in addition the speaker relates to the implementers need to ' . . . tailor a solution to a specific problem'. Here, the use of medicine as a reference point is powerful since it cuts right to the heart of the problem facing ERP implementers. Implementers perform an act of diagnosis of the client organisation, and, like a physician, in order to diagnose they need to extract vital information from the clients' employees. This knowledge, just as in the case of medicine, is highly contextual and local in nature. The real challenge facing the implementer is to understand the 'problem', which in reality is the previous workflow in the client organisation, in order to customise the DAL ERP menus to fit the specific needs of the client. This aspect of implementation work can be described as translation: understanding the meaning of local and often chaotic realities of work in the client organisation, and transforming them into more structured workflows which could then be re-structured according to an existing and boxed workflow within the software. As examples studies within Science and Technology Studies teach us (Law and Hassard 1999), translation involves the application of power and the balancing of social interests. The implementers employ their brokering position between the client and the software and while translating actual work realities into software capabilities, actually convinced the key users of the software's superiority. Interestingly, ERP implementers talk about the DAL language and logic and their need to convince the key users to adopt this language and logic.

To perform their important role as translators, the implementers had to master a set of service and social skills which allowed them to extract the vital knowledge and knowhow from key users in the client organisation. Importantly, the aim of extracting local information about workflows and administrative logic of the client organisation is not to adjust the software to the client's needs but instead to adjust the client to the capabilities of the organisational software.

An important function of the implementers, I claim, is to perform what I will call 'reverse customisation'. Customisation, by definition, is the adaptation of a product to the specific needs of a client. Here, the emphasis in on the producers' willingness to re-design their product according the client specifications. When the producers and implementers of the DAL ERP system maintain that their software is adaptive and highly flexible, they mean within the readymade menus and workflows defined as 'best practice'. In reality they hardly modify any of the menus or workflows boxed within the software. The efforts to convince the potential buyers that DAL ERP encapsulates the most up-to-date work procedures within a wide range of subject areas begin in special promotional events which take place in hotel lobbies even before contract negotiations. But most of the reverse customisation is built into the frequent social interaction between the implementer of a specific module and the key user appointed by the client organisation. Extraction of vital information from the key user and the act of persuasion of software superiority are intertwined.

Reverse customisation requires the implementers to do more than simply learn the ways of the client organisation. A major role they play is in convincing the key users to think within the envelope, broad and flexible as it may be, offered by the ERP software. This means that as part of the social and service skill they need to master the art of persuasion. To be convincing the implementers need to present themselves to the clients' key users as experts in their field, to demonstrate an excellent understanding of the existing workflow in the client organisations, to have a very good command of the software, and to be able to persuade the key users that the software solution is indeed superior to the previous way of conducting business. All these skills converge in practice. For example, the presentation of the software options and the effort to convince the client are done simultaneously as part of the interaction between the implementer and the key user. Here is a short quote from an interview with a key user in the HR department of an Israeli university, who was convinced to adapt the DAL way of thinking:

> During the first stage I'm supposed, in HR for example, to know all the work in our [the client organization] department and who one should speak with [when encountering a problem]. I need to know what other departments are connected to the HR department, what applications they might have, and I need to provide this information to the implementation company. I need to provide them with the broad picture. When we start working with the software, I need to understand how it works and to start thinking more in the 'DAL way'.

This interview excerpt provides an indication that in reality the users are required to adapt themselves to the software capabilities rather than the other way around.

To sum up, in this paper I identify three important types of skills which the implementers see as central to their work: technical, content, and interactive social skills. Implementers and their managers have a developed vocabulary for the required technical skills, and also detailed descriptions of how these skills are learned and transferred. This is also true for the so-called 'content' skills, namely experience in a specific subject matter acquired prior to their employment as implementers through professional training and practice in field such as engineering and accounting. Yet all those involved in ERP implementation find it much harder to discuss the interactional social skills which they employ while extracting vital information from key users, convincing them of the superiority of their product, and presenting themselves as experts in their field. Some of the informants describe these skills as qualities that a person either has or does not have. Others said that these interactive skills could be learned, but failed to specify how. The difficulty in discussing the required interactional skills is also related to the traditional cultural separation between knowledge and service work which I highlighted at the beginning of this paper. In the daily work practice of the ERP implementers, service and the technical elements are combined as part of social interactions, and together they comprise a distinct set of skills different from the sum of their parts.

## 7. Discussion and conclusions

The growing digitalisation of production has created the flow of technical experts from the R&D labs and into the service and sales functions, where they customise innovative products according to clients' needs (Darr 2006). In the case of ERP, we see the central role of expert knowledge in the implementation teams, as 'content' experts engage in 'reverse customisation'. As the technical complexity of sales and service increases, I argue, so does the need of so-called 'knowledge workers' to depend on interactive social skills. The growing convergence of service and technical skills is rooted in a shift in advanced economies from sales of a product to sales of a process, and carries important implications for cultural categories, work organisation, and educational programmes. While the separation between knowledge and service work is fundamental to our society, in the daily work of ERP implementers this analytic separation is all but meaningless.

Governments and economic institutions have long tried to measure and quantify types of skills and the complexity of different lines of work. The analytical distinction between technical and social skills underpins some of these attempts. For example, much of the sociological research on the skill levels of different jobs, which is based on the American *Dictionary of Occupational Titles*, combines three main dimensions: complexity in dealing with things, with people, and with data, to create an overall measure of job complexity (Atttewell 1990, p. 426). Technical skills are associated mainly with the manipulation of things, while social skills are related mostly to the complexity of dealing with people. This basic separation is challenged by the rise of techno-service workers, and might point to a need to re-evaluate the way we classify and quantify our contemporary world of work.

What exactly does the growing convergence and the interdependency of knowledge (or technical) work and service (or sales) work mean? On one level, it means that the service elements and the technical elements of ERP work are not separated in temporal terms, but are instead performed simultaneously. The interactive social skills employed by ERP implementers include the development of what Pacey (1992, pp. 146–147) calls a 'technological dialogue' with the key users. The creation of such dialogue requires building rapport and professional trust, as well as the interactive exchange of technical, political, and social information. The ERP implementers also conduct technological interviews with the key users, in order to extract vital information from them. Here, knowledge and service work are intertwined in temporal terms.

The blurring of boundaries between knowledge and service in the techno-service sector is, in a deeper sense, an indication of the growing penetration of professional work into the heart of the industrial enterprise. The separation of knowledge and service work has historically been supported by work organisations, through the creation of separate departments and a clear division of labour between knowledge and service workers. Yet, this distinction between knowledge and service work has never existed within the professions. In medicine, law, and accountancy, this distinction carries little meaning, and professionals will find it very difficult to separate the knowledge and service aspects of their work.

As professionals enter sales and service positions, they carry with them the blending of these two types of skills, which is part and parcel of their long professional socialisation. Since organisations, unlike the professions, think with categories which better fit the logic of the industrial era, they find it hard to conceptualise the skills employed by techno-service workers, and to tailor effective training programmes for them.

One practical implication of this study is that the enhancement of the *interactive socio-technical skills* of the ERP implementers could greatly improve their chances of success. Formal training which effectively combines technical and service skills is neglected today. Good communication skills could improve knowledge and skill transfer within project teams, and between the teams and the key users. ERP implementers should learn how to manage a *technological interview*, specifically structured to extract vital technological information about the client's organisations. Formal training and informal training which require students to confront the growing interdependencies between social and technical skills will support an emphasis on value-added processes and will improve the competitiveness of enterprises in the emerging techno-service sector.

## Acknowledgments

I would like to thank my research assistants Liora Shakked and Sharon Kolski-Rosenthal.

## Funding

The study has been supported by the Israel Science Foundation.

## References

Atttewell, P. (1990), 'What is skill?', *Work and Occupations*, 17, 422–448.
Autor, D.H., Katz, L.F., and Kearney, M.S. (2006), 'The polarization of the U.S. Labor Market', NBER Working Paper.
Barley, S.R., and Bechky, B.A. (1994), 'In the backrooms of science: the work of technicians in science labs', *Work and Occupations*, 21, 85–126.
Barley, S.R., and Orr, J. (1997), 'Introduction: the neglected workforce', in *Between Craft and Science: Technical Work in U.S. Settings*, eds. S.R. Barley and J. Orr, Ithaca, NY and London: Cornell University Press, pp. 1–19.
Blair, T. (1998), *The Third Way*, London: Fabian Society.
Castells, M., and Aoyama, Y. (1994), 'Paths towards the informational society: employment structure in G-7 countries', *International Labor Review*, 133(1), 5–33.
Darr, A. (2002), 'The technicization of sales work: an ethnographic study of the US electronics industry', *Work, Employment and Society*, 16(1), 47–65.
Darr, A., (2006), *Selling Technology: The Changing Shape of Sales in an Information Economy*, Ithaca, NY: Cornell University Press.
Freidson, E. (1970), *Profession of Medicine: A Study of the Sociology of Applied Knowledge*, Chicago and London: The University of Chicago Press.
Hatoni, Y. (2013), 'The Israeli IT market is in decline', *PC Computers and People*, March 19.
Hecker, D.E. (2005), 'Occupational employment projections to 2014', *Monthly Labor Review*, 70–101.
Law, J., and Hassard, J. (1999), *Actor Network Theory and After*, Oxford: Balckwell.
Lee, K.-R. (2004), 'Utilization of knowledge intensive services for the innovation manufacturers in Korea', *Asian Journal of Technology Innovation*, 12(2), 209–225.
Miles, I. (2005), 'Knowledge intensive business services', *Foresight*, 7(6), 39–63.
Miozzo, M., and Grimshaw, D. (2005). 'Modularity and innovation in knowledge-intensive business services: IT outsourcing in Germany and the UK', *Research Policy*, 34, 1419–1439.
Pacey, A. (1992), *The Maze of Ingenuity: Ideas and Idealism in the Development of Technology*, Cambridge, MA: MIT Press.
Pentland, B. (1997), 'Bleeding edge epistemology: practical problem solving in software support hot lines', in *Between Craft and Science: Technical Work in U.S. Settings*, eds. S. Barley and J. Orr, Ithaca and London: Cornell University Press, pp. 113–128.
Pine, J. (1993), 'Mass customizing products and services', *Planning Review*, 21(4), 6–55.
Reich, R. (1993), *The Work of Nations*, London: Simon & Schuster.
U.S. Department of Labor, Bureau of Labor Statistics (1985), *Occupational Employment in Manufacturing Industries*, Washington, DC: U.S. Government Printing Office.
U.S. Department of Labor, Bureau of Labor Statistics (1988), *Occupational Employment in Manufacturing Industries*, Washington, DC: U.S. Government Printing Office.
U.S. Department of Labor, Bureau of Labor Statistics (1991), *Occupational Employment in Manufacturing Industries*, Washington, DC: U.S. Government Printing Office.

# A semantic network analysis of technological innovation in dentistry: a case of CAD/CAM

Jang Hyun Kim[a] and Jinsuk Lee[b]

[a]Department of Interaction Science, Sungkyunkwan University, Jongno-Gu, Seoul, South Korea
[b]Proths-line Dental Institute, Suseong-gu, Daegu, South Korea

Diffusion of innovations in dentistry has rarely been studied. This study tracked the usage of computer-aided design/computer-aided manufacturing or machining (CAD/CAM) in general public's search query patterns and academic journal articles to find the terminology's diffusion in society and dentistry. Data were retrieved from Google Trends and Web of Science database, and the authors reorganised the search results and examined structural pattern of them. Results show that CAD/CAM technology is influenced by and interacting with relevant technologies and social arrangements. The emergence of CAD/CAM in dentistry was delayed than that of general public's perception, but the terminology established itself as a fundamental condition and simultaneously an outcome of dental materials development, medical/dental science, clinical techniques, and social trends.

## 1. Introduction

Studies have reported that technology is permeating into society or a part of it, through consistent or (a) typical diffusion processes. Such a process has been called, 'diffusion of innovations', and has been studied since the time of Everett Rogers (e.g. Rogers 1995). This study uses a case of computer-aided design/computer-aided manufacturing or machining (CAD/CAM) technology in dentistry to examine the changing perception of the technology among scholars in dentistry for several reasons. One, technology adoption in dentistry has been studied rarely. This problem has hindered proper growth of technological understanding and enhancement of dental (clinical) processes. Two, CAD/CAM has been popular in society since the 1980s, but in dentistry, the diffusion has not been tracked and recorded properly. Three, CAD/CAM may stand for a core technology for clinical innovation for dentistry as the prosthetic process requires automation of diagnosis, clinical planning, and clinical procedures. However, there are scarce studies dealing with such an aspect.

Innovation processes can occur in production, process, consumer's choice, and organisational aspects (Lundvall 1995). Innovation is considered as a continual process of learning, searching, and exploring, which results in new products, techniques, organisational forms, and markets (Lundvall 1995). Innovation in dentistry such as implant in prosthetic dentistry has evolved with the help of new technology such as CAD/CAM for scanning teeth and oral structure, and milling prosthetic appliances. Overall, innovations in dentistry, especially in prosthodontics and dental materials, have emerged as a result of the interplay of computing technology, material development, and clinical accumulation of cases. First, CAD/CAM was introduced and explored as a breakthrough for dentistry in the 1960s with the emergence of computing technology. Second, introduction of new-type ceramics such as aluminium-based ceramics and zirconia-based ceramics provoked debates on which one is better in terms of durability, safety, and cost than others.

This study aims at tracking and understanding the perception of CAD/CAM in dentistry, which may serve as an exemplary case of technology diffusion in the field. Specifically, it examines scholarly works retrieved from Thomson Reuter's Web of Science database over time, as well as Googol Trends results.

The current study utilises systematic data analysis and semantic network analysis to achieve the purpose of this study. The former is used to describe (1) general tendency of CAD/CAM use and (2) academic approaches to CAD/CAM in dental science. The latter is employed to retrieve semantic clusters of words by examining co-occurrence of and distances between words.

This study is organised as the following: Literature review section provides a systematic review of innovations related to CAD/CAM technology. Methodology section explicates the data and analytic method used in this study. Results section reports the findings from this study. Discussion section elaborates and interprets the findings and retrieves theoretical implications and clinical implications. Furthermore, it presents limitations of this study and suggestions for future research. Conclusion section offers a summary of this study and concludes it.

## 2. Literature review

### 2.1. *Development of CAD/CAM technology*

According to CADAZZ.com (2014), 'Sketchpad' was the first software for CAD, produced in the 1960s by an MIT graduate student Ivan Sutherland. The software is considered still innovative as it offered direct interface between a user and computer, using a light pen for drawing on the computer's display. In the 1960s, forerunners of CAD/CAM including Patrick J. Hanratty, Ivan Sutherland, and Charles Lang appeared and their works are still influential in the field. Before the emergence of CAD/CAM, in the 1950s, the US Air Force tested an air defense system called Semi-Automatic Ground Environment for compiling and rendering information from multiple radars. This system was also developed by MIT (Arabe 2001).

In the 1970s, large manufacturing companies such as Ford, General Motors, Mercedes-Benz, Nissan, and Toyota developed different kinds of CAD software for their process innovation (Arabe 2001). These pieces of software were used for designing automobile body structure and its components. The market size of CAD software grew from $25 million USD to 1 billion USD in 1979.

In 1982, Autodesk released the first version of AutoCAD which made a first and great success as commercial software (Arabe 2001). UNIX work station that introduced in the early 1980s opened a new horizon in CAD/CAM market for its easy maintenance, low cost, and advanced performance for distributed networks. At that time, 3D rendering was also becoming an industrial standard for CAD/CAM software market. Pro/Engineer by Parametric Technology Corp was the first CAD software that had both 3D rendering capability and UNIX-OS compatibility.

In the 1990s, personal computer (PC) users were able to use 3D rendering capability for cheap price. Microsoft Windows NT and Intel's Pentium processors were underlying conditions for such changes. Since late 1990s, CAD/CAM has not been just a solution for corporations. With the introduction of World Wide Web, people were able to collaborate easier than before, as the web enabled them to work together regardless of their geographical locations. CAD/CAM was accessible to anyone who had PCs (Arabe 2001; CADAZZ.com 2014).

### 2.2. *CAD/CAM as an innovation and its major actors*

CAD/CAM in this paper is considered as an innovation, as it has been one of major technological changes in dentistry. Dental medicine industry is a complex and dynamic system with many vertical and horizontal relationships among many actors such as dentists, patients, insurance companies, dental hygienists, pharmaceutical companies, IT (information technology) developers, and researchers in relevant fields (e.g. Sarkar and Costa 2008; Kim 2012; Kim and Park 2014). These actors are interacting with each other, and the process of innovation necessarily involves at least some of these actors. Innovation processes may take place within a company's boundaries (closed innovation) or outside (open innovation), according to Chesbrough (2003).

Leydesdorff and Meyer (2003) compared two systematic approaches to technological innovation and its diffusion processes. First, discipline-based knowledge generation, the so-called 'Mode 1', has been a mainstream approach to innovation. Such an approach has helped differentiate between labours and expertise, and has increased efficiency and depth of knowledge in each 'field'. Second, 'Mode 2' scholars have posited that the role of science, technology, and society has become less differentiated than before and disciplines are disappearing (Shinn 2003). Leydesdorff and Etzkowitz (1996) proposed the triple helix (TH) model. The model presents that three helices, university–government–industry (UGI), 'communicate with each other and can occasionally and partially, take on each other's role if needed (Kim, 2012, p. 154)'. The TH model has helped to find why researchers and universities are trying to assimilate the behavioural patterns of corporations. In the TH structure, globalisation is another thing to consider. Park and Leydesdorff (2010), interestingly, found that Korean government's policy of promoting international publications discouraged domestic UGI cooperation.

Arora, Youtie, Shapira, Gao, and Ma (2013) reported that (web) content analysis is a valid strategy of evaluating the diffusion of emerging technology. Through web analysis, they found three groups of graphene enterprises, respectively, focusing on product development, materials development, and integration into extant product portfolios. They compared companies in China, the USA, and the UK and found that country-level factors are important in understanding the emerging technology (graphene) and diverging commercial approaches to its market (Arora et al. 2013). The current study collected research abstracts globally in order to trace the research trends of the world, not a single country.

In this context, Lee (2014) found that the nationalities and affiliations of innovation research authors are rapidly being diversified and globalised. Research articles in innovation studies increasingly adopt sophisticated research method. In addition, the sample size of these studies in the field is getting larger, and their research coverage is becoming longitudinal, not short-term.

Kang, Gwon, Kim, and Cho (2013) tracked the determinants influencing commercialisation of new technology by firms including the firm size and the degree of Korean Government's support of it. The appropriability, innovative capabilities, and investment in external research and development (R&D) are found to exert positive impact on small and medium-sized enterprises (SME) commercialisation, that is, diffusion in market sector. The study confirmed the effect of government support on the formulation of commercialisation strategies.

Fujita (2012) reported the case of Vietnamese automobile industry in regard to innovation systems. The study provided detailed first-hand accounts of how local firms contributed to form and utilise the emerging sectoral system of innovation including production and logistics to acquire needed capabilities. The current study examined dental scholarship and general publics' approach to CAD/CAM technology.

In addition, Martinez-Torres (2014) researched how an open-source software project is associated with the organisation and development of the underlying virtual community. Although the present study is not directly linked to virtual community, examining the linkages among extant studies provides an insight to identify de facto community of scholars sharing similar perspectives on CAD/CAM in dentistry. Martinez-Torres (2014) analysed the online participation in virtual communities using (social) network analysis. The researcher reported that participation inequality, hierarchy, and the cohesion of the community constitute the core factors of the participation mechanism within communities.

### 2.3. *Convergence theory*

In the case of CAD/CAM technology, its diffusion may be interpreted as a result of convergence. Conversions theory (Rogers and Kincaid 1981; Rogers 1995; Kincaid 2002; Barnett 2008) posits that if an actor (agent) is located in a closed system, the continuing exchange of information is likely to lead to 'value set convergence' (Kim 2012, p. 154). Such value sharing may lead to facilitate the interchangeability of the role and function of participating actors. For example, rapidly growing CAD/CAM technology for dentists is an external stimulus to their profession. Dentists may examine the possible applications of the technology to their clinical practices; simultaneously, researchers in the field may try to find academic implications of the technology; and engineers may try to find a way to utilise CAD/CAM in developing hardware or software solutions for dentists. Throughout these possible endeavours, communication within each profession (e.g. dental medicine researchers) and inter-profession communication (e.g. communication among dentists, hygienists, and engineers) may lead to convergence of their thoughts and values on the meaning and applicability of CAD/CAM technology.

Citing convergence theory, Chung et al. (2014) examined international hyperlink networks and their content in terms of .com domain. The results indicated that the hyperlink network of websites with outward hyperlinks to .com websites confirmed the dominant centrality of the USA. In addition, incoming hyperlinks from .com websites revealed a core–periphery structure centring around the USA and other superpowers. Convergence theory deals with cultural assimilation and dissimilation due to communication flows and the study relied on the theory for interpreting the results.

According to Figueroa, Kincaid, and Hurley (2014), convergence theory was supported in their anti-multiple and concurrent sexual partnerships (MCP) campaign to lower the occurrences of human immunodeficiency virus infection. Through multivariate causal attribution analysis, they found that their campaign to promote convergence demonstrated a significant indirect impact on MCP through its prohibitive effect on attitudes that favour MCP, and its positive influence on knowledge and discussion of MCP risk with sex partner(s).

Kim (2012) and Kim and Park (2014) have attempted to apply convergence theory to understand innovation (technology) and its diffusion over time. Barnett (2008) argued that two additional propositions could be added to convergence theory:

> First, the stronger the link between individual nodes or organizations, the greater their reciprocal influence will become. They will converge faster on a common set of beliefs. Second, the greater the proportion of messages initiated by an individual node or organization, the more similar the [ultimate] equilibrium will be to that of the initial state of beliefs. (Barnett 2008 summarized in Kim 2012, p. 154)

Even if dentistry has differentiated specialties and interests, existing studies have not tracked the introduction and growth of CAD/CAM technology in the field. This lack is salient when the authors of this paper searched Google Trends and Web of Science database as reported in the following sections.

Given the above-mentioned theoretical discussions, the authors formed two research questions for this study:

RQ1. How have general publics and researchers in dentistry perceived CAD/CAM technology in terms of utility in dental medicine?

RQ1-1. In view of word usage frequency, what were the characteristics found in Google Trends results for 2005–2014 years?

RQ1-2. In view of word usage frequency and semantic networks, what were the characteristics found in Web of Science database for 1995–2014 years?

RQ2. What are theoretical and practical implications of the findings of this study?

## 3. Methodology

### 3.1. *Data and systematic data analysis*

Two data sets were constructed from two sources. One, the authors collected people's search query data from Google Trends (http://www.google.com/trends/) in December 2014. The two sessions of queries were conducted using two sets of words: (1) CAD/CAM and (2) CAD/CAM dental. Google search engine is used by general publics including scholars, but this study assumes that a majority of the users are non-scholar users, and Google Trends is a good way of tracking general publics or non-experts' information-seeking behaviour.

Two, the authors used 'CAD/CAM dental' to retrieve the studies using the words in their texts from Web of Science database. By the search, more than 560 studies were retrieved, and the details are included in the following section. Google Trends data covered from 2005 to 2014, whereas Web of Science data covered from 1995 to 2014. Web of Science data were split into four groups after the analysis of the whole data. The four groups are: 1995–1999; 2000–2004; 2005–2009; and 2010–2014. Compared to Google Trends data, Web of Science is dedicated to scholarly and research-related purpose. Therefore, the authors of this study assume that Web of Science database is a key indicator of scholarly interests in both demand and supply aspects of information. Specifically, demand side is possible information search of relevant studies; supply side is that most of the Web of Science results are academic research papers authored by scholars. Technically, the results were analysed in depth using Microsoft Excel 2007 software. The information examined for this study included authors and their affiliations, publication details (e.g. date, publisher and abstract), and other information provided by the database. The search results were compiled and reorganised to serve for the purpose of this study.

### 3.2. *Semantic network analysis*

This study used semantic network analysis for analysing research abstracts retrieved from the Web of Science database. Semantic network analysis is 'a structure of analysis based on shared meaning' through computational text analysis tools (Doerfel and Barnett 1999, p. 589). The analysis as a spatial model representing relationship of words in terms of co-occurrence, frequency, and distance can increase understanding of the text's meaning and its structure as well (Doerfel and Barnett 1999). For this process in the present study, computational content analysis software 'WORDij' (Danowski 2010) is used. WORDij is a word-pair-based software for semantic structure retrieval without any prior categories (Danowski 2010). With the software, any text sample in the UTF-8 format can be analysed with computer algorithms that search for any patterns that are found from the text. This is possible with co-occurrence models and neural networks supported by WORDij (Danowski 2010).

Instead of categorising messages, with a network perspective one can capture the relationships among words within the messages. Defining word-pair link strength as the number of times each word occurs closely in text with another, all possible word pairs have an occurrence distribution whose values range from zero on up. This ratio scale of measurement allows the use of sophisticated statistical tools from social network analysis toolkits. These enable the mapping of the structure of the word network (Danowski 2013).

WORDij also enables researchers to obtain graphical representation (multi-dimensional scaling, MDS) of word structure (meaning structure) of the sampled text. The coordinates retrieved from MDS for each group of text were compared.

MDS was used to represent comparative locations of words in a form of semantic network data matrix. UCINET 6 was used for matrix calculation, and NETDRAW (Borgatti 2002) was used for MDS presentation. Among many centrality indicators available, betweenness centrality was employed for the analysis (Freeman 1979; Richards 1995). Betweenness centrality is explained by Hanneman and Riddle (2005) as

> Using the computer, it is quite easy to locate the geodesic paths between all pairs of actors[words], and to count up how frequently each actor[word] falls in each of these pathways. If we add up, for each actor, the proportion of times that they are 'between' other actors for the sending of information in the … data, we get the measure of actor centrality. We can norm this measure by expressing it as a percentage of the maximum possible betweenness that an actor could have had. (Hanneman and Riddle 2005, [ … ] by the authors)

## 4. Research results

### 4.1. *Descriptive indicators of studies on CAD/CAM*

There were 563 studies retrieved when the authors typed 'CAD/CAM' and 'dental' as a query in Web of Science database. The database covered January 1995–November 2014. As Figure 1 indicates, the number of studies which included the words searched has increased rapidly. In particular, since 2011, the increase showed a big leap from 50 to 99 in just two years.

The aggregated number of citations of the papers which included 'CAD/CAM' and 'dental' has shown exponential growth as Figure 2 shows. Such trend is a typical case of continual and strong growth in technology diffusion. To be brief, CAD/CAM technology in dentistry has shown a salient growth.

However, according to the Google Trends results, the word 'CAD/CAM' itself is not new and losing ground in general search query, while 'CAD/CAM dental' is not variant over time, as Figure 3(a) indicates. Figure 3(b) has background lines, and each line denotes 20 compared to the highest frequency in January 2004–December 2014. For instance, in October 2007, 'CAD/CAM dental' showed the highest search query frequency and its score is assigned 100. All other months are assigned comparative ratio (0–100) compared to the number of October 2007.

Location of searching in Figure 3(c) saliently demonstrates that dental usage of the word CAD/CAM is US-centric, compared to the distribution of CAD/CAM search locations. It supports the trend that USA is dominating the research of CAD/CAM in the area of dentistry.

By reorganising the Web of Science database results, the authors compiled 30 most cited papers (Table 1). Twelve out of 30 were from *Dental Materials* journal. There were two *Dental Materials Journal* articles, but these should not be confused with the articles from the journal *Dental Materials*. Among the 30, three papers are review papers, while the others are

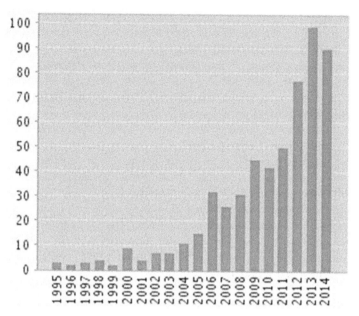

**Figure 1:** The number of papers dealing with CAD/CAM in dentistry (1995–2014).
Source: Thomson Reuters Web of Science database. Retrieved December 18, 2014.

all research articles. Interestingly 12 out of 30 papers were published in 2007–2009, which is congruent with the 'spike' of search queries found in Figure 3(b). The most cited article was written by Denry and Kelly. The paper is entitled, 'State of the art of zirconia for dental applications', and was published in 2008. The second and fourth papers were review papers. The former is entitled, 'Review of the clinical survival of direct and indirect restorations in posterior teeth of the

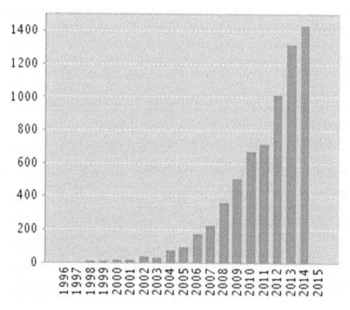

**Figure 2:** The number of citations of the papers dealing with CAD/CAM in dentistry (1995–2014).
Source: Thomson Reuters Web of Science database. Retrieved December 18, 2014.

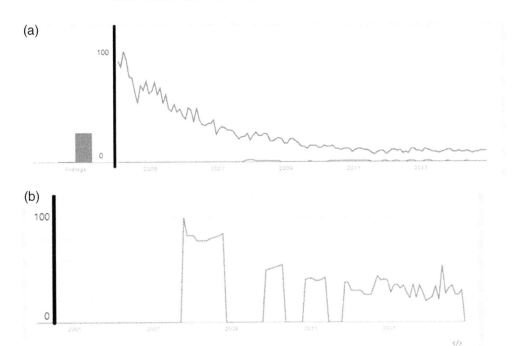

(c)

| Region | cad/cam dental | cad/cam |
|---|---|---|
| United States | 100 | 13 |
| Brazil | 0 | 9 |
| Canada | 0 | 12 |
| China | 0 | 20 |
| Germany | 0 | 20 |
| Spain | 0 | 10 |
| United Kingdom | 0 | 32 |
| India | 0 | 100 |
| Italy | 0 | 10 |
| Japan | 0 | 8 |
| Mexico | 0 | 16 |
| Netherlands | 0 | 14 |
| Poland | 0 | 23 |
| Turkey | 0 | 10 |
| Vietnam | 0 | 33 |

**Figure 3:** Comparative query frequency analysis retrieved from Google Trends. (a) Contrast of worldwide query frequency of 'CAD/CAM' in red and 'CAD/CAM dental' in blue lines. (b) Detailed analysis of 'CAD/CAM dental' frequency. (c) Location of searching 'CAD/CAM' and 'CAD/CAM, dental'.
Note. Each line denotes 20 compared to the highest frequency (=100) during the period 2004–2014. Retrieved December 24, 2014, from http://www.google.com/trends/explore?hl=en-US#q=cad%2Fcam%20dental%2C%20cad%2Fcam&cmpt=q

permanent dentition', coauthored by J. Manhart, H.Y. Chen, G. Hamm, and R. Hickel. The latter was printed in 2006 and was entitled, 'Ceramics in dentistry: Historical roots and current perspectives'. The authors of the paper were J.R. Kelly, I. Nishimura, and S.D. Campbell.

**Table 1:** Top 30 most cited papers in the area of dentistry using CAD/CAM.

| Authors | Year | Title | Type | Journal name (Abbreviated ISO) | Times cited |
|---|---|---|---|---|---|
| Denry, I. and Kelly, J.R. | 2008 | State of the art of zirconia for dental applications | Article | *DENT MATER* | 334 |
| Manhart, J., Chen, H.Y., Hamm, G. and Hickel, R. | 2004 | Review of the clinical survival of direct and indirect restorations in posterior teeth of the permanent dentition | Review | *OPER DENT* | 268 |
| Tinschert, J., Zwez, D., Marx, R., and Anusavice, K.J. | 2000 | Structural reliability of alumina-, feldspar-, leucite-, mica- and zirconia-based ceramics | Article | *J DENT* | 194 |
| Kelly, J.R., Nishimura, I., and Campbell, S.D. | 1996 | Ceramics in dentistry: Historical roots and current perspectives | Review | *J PROSTHET DENT* | 178 |
| Sarment, D.P., Sukovic, P., and Clinthorne, N. | 2003 | Accuracy of implant placement with a stereolithographic surgical guide | Article | *INT J ORAL MAX IMPL* | 174 |
| Raigrodski, A.J. | 2004 | Contemporary materials and technologies for all-ceramic fixed partial dentures: A review of the literature | Article | *J PROSTHET DENT* | 149 |
| Hikita, K., Van Meerbeek, B., De Munck, J., Ikeda, T., Van Landuyt, and three others | 2007 | Bonding effectiveness of adhesive luting agents to enamel and dentin | Article | *DENT MATER* | 140 |
| Aboushelib, M.N., de Jager, N., Kleverlaan, C.J., and Feiler, A.J. | 2005 | Microtensile bond strength of different components of core veneered all-ceramic restorations | Article | *DENT MATER* | 113 |
| Luthardt, R.G., Holzhuter, M.S., Rudolph, H., Herold, V, and Walter, M.H. | 2004 | CAD/CAM-machining effects on Y-TZP zirconia | Article | *DENT MATER* | 100 |
| Tinschert, J., Natt, G., Mautsch, W., Spiekermann, H., and Anusavice, K.J. | 2001 | Marginal fit of alumina- and zirconia-based fixed partial dentures produced by a CAD/CAM system | Article | *OPER DENT* | 90 |
| Curtis, A.R., Wright, A.J., and Fleming, G.J.P. | 2006 | The influence of surface modification techniques on the performance of a Y-TZP dental ceramic | Article | *J DENT* | 76 |
| Guess, P.C., Kulis, A., Witkowski, S., Wolkewitz, M., Zhang, Y., and Strub, J.R. | 2008 | Shear bond strengths between different zirconia cores and veneering ceramics and their susceptibility to thermocycling | Article | *DENT MATER* | 70 |
| Wang, H., Aboushelib, M.N., and Feilzer, A.J. | 2008 | Strength influencing variables on CAD/CAM zirconia frameworks | Article | *DENT MATER* | 70 |

*(Continued)*

**Table 1:** Continued.

| Authors | Year | Title | Type | Journal name (Abbreviated ISO) | Times cited |
|---|---|---|---|---|---|
| Beuer, F., Schweiger, J., and Edelhoff, D. | 2008 | Digital dentistry: an overview of recent developments for CAD/CAM-generated restorations | Article | *BRIT DENT J* | 67 |
| Ortorp, A., Kihl, M.L., and Carlsson, G.E. | 2009 | A 3-year retrospective and clinical follow-up study of zirconia single crowns performed in a private practice | Article | *J DENT* | 64 |
| Miyazaki, T., Hotta, Y., Kunii, J., Kuriyama, S., and Tamaki, Y. | 2009 | A review of dental CAD/CAM: current status and future perspectives from 20 years of experience | Article | *DENT MATER J* | 64 |
| De Jager, N., Pallav, P., and Feilzer, A.J. | 2005 | The influence of design parameters on the FEA-determined stress distribution in CAD–CAM produced all-ceramic dental crowns | Article | *DENT MATER* | 63 |
| Beuer, F., Schweiger, J., Eichberger, M., Kappert, H.F., Gernet, W., and Edelhoff, D. | 2009 | High-strength CAD/CAM-fabricated veneering material sintered to zirconia copings – A new fabrication mode for all-ceramic restorations | Article | *DENT MATER* | 60 |
| Chen, H.Y., Hickel, R., Setcos, J.C., and Kunzelmann, K.H. | 1999 | Effects of surface finish and fatigue testing on the fracture strength of CAD–CAM and pressed-ceramic crowns | Article | *J PROSTHET DENT* | 60 |
| Beuer, F., Aggstaller, H., Edelhoff, D., Gernet, W., and Sorensen, J. | 2009 | Marginal and internal fits of fixed dental prostheses zirconia retainers | Article | *DENT MATER* | 56 |
| Lohbauer, U., Petschelt, A., and Greil, P. | 2002 | Lifetime prediction of CAD/CAM dental ceramics | Article | *J BIOMED MATER RES* | 56 |
| Vercruyssen, M., Jacobs, R., Van Assche, N., and Van Steenberghe, D. | 2008 | The use of CT scan based planning for oral rehabilitation by means of implants and its transfer to the surgical field: a critical review on accuracy | Review | *J ORAL REHABIL* | 55 |
| Guess, P.C., Zavanelli, R.A., Silva, N.R.F.A., and Bonfante, E.A., Coelho, P.G., and one other | 2010 | Monolithic CAD/CAM Lithium Disilicate Versus Veneered Y-TZP Crowns: Comparison of Failure Modes and Reliability After Fatigue | Article | *INT J PROSTHODONT* | 54 |
| Edelhoff, D., Beuer, F., Weber, V., and Johnen, C. | 2008 | HIP zirconia fixed partial dentures - Clinical results after 3 years of clinical service | Article | *QUINTESSENCE INT* | 50 |

(*Continued*)

**Table 1:** Continued.

| Authors | Year | Title | Type | Journal name (Abbreviated ISO) | Times cited |
|---|---|---|---|---|---|
| Sjogren, G., Molin, M., and van Dijken, J.W.V. | 1998 | A 5-year clinical evaluation of ceramic inlays (Cerec) cemented with a dual-cured or chemically cured resin composite luting agent | Article | *ACTA ODONTOL SCAND* | 49 |
| Cehreli, M.C., Kokat, A.M., and Akca, K. | 2009 | CAD/CAM zirconia vs. slip-cast glass-infiltrated alumina/zirconia all-ceramic crowns: 2-year results of a randomized controlled clinical trial | Article | *J APPL ORAL SCI* | 47 |
| Sundh, A. and Sjogren, G. | 2006 | Fracture resistance of all-ceramic zirconia bridges with differing phase stabilizers and quality of sintering | Article | *DENT MATER* | 47 |
| de Jager, N., Feilzer, A.J., and Davidson, C.L. | 2000 | The influence of surface roughness on porcelain strength | Article | *DENT MATER* | 46 |
| Bindl, A., Luthy, H., and Mormann, W.H. | 2006 | Strength and fracture pattern of monolithic CAD/CAM-generated posterior crowns | Article | *DENT MATER* | 45 |
| Zarone, F., Russo, S., and Sorrentino, R. | 2011 | From porcelain-fused-to-metal to zirconia: Clinical and experimental considerations | Article | *DENT MATER* | 44 |

### 4.2. *Semantic network analysis of abstracts of the studies on CAD/CAM*

Figure 4 shows semantic networks of the paper abstracts during the whole research period: 1995–2014. *Zirconia*, *CAD/CAM*, *dental materials*, *restorations*, and *in vitro* were the word nodes with the highest betweenness centrality. These words denote materials (*Zirconia* and *dental materials*) and therapeutic processes (*restorations*). Other words with moderately high between centrality include also the words of materials (*dental ceramics*) and prosthetic dental processes (*marginal fit, frameworks, accuracy, flexural strength, internal fit, systems,* and *partial dentures*). These words comprehensively reflect the development of CAD/CAM-related clinical techniques and materials.

The following four diagrams represent changing foci of CAD/CAM-based dentistry. Figure 5(a) shows that, in 1995–1999, the most central word is *dental porcelain*, which indicates the material used for prosthetic dentistry at that time. The words reflecting changing technological trends such as *future trends, computer aided manufacturing, data exchange, surgical template, CT image, computer, scanning software, three-dimensional measurements,* and *computer-aided design* were proximately located near the word CAD/CAM or clustered altogether in the diagram. Also, the words related to prosthetic dental processes including *indirect restorations, dental impression materials, dental implant, cementation, dental crown, dental ceramics,* and *dental restoration* indicated moderate betweenness centrality.

Figure 5(b) denotes the semantic structure of paper abstracts in 2000–2004. The figure indicates that, in 2000–2004, the word *porcelain* lost its dominant centrality. Instead, *dental*

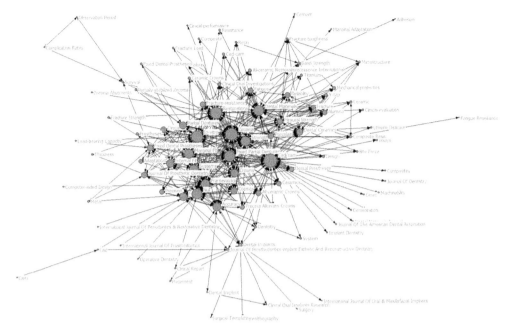

**Figure 4:** Semantic network of CAD/CAM DENTAL research abstracts 1995–2014.
Note. Node size: Betweenness centrality.

*materials* and *machining* are two keywords of the time period. Other words with moderate centrality include *zirconia ceramic, inlay-retained, crowns, guided surgery, computer aided manufacturing, fracture,* and *bond strength*. These words represent dental materials (*zirconia ceramic*) and possible utilities of CAD/CAM (e.g. *computer aided manufacturing, guided surgery, fracture,* and *bond strength*). Dental materials, one of the two core words, was surrounded by examples of dental materials including *porcelain, glass-ceramic, zirconia crown, crowns, dental crown,* and relevant processes (e.g. *grinding* and thermocycling and mechanical loading (*TCML*)).

Figure 5(c) demonstrates that, in 2005–2009, the words *image processing, occlusal surface,* and *3d object* retain the highest betweenness centrality and are interlinked among themselves. In particular, *image processing* is linked to *occlusal surface, 3d object, glass-ceramic, TCML, CAD/CAM implant crowns, crown penetration,* and many others. The word *3D object* is closely linked to *occlusal surface, surface, modification, ceramic dental crowns,* and so on. Other words surrounding the three core words include: *Mathematical analysis, bioceramics, Esthetics, dental education, nurbs surface, zirconia, data exchange,* and *CAD/CAM implant crowns*. CAD/CAM is linked to *three-dimensional measurements, dental impression materials, computer-aided analysis, fracture, machinability, Vickers hardness,* and so on. These words represent the increasing importance of 3D and CAD/CAM technology in prosthetics, clinical processes relating to prosthetics, and the importance of surface (modification) in clinical processes. Figure 5(d) indicates the semantic network of 2010–2014 data. Most salient finding from the figure is that *CAD/CAM* is the word with the highest betweenness centrality, followed by *Zirconia, dental ceramics,* and others. Interestingly, other pairs of words such as *adhesive* and *polymeric CAD/CAM materials, retentive force,* and *zirconia coping* have their own respective small clusters. The words surrounding *CAD/CAM* and *zirconia* include *chipping, fracture, fracture load, replica technique, FDP, overdenture, dental crown, try-in, three-dimensional process,* and many others. As previous figures supported, in dentistry, *CAD/CAM* increasingly gained its presence

(a)

(b)

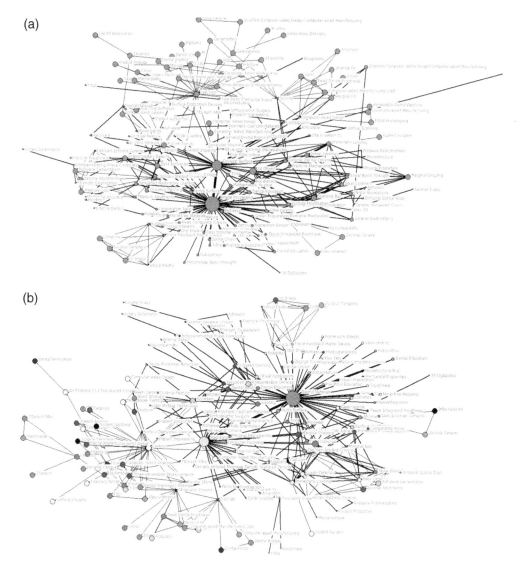

**Figure 5:** Semantic network of CAD/CAM dental research abstracts: Time split. (a) 1995–1999. (b) 2000–2004. (c) 2005–2009. (d) 2010–2014.

and importance over the past 20 years, which is relatively delayed compared to Google Trends results.

## 5. Discussion (RQ2)

### 5.1. *Theoretical implications*

This study was intended to track the perception of CAD/CAM in society (represented by Internet users) and dentistry by (1) general public's search query record from Google Trends and (2) scholars' research articles and their records archived in Web of Science database. There are four theoretical implications from the analysis.

(c)

(d)

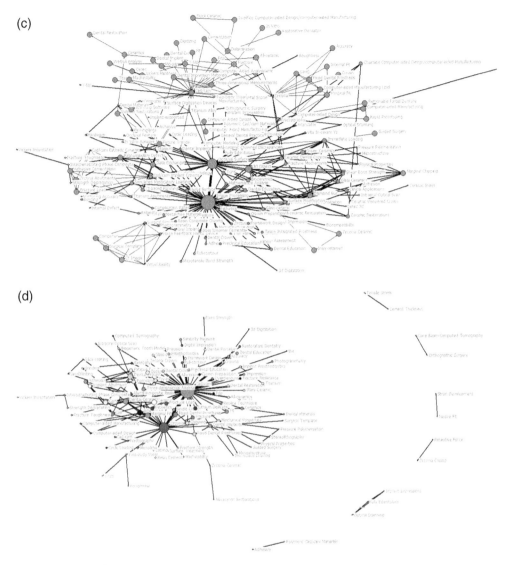

**Figure 5:** Continued.

First, there is a time gap between general public's interest in CAD/CAM technology and the people with a specialty, dentistry. The time difference could seem not unnatural at first sight, but if we look at other cases, there is a clear discrepancy between the CAD/CAM case here and others. In particular, the word sustainable development (or sustainability) was raised and applauded by a small group of people such as environment activists, environment or policy specialists, and educated people in the 1980s or earlier. Since the wave of globalisation, more people got interested in the sustainability issue, and as of 2015, most people are aware of the issue and request their government or parliament to pass a bill enforcing sustainable development.

On the contrary, the peak of 'CAD/CAM' search in Google was the first year of data sampling period (2005), according to the results in Figure 3. There was a continual decrease in the word search to 2014. This result was in contrast to 'CAD/CAM dental' query frequency. There were several spikes of the words search and such hike was getting frequent as time goes close to the year 2014.

This finding is interesting, but there may be several ways to explain it. First, dentistry may be slower in adopting CAD/CAM technology than other areas as it is not so much useful to adapt the technology to the clinical process of dentistry. Rogers (1995) argued that about 45–87% of variance of rate of adoption can be attributed to perceived characteristics of each innovation. There are five of them: (1) relative advantage; (2) compatibility; (3) complexity; (4) trialability; and (5) observability. In addition to these five traits, type of decision for adoption, communication channel, social system (e.g. democratic or dictatorial), and intensity of endeavour for adoption are important (Rogers 1995). Rogers's position suggests us that (1) we should look at the innate traits of innovation itself, and that (2) we should consider other factors influencing the rate of adoption.

In the case of CAD/CAM, relative advantage may not be so evident until (1) the price of CAD/CAM got lowered due to the emergence of CAD/CAM software for PC and World Wide Web; (2) the technology became simple enough for many dentists to learn it; (3) trialability may be limited due to high cost for buying CAD/CAM system. These possible reasons should be further examined by future research.

Second, CAD/CAM technology was influenced by or at least associated with the availability of proper materials to enhance clinical outcome in dental medicine. As Figure 5(a) indicates, changes in dental materials from glass-ceramic to alumina and zirconia are associated with the increasing use of CAD/CAM technology. For instance, a type of zirconia use is closely linked to CAD/CAM technology:

> Y-TZP(Yttrium-oxide partially stabilized zirconia) can be manufactured through 2 methods through computer-aided design/computer-aided manufacturing(CAD/CAM) technology. First, enlarged coping/framework can be designed and milled from a homogeneous ceramic soft green body blank of zirconia ... Other CAD/CAM systems are also available for designing and milling zirconia restorations. [Cerkon, DCS President, Denzir, ... ]. (Conrad, Seong, and Pesun 2007, p. 394)

Therefore, throughout the 20-year sampling period, CAD/CAM-related words were co-occurring with the words standing for dental materials. Earlier materials such as dental porcelain and glass-ceramic were salient nodes in Figure 5(a) covering 1995–1999, while zirconia and its adapted version are frequently revealed in Figure 5(d) covering 2009–2014. This finding reminds us that innovation in most cases is not an independent phenomenon. Rather, it involves an interaction with circumstances, potential adopter's readiness, and other innovations (e.g. innovation in dental materials in the current study). Such a perspective is getting more prominent as many scholars in innovation studies are approaching innovation phenomenon as a part of complexity system. As Leydesdorff and Eskowitz (1996) pointed out, from the evolutionary perspective, R&D is an institutionalised source of change (variation), and such a change is selected in market from diverse platforms such as local or global, private or public, and national or regional. This complex system can be understood from the dynamics of multilateral interactions, as such systems or components of them are interactive, transient, and 'understandable only in terms of fluxes' (Leydesdorff and Eskowitz 1996, p. 201).

Third, CAD/CAM is unique in that its characteristic as a kind of innovation is changing continually. When CAD/CAM was introduced in the 1960s, there was even no distinction between PC and mainframe (large-capacity servers). Furthermore, there was no operating system working for either mainframe (e.g. UNIX) or PCs (e.g. Windows NT and Linux). CAD/CAM in the 1960s was just a pen-based interface which had great potential for 3D design use. Later, the definition of CAD/CAM was changed to a system for plant reengineering as automobile corporations invested their money and labor forces in developing their own CAD/CAM system. Since the 1980s, CAD/CAM became more user-friendly than before because of the rapid diffusion of PC and operating system based on graphical user interface (GUI). Since the 2010s, CAD/CAM stands for balanced meaning of scanning, designing, and manufacturing as 3D scanners and 3D printers are emerging as a new device. CAD is considered as a possible step for 3D printing.

Inherently, CAD/CAM is not a static concept. It reflects technological advancements in software and hardware. In addition, the development of dental materials was another factor influencing the nature of CAD/CAM. Longevity of the terminology ironically is due to its versatility, applicability, and breadth of meaning. Changing foci of the meaning revealed in Figure 4 clearly support the flexible and fluidic meaning of CAD/CAM.

### 5.2. *Practical implications*

Innovations in dental medicine have been a result of complex dynamics of clinical techniques, material development, appliance/device development, software enhancement, information technology, and better understanding of human body. CAD/CAM in this study represents an exemplary case of continual innovation with broadened and changed meaning due to the development of relevant technologies.

Convergence theory posits that communication among certain group of people homogenises thought of the constituents. Myths and beliefs in CAD/CAM may reflect such a theory because CAD/CAM has been considered important in some time frame, but in others it was not the case. Specifically, the betweenness centrality of CAD/CAM word in 2010–2014 was at the highest compared to the other time frames (Figure 5). It was congruent with the results from Google Trends data shown in Figure 3(b). The importance of CAD/CAM is increasing at the same time with the innovation of zirconia (Yttrium tetragonal zirconia polycrystals, as shown in Figure 5(d)), 3D CT, and 3D printers in the 2010s, and emergence of diverse techniques of dental implants.

After all, the results here support the position of the TH approach: They demonstrate that agents of innovation are not limited to a certain group of people. From a complexity systems perspective, TH scholars argue that three sectors (helices), UGI or UIG communicate with one another and may assimilate one another's orientations, priorities, and values. The keywords retrieved through semantic network analysis reflect both sides: surroundings and technology itself. For instance, changes in materials, diffusion of PC, and operating system as an external stimuli enhanced the potential of CAD/CAM in dentistry. On the other hand, inherent changes of CAD/CAM technology such as the introduction of GUI for CAD/CAM software possibly increased consumers' intent to purchase the technology. The results in this research hint that the meanings and utilities of CAD/CAM have been expanded through the interactions of the three helices, and the expansion promoted the growth of and changes in the meaning of CAD/CAM over time (see Etzkowitz and Leydesdorff 2000; Leydesdorff and Meyer 2003; Park and Leydesdorff 2010; Kim 2012, Kim and Park 2014 for other industry's cases).

One of current and salient findings of TH approach is that government and university sectors are trying to apply their own behavioural patterns and institutional arrangements to those of industry sector. Although the benefit of such a trend is still uncertain, future research should determine the nature of interactions of the three sectors in dentistry. CAD/CAM could be a good starting point of testing and evaluating TH approach in dentistry.

### 6. Conclusions

This paper tracked the word usage of CAD/CAM in general publics' information-seeking records in 2005–2014 and researchers' perceptions in dental medicine research paper abstracts in 1995–

2014. The data retrieved clearly demonstrated that innovation (CAD/CAM here) is influenced by and interacting with relevant technologies and social arrangements. The emergence of CAD/CAM in dentistry was lagged behind compared to that of general public's perception, but the terminology established itself as a fundamental condition and simultaneously an outcome of dental materials development, information technology, medical science, clinical techniques, and social trends.

Future studies are called for to find the dynamics of these relevant UGI sectors and their interactions and forces. The TH approach could be a possible theoretical lens for doing such future research. This paper may not be directly measuring the processes of innovation, but it was able to show how general publics and dental medicine scholars accepted and adopted the 'new' technology, CAD/CAM.

## Funding

The first author acknowledges the financial support received from BK 21+ administered by Sungkyunkwan University, funded by Ministry of Education, Republic of Korea.

## References

Arabe, K.C. (2001), 'CAD/CAM: Past, Present and Future', Retrieved December 15, 2014, from http://news.thomasnet.com/imt/2001/02/23/cadcam_past_pre

Arora, S.K., Youtie, J., Shapira, P., Gao, L., and Ma, T. (2013), 'Entry strategies in an emerging technology: a pilot web-based study of graphene firms', *Scientometrics*, 95(3), 1189–1207.

Barnett, G.A. (2008), 'The role of the Internet in cultural identity', in *Embedding into Our Lives: New Opportunities and Challenges of the Internet*, eds. L.W. Leung, A.Y.H. Fung, and P.S.N. Lee, Hong Kong: The Chinese University Press, pp. 347–368.

Borgatti, S.P. (2002), *NetDraw: Graph Visualization Software*, Harvard: Analytic Technologies.

CADAZZ.com. (2014), 'CAD software: history of CAD/CAM', Retrieved December 15, 2014, from the World Wide Web, http://www.cadazz.com/

Chesbrough, H.W. (2003), *Open Innovation: The New Imperative for Creating and Profiting from Technology*, Boston, MA: Harvard Business Press.

Chung, C.J., Barnett, G.A., and Park, H.W. (2014), 'Inferring international dotcom Web communities by link and content analysis', *Quality & Quantity*, 48(2), 1117–1133.

Conrad, H.J., Seong, W.J., and Pesun, I.J. (2007), 'Current ceramic materials and systems with clinical recommendations: a systematic review', *The Journal of Prosthetic Dentistry*, 98(5), 389–404.

Danowski, J.A. (2010), *WORDij 3.0 [Computer Program]*, Chicago: University of Illinois at Chicago.

Danowski, J.A. (2013), 'Conceptualizing semantic networks', Retrieved December 1, 2014, from http://wordij.net/about.html

Denry, I., and Kelly, J.R. (2008), 'State of the art of zirconia for dental applications', *Dental Materials*, 24(3), 299–307.

Doerfel, M.L., and Barnett, G.A. (1999), 'A semantic network analysis of the international communication association', *Human Communication Research*, 25(4), 589–603.

Etzkowitz, H., and Leydesdorff, L. (2000), 'The dynamics of innovation: from national systems and Mode 2 to a Triple Helix of University-Industry-Government relations', *Research Policy*, 29(22), 109–123.

Figueroa, M.E., Kincaid, D.L., and Hurley, E.A. (2014), 'The effect of a joint communication campaign on multiple sex partners in Mozambique: the role of psychosocial/ideational factors', *AIDS Care*, 26, S50–S55.

Freeman, L.C. (1979), 'Centrality in social networks: conceptual clarification', *Social Networks*, 1, 215–239.

Fujita, M. (2012), 'How sectoral systems of production promote capability building: insights from the Vietnamese motorcycle industry', *Asian Journal of Technology Innovation*, 20, 111–131.

Hanneman, R.A., and Riddle, M. (2005), 'Introduction to social network methods', Retrieved April 4, 2014, from http://faculty.ucr.edu/~hanneman/nettext/

Kang, J., Gwon, S.H., Kim, S., and Cho, K. (2013), 'Determinants of successful technology commercialization: implication for Korean Government-sponsored SMEs', *Asian Journal of Technology Innovation*, 21(1), 72–85.

Kim, J.H. (2012), 'A hyperlink and semantic network analysis of the triple helix (university-government-industry): the interorganizational communication structure of nanotechnology', *Journal of Computer-Mediated Communication*, 17(2), 152–170.

Kim, J.H., and Park, H.W. (2014), 'Food policy in cyberspace: a webometric analysis of national food clusters in South Korea', Government Information Quarterly, 31(3), 443–453.

Kincaid, D.L. (2002), 'Drama, emotion, and cultural convergence', *Communication Theory*, 12(2), 136–152.

Lee, K.R. (2014), '10 years of innovation studies in Asia through the Asian Journal of Technology Innovation', *Asian Journal of Technology Innovation*, 22(1), 168–184.

Leydesdorff, L., and Etzkowitz, H. (1996), 'Emergence of a triple helix of university-industry- government relations', *Science and Public Policy*, 23, 279–286.

Leydesdorff, L., and Meyer, M. (2003), 'The triple helix of university-industry-government relations: guest editorial', *Scientometrics*, 58(2), 191–203.

Lundvall, B. Å. (ed.) (1995), *National Systems of Innovation: Toward a Theory of Innovation and Interactive Learning*, London: Biddles.

Martínez-Torres, M.D.R. (2014), 'Analysis of activity in open-source communities using social network analysis techniques', *Asian Journal of Technology Innovation*, 22(1), 114–130.

Park, H.W., and Leydesdorff, L. (2010), 'Longitudinal trends in networks of university–industry–government relations in South Korea: the role of programmatic incentives', *Research Policy*, 39(5), 640–649.

Richards, W.D. (1995), *NEGOPY 4.30 Manual and User's Guide*, Burnaby: School of Communication, Simon Fraser University.

Rogers, E.M. (1995), *Diffusion of Innovations*, New York, NY: Simon and Schuster.

Rogers, E.M., and Kincaid, D.L. (1981), *Communication Networks: Toward a New Paradigm for Research*, New York: Free Press.

Sarkar, S., and Costa, A.I. (2008), 'Dynamics of Open Innovation in the Food Industry', *Trends in Food Science & Technology*, 19(11), 574–580.

Shinn, T. (2003). 'The 'Triple Helix' and 'new production of knowledge' as socio-cognitive fields'. In *Social Studies of Science and Technology: Looking Back, Ahead*, eds. B. Joerges & H. Nowotny, Dordrecht: Springer, pp. 103–116.

# Convergence innovation of the textile machinery industry in Korea

Kong-rae Lee[a], JinHyo Joseph Yun[a] and Eui-Seob Jeong[b]

*[a]DGIST, Techno Jungang Daero, Hyeonpung-myeon, Dalseong-gun, Daegu Korea*
*[b]KISTI, Dongdaemun-gu, Seoul, Korea*

This paper aims to explore why the Korean textile machinery industry failed in competence building although its strong user sector, the textile industry of Korea, was once ranked high with strong competence. It argues that local user firms of the textile machinery industry did not play a role in building up the competence of specialised suppliers through convergence innovation. The diversity of textile machinery is so large that their convergence types of innovation are distinctive in creating new functions and products. The convergence innovation between the two industries and the resultant positive synergy has not been generated much in Korea. Strong user firms rather escaped from cooperative work with specialised suppliers, which otherwise may have generated convergence innovation and strengthened their competence. Weak convergence innovation by both textile firms and specialised suppliers caused their economic activities concurrently downturned. The Korean textile machinery industry and its user sector have lost their competence in relatively short period.

## 1. Introduction

It may be easily assumed that Korea would have a strong textile machinery industry since she had once the world's top-class textile industry that is a distinctive user sector of textile machines in 1970s. Many of industry analysts still believe that the Korean textile machinery industry is competitive due to the fact that its backward and forward industries are strong. This belief, however, is not true anymore. According to the geese theory that explains a step-by-step industrial development, in which one industry first develops and accumulates capability to enter into another industry that requires higher technological capability (Lee 1981), the Korean textile industry should have shown such development path so as to have a strong textile machinery industry.

Moreover, information and telecommunication industry as well as electronic industry overall has a strong innovation capability to support the innovation of related industries in Korea. IT technology is in fact very important in the innovation of textile machines. Textile production has been to large extent automated due to rapidly rising wages even in low-waged countries. As a result, local specialised suppliers have had good opportunities to supply highly automated and innovated machines by applying IT technologies to their user firms. However, statistics show that the Korean textile machinery industry has failed in doing so. The industry has continued to fall in terms of the number of firms, employees, sales, and patenting over the last decade.

As a result of this failure, the Korean textile machinery industry has continued to decline over the last decade. The number of employees of the industry remarkably decreased from 9063 in 2000 to 3235 in 2010, almost one-third of the previous number in 2000. Daegu and Gyeongbuk regions that have been well known for textile clusters also showed a significant employment loss for the same period. Especially, Daegu region maintains a minimum level of employment in the textile machinery industry, just 593 in 2010, which was 3016 in 2000 and 3019 in 2002 as seen in Figure 1. Its share out of national total number of employees in the industry decreased by almost half from 33.2% to 18.3% for the same period. Both Daegu and Gyeongbuk regions were once well known as the hub of textile industries and a textile machinery cluster.

The fall of the Korean textile machinery industry was not limited to employment only. Along with the decrease of employment, the number of specialised textile machinery suppliers reduced from 521 in 2000 to 129 in 2010. Daegu region showed a similar trend as the number of specialised suppliers reduced from 199 in 2000 to just 31 in 2010 (Korean Statistical Information Service 2013). Sales data of the Korean textile machinery industry showed more or less the same trend in the number of firms and employment. Its sales were 1045 billion won in 2000, which decreased to 619 billion won in 2010. The sales trends of the two regions are similar to the national trends. For instance, the sales of Daegu region were 366 billion won accounting for 24.7% of the national total in 2000. However, it has fallen to 12.8 billion won taking just 2.1% out of the national total in 2010 (Korean Statistical Information Service 2013). Therefore, it would be worth exploring why the Korean textile machinery industry, with such a strong and large user sector, once a world-class textile industry in terms of sales volume, has failed in building up competence and so its business.

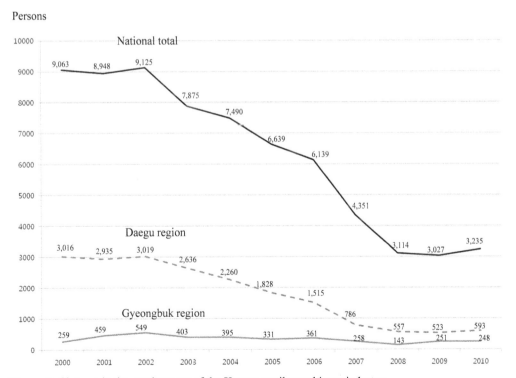

**Figure 1:** Changes in the employment of the Korean textile machinery industry.
Source: Website of Korean Statistical Information Service (http//kosis.kr).

This paper aims to explore what kind of obstacles existed and what kind of innovation sources were lacking behind this noticeable decline of the Korean textile machinery industry. It specifically tries to find out the main causes of the shrink, the degree of convergence innovation of the industry, and the factors that were lacking in the competence building of the textile machinery industry. In the process of exploration, we speculate that the Korean textile firms have not sufficiently carried out R&D work to generate ideas for the convergence innovation of textile machines because they were not interested in the exploitation of the commercial value of the textile machinery. It is also assumed that the innovation of textile machinery holds typical characteristics of convergence innovation. Our hypothesis, however, is that the Korean specialised suppliers were not able to make success in this kind of convergence innovation and, as result, have lost their competence due to the lack of knowledge input from their user firms, the textile firms.

## 2. Conceptual framework and research methodology

### 2.1. *Processes of convergence innovation*

Technology convergence increasingly appears in the modern innovation scene. The article on 'Technological change in the machine tool industry, 1840–1910' by Rosenberg (1963, 1982) explains that, at the end of the nineteenth century, all machines confronted a similar collection of technological problems dealing with such matters as power transmission, control devices, feed mechanisms, friction reduction, and a broad array of problems connected with the properties of metals. These problems became common to the production of a wide range of commodities. These were apparently unrelated from the point of view of the nature of the final product. The uses, however, of the final product were very closely related on a technological basis. Rosenberg called this phenomenon as technological convergence and argued that the intensive degree of specialisation which developed in the second half of the nineteenth century owed its existence to a combination of this technological convergence.

Similar to technological convergence, the term 'technological fusion' has been once used by some innovation scholars (Kodama 1986, 1991, 1994; Lee 2007; Lee, Kang, Hwang, and Lee 2010). Kodama (1986) argued that there are two fundamental types of innovation: one is the technological breakthrough and the other is a technology fusion. According to Kodama, breakthrough innovations are associated with strong leadership in a particular technology, and technology fusion can be possible through concerted efforts by several different actors. He empirically observed a phenomenon of technology fusion that occurred first between machinery industries and electronic industries in 1970, and later among variety of industries including chemicals, foods, and pharmaceutical industries in 1974.

Recently, there has been growing trends of innovation studies on the process of convergence innovation, particularly at the micro level. Kim (2014) studied the convergence innovation between printing technology and electronic technology and argued that there is continuous disequilibrium between converging technologies which are divided into two types: reference technology and matching technology. Two types of converging technologies tend to innovate at differing degrees of speed in such a manner that when one technology (reference technology) is innovated generating disequilibrium, the other technology, called as matching technology, necessarily innovates to match or adjust optimal balance between the functions of the two technologies. He stated that the process of tuning involving mutual matching and minute adjustment across disparate technologies to achieve a target performance is one of the most critical attributes in convergence innovation.

As such, the processes of convergence innovation can be found in many innovations not only in the twentieth century but also in current times. That is, the convergence between many user sectors and machining technology explored by Rosenberg (1963) is still going on in current times. It is also perceived that such processes of convergence innovation are universally applied in all technological fields and industrial areas (OECD 1993; Roco and Bainbridge 2002; Rafols and Meyer 2006). As seen in Figure 2, technology A1 and technology B2 converge to create technology C1, which is a new innovation creating new functions, new products, or new processes. During the process of convergence, technology A can be reference technology or matching technology to match or adjust optimal balance between the functions of the two technologies as explained by Kim (2014). In that sense, both technology A and technology B may have certain degree of tuning capability in the process of matching or adjusting an optimal balance. Tuning capability may imply technological opportunity to make an innovation of individual technology and convergence innovation of the two technologies involved.

### 2.2. *Application to the case of textile machinery*

The process of convergence innovation mentioned above can be applied to the case of textile machinery along with textile technology. Past innovation studies have explored part of such convergence innovation, for instance, case exploration on machine tools (Lee 1996), intelligence robots (Lee 2007), printing technology (Lee and Seong 2009), printed electronics (Kim 2014), robotics (Kumaresan 2001), and so on. Textile machinery technology is likely to be closely linked to textile technology through a typical process of convergence innovation. In fact, many international patent codes (IPCs) associated with textile technologies are mixed with textile machinery technologies so as to unable to distinguish two technologies. We regarded these cases as textile machinery technologies.

Component technologies affecting the convergence innovation of textile machinery can be grouped into two types. The one is user sources such knowledge about fibres as super fibres (U1), high-performance fibres (U2), industrial material fibres (U3), high functional fibres (U4), and cloth and life material fibres (U5) as shown in Figure 3. They are basically embedded in

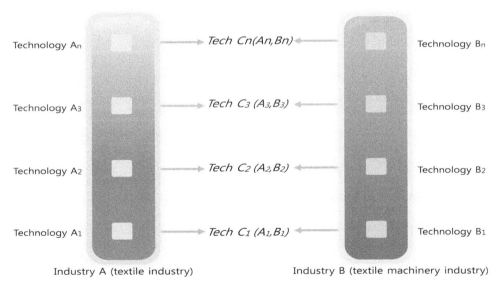

Technology An — Tech Cn(An,Bn) — Technology Bn

Technology A3 — Tech C3 (A3,B3) — Technology B3

Technology A2 — Tech C2 (A2,B2) — Technology B2

Technology A1 — Tech C1 (A1,B1) — Technology B1

Industry A (textile industry)        Industry B (textile machinery industry)

**Figure 2:** Processes of convergence innovation between industry A and industry B.

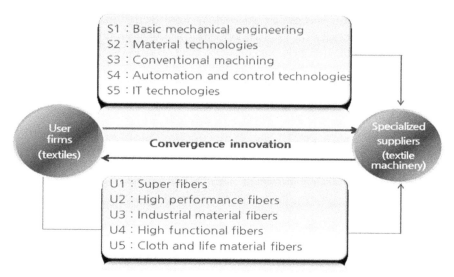

**Figure 3:** Sources of convergence innovation between textile firms and textile machinery firms.

experts of user firms, that is, textile firms. The other is such machinery technology as basic mechanical engineering (S1), material technologies (S2), conventional machining (S3), automation and control technologies (S4), and IT technologies (S5). They are obviously embedded in experts of specialised textile machinery suppliers or vast areas of related suppliers.

Many CEOs of textile firms would not have known how to deal with convergence innovation that requires diverse knowledge and technologies. They would have sought to escape from the textile business or invest in less developed countries with cheaper wages. Technological problems were solved and shared among different types of textile machinery manufacturers. Technological convergence has prevailed in the contemporary innovation of textile machinery which adopted information and telecommunication technology as has been the case in many other technology fields. It has evolved up to the point that different technologies are deeply integrated and even chemically mixed, resulting in completely new types of products.

### 2.3. *Research questions and methodology*

Research method has been chosen for fulfilling the objectives of research. Our research objective is to explore why the Korean textile machinery industry could not build up competence although its user sector, the textile industry, was once competitive ranked the second in the world textile market. Related research questions to explore the objective include: (a) What was the main cause of the shrink and the loss of competence? (b) To what extent convergence innovation of the industry has been taking place in Korea? and (c) What was lacking in the competence building of the textile machinery industry?

The research method adopted in this paper is an archival analysis mixed with field survey. The first kind of archival data used are economic indicators such as outputs, sales, exports, imports, and employees of the textile industry and the textile machinery industry. These data are necessary to answer the first research question. The second type of data includes innovation indicators such as patent application and patent registration, which are also required to answer the third research question. The data were collected at the national level as well as at the regional level. Regional level data are mostly that of Daegu and Gyeongbuk regions, where both the textile industry and the textile machinery industry once flourished.

Together with the archival analysis, we utilised stories of firms obtained through field survey with companies running textile business or textile machinery business in Daegu and Gyeongbuk regions. Among interviewees are CEOs of Keumyong Co. and Ilsin Machine Co. as specialised textile machinery suppliers, CEO of Hwa Sun Co. as a user of textile machinery, and lastly CEO of Korea Textile Machinery Research Institute (KTMRI) which has been an important player in the Korean textile machinery industry as a liaison and coordinator of the textile machinery innovation system in Korea.

## 3. Convergence innovation in textile machinery industry in Korea

### 3.1. *Patenting in textile machinery by types of firms*

Patenting data are good indicators to see overall trends of innovation activities, especially at the industry level. As shown in Table 1, in textile machinery patenting in Korea, there were totally 20,826 patent applications by local firms and individuals for the last 12 years from 2000 to 2011. Forty-eight per cent (9999 applications) out of total textile machinery patents were accounted for by users. Among users who have generated patents, 32.3% were from textile firms and the remaining 67.7% were from individuals (Korea Intellectual Property Rights Information Service 2013). An interesting observation from these data is that individuals are the largest contributor in patenting activities of the Korean textile machinery industry (Kore Intellectual Property Rights Information Service 2013).

Specialised textile machinery suppliers have submitted 698 patent applications taking 2.4% out of the national total. It is surprising that specialised suppliers show such an extremely low level of patent applications. This implies that the Korean textile machinery industry has lost its

**Table 1:**  Patenting trends in textile machinery by users and suppliers in Korea.

| Classification | 2000–2003 | 2004–2007 | 2008–2011 | Total (%) |
|---|---|---|---|---|
| National total (A) | 5186 | 7752 | 7888 | 20,826 (100.0) |
| User firms (C) | 2175 | 3405 | 4419 | 9999 (48.0) |
| Users: textile firms (C1) | 66 | 192 | 1682 | 3233 (15.5) |
| Other users (individuals) (C2) | 2109 | 3213 | 2737 | 6766 (32.5) |
| Specialised textile machine suppliers (D) | 66 | 192 | 440 | 698 (3.4) |
| Other related suppliers (R) | 2945 | 4155 | 3029 | 10,129 (48.6) |
| Electronics | 2159 | 3333 | 1909 | 7401 (35.5) |
| Chemical | 331 | 351 | 410 | 1092 (5.2) |
| Metal products | 125 | 183 | 194 | 502 (2.4) |
| Electrical appliances | 206 | 5 | 26 | 237 (1.1) |
| Paper products | 23 | 67 | 92 | 182 (0.9) |
| Motors | 13 | 43 | 92 | 148 (0.7) |
| Machinery industry | 29 | 79 | 125 | 233 (1.1) |
| Construction | 9 | 30 | 67 | 106 (0.5) |
| Materials | 16 | 25 | 52 | 93 (0.4) |
| Food, medical, and pharmaceutical | 17 | 24 | 36 | 77 (0.3) |
| Others | 17 | 15 | 26 | 58 (0.3) |
| Ratio of user firms (C/A) | 41.9 | 43.9 | 56.0 | 48.0 |
| Ratio of specialised suppliers (D/A) | 1.3 | 2.5 | 5.6 | 3.4 |
| Ratio of related suppliers ((D + R)/A) | 58.1 | 56.1 | 44.0 | 52.0 |

Source: Website of Korea Intellectual Property Rights Information Service (http//kipris.or.kr).

competence not only in the creation of value added but also in innovation activities in terms of patenting. When we include other related suppliers into the category of textile machinery suppliers, their patent applications total to 10,827, accounting for 52.0% out of the national total for the last 12 years from 2000 to 2011. This patenting trend implies that the innovation source of textile machinery largely came from related suppliers such as suppliers of electronics, chemicals, metal products, electrical appliances, paper products, motors, machinery, construction, materials, and so on.

Among related suppliers, the electronics sector accounted for 35.5%, clearly distinguished from other related suppliers. This obviously shows that information, communication and telecom (ICT) technologies are reference technology in the convergence innovation of the textile machinery over the last 10 years. The ICT technology has been greatly integrated into textile machinery for their automation and communication, followed by chemical technology (5.2%) which may have generated the innovation of textile materials. It may be associated with treatment technology of threads, yarns, fabrics, or fibrous goods by chemical, biochemical or physical means, or fibrous goods made from such materials. With minor portions, metal products (2.4%) and electrical appliances (1.1%) seem to have affected the innovation of the textile machinery industry to some extent as shown in Table 1.

Figure 4 depicts the trend of shares of textile machinery patents by three types of firms: related suppliers, textile firms, and specialised textile machinery suppliers. By 2004, related suppliers dominated patenting in textile machinery as they accounted for 85.7% in 2004 though they declined afterwards. The declining trend of the related suppliers after 2004 was due to the recession of the industry. Domestic textile machinery suppliers suffered from the entries of the Chinese

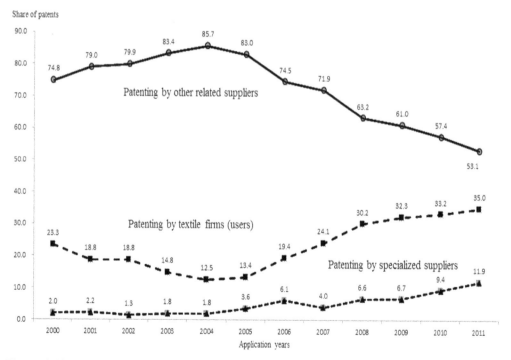

**Figure 4:** Shares of textile machinery patents by type of firms in Korea.
Source: Website of Korea Intellectual Property Rights Information Service (http//kipris.or.kr).

textile machinery suppliers with cheap prices into global market since 2004. Many Korean suppliers exited the textile machinery markets, resulting in a rapid contraction of the industry size.

The share of textile machinery patents taken by textile firms who are users of textile machinery had decreased until 2004, which jumped back quickly from 13.4% in 2005 to 35.0% in 2011. Increasing share of user firms in textile machinery patents is a desirable trend for the textile machinery industry, because active engagement of user firms in the innovation of textile machinery will ultimately lead to strong competence building of the textile machinery industry (Lee 1998).

Looking at firm-level data on patenting in textile machinery by user firms, we have identified top 10 user firms as seen in Table 2. One who ranked the first was Hyo Sung Co. with 649 patents for 12 years from 2000 to 2011. The 2nd was ranked by Kolon Industries, Inc. followed by Kolon Co. (3rd with 184), Woongjin Chemical Co. (4th with 164), Kolon Gloth Co. (5th with 149), Korea Textile Development Institute (KTDI) (6th with 65), Toray Advanced Materials Korea (7th with 52), Kolon Fashion Material, Inc. (8th with 51), Dyetec Center (9th with 50), and Hubis Co. (10th with 39). Interestingly, four affiliate companies of Kolon Group are included in the top 10 patenting user firms. Kolon Group has been a well-known conglomerate specialised in textile business in Korea. It appears that affiliate companies of Kolon Group are leading innovators of the Korean textile industry as well as the Korean textile machinery industry.

Patenting by specialised textile machinery suppliers are not impressive compared with that of user firms. Top 10 patenting specialised suppliers are listed in Table 3. The first is Sunster Co. with 87 patents, followed by Sunstar Precision Co. with 69 patents. The third was KTMRI with 28 patents, followed by Inbro Co (4th with 26 applications), Sunstar R&C Co. (5th with 14), Dae Hung Hitech Co. (6th with 14), Daelim Starlet Co. (7th with 10), Ilsung Machine Industry Co. (8th with 9), Ssangyong machinery Co. (9th with 9), and lastly Dae Kwang Co. (10th with 6). Two affiliate companies of Sunstar appeared to be the most innovative specialised suppliers in Korea. Interestingly, the KTMRI and Dyetec Center, government sponsored research institutes, took a leading position in patenting activities. Ssangyong Machinery Co. was once a well-known specialised textile machinery supplier, but it has recently lost its drive in patenting activities.

### 3.2. *Convergence innovation in textiles machinery in Korea*

The innovation of textile machinery seems to have typical characteristics of convergence innovation similar to that of machine tools, intelligence robots, printed electronics, and robotics. As seen in Figure 5, textile machinery patents with two IPCs appeared to be 5821 (32.7%) out of total patents. In the same way, it is discovered that textile machinery patents with three IPCs

**Table 2:** Top 10 patenting user firms in textile machinery fields in Korea.

| Ranks | Name of firms | 2000–2003 | 2004–2007 | 2008–2011 | Total |
|---|---|---|---|---|---|
| 1 | Hyo Sung Co., Ltd | 176 | 220 | 253 | 649 |
| 2 | Kolon Industries, Inc. | 0 | 56 | 221 | 277 |
| 3 | Kolon Co., Ltd | 106 | 65 | 13 | 184 |
| 4 | Woongjin Chemical Co. | 4 | 39 | 121 | 164 |
| 5 | Kolon Glotech Co. | 1 | 38 | 110 | 149 |
| 6 | KTDI | 23 | 12 | 30 | 65 |
| 7 | Toray Advanced Materials Korea, Inc. | 8 | 10 | 34 | 52 |
| 8 | Kolon Fashion Material, Inc. | 0 | 9 | 42 | 51 |
| 9 | Dyetec Center | 3 | 4 | 43 | 50 |
| 10 | Hubis Co. | 23 | 5 | 11 | 39 |

**Table 3:** Top 10 patenting specialised suppliers in textile machinery in Korea.

| Ranks | Name of firms | 2000–2003 | 2004–2007 | 2008–2011 | Total |
|---|---|---|---|---|---|
| 1 | Sunstar Co., Ltd | 11 | 43 | 33 | 87 |
| 2 | Sunstar Precision Co. | 30 | 31 | 8 | 69 |
| 3 | KTMRI | 0 | 6 | 22 | 28 |
| 4 | Inbro Co., Ltd | 12 | 14 | 0 | 26 |
| 5 | Sunstar R&C Co., Ltd | 0 | 0 | 14 | 14 |
| 6 | Dae Hung Hitech Co., Ltd | 4 | 2 | 6 | 12 |
| 7 | Daelim Starlet Co., Ltd | 3 | 3 | 4 | 10 |
| 8 | Ilsung Machine Industry Co., Ltd | 3 | 1 | 5 | 9 |
| 9 | Ssangyong Machinery Co., Ltd | 5 | 3 | 1 | 9 |
| 10 | Dae Kwang Co., Ltd | 0 | 0 | 6 | 6 |

are 4451 (25.1%), and that with four IPCs are 3071 (17.3%). As a result, textile machinery patents with more than two IPCs that indicate convergence innovation accounted for 50.1% out of total patents. This kind of patenting pattern can be drawn as a convex curve like a left-side diagram of Figure 5. In other words, it can be said as the pattern of convergence innovation in the textile machinery industry, which is similar to that of intelligent robots seen in the right-side diagram of Figure 5 (Lee 2007).

One question arises regarding convergence innovation of the textile machinery industry. What are key component technologies that can be reference or matching technology in the convergence innovation of textile machinery? We distinguished 10 key component technologies from whole number of IPCs in textile machinery field by matrix comparison. Eight key component technologies based on IPCs were chosen, with which more than 1000 patents exist as shown in Table 4. They are D06F (laundering technologies), D01F (fibres technology), D06M (treatment technology), D21H (pulp composition), D04B (knitting), D01D (mechanical methods), D03D (weaving), and D05B (sewing). With eight component technologies, we made a convergence innovation matrix related to textile machinery technology as seen in Table 4.

The convergence innovation matrix tells us component technologies which are frequently converging on each other. It indicates, however, convergence innovation takes place within textile machinery clusters. Component technologies included in the matrix are highly possible to be reference technology that is converged or matching technology that is converging. As shown in Table 4,

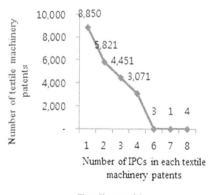

Textile machinery

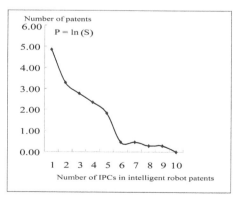

Intelligent robots

**Figure 5:** Patterns of convergence innovation in textile machinery.

**Table 4:** Convergence innovation matrix of textile machinery technologies.

|  | D06F | D01F | D06M | D21H | D04B | D01D | D03D | D05B |
|---|---|---|---|---|---|---|---|---|
| D06F | 8484 |  |  |  |  |  |  |  |
| D01F |  | 2268 | 114 | 15 | 24 | 619 | 100 |  |
| D06M |  | 114 | 2049 | 14 | 31 | 47 | 158 | 3 |
| D21H |  | 15 | 14 | 1729 |  | 5 | 2 |  |
| D04B |  | 24 | 31 |  | 1315 | 10 | 66 | 6 |
| D01D |  | 629 | 47 | 5 | 10 | 1131 | 28 |  |
| D03D |  | 100 | 158 | 2 | 66 | 28 | 1096 | 5 |
| D05B |  |  | 3 |  | 6 |  | 5 | 1078 |

Notes: D06F (technology related to laundering, drying, ironing, pressing, or folding textile articles), D01F (chemical features in the manufacture of artificial filaments, threads, fibres, bristles, or ribbons, apparatus specially adapted for the manufacture of carbon filaments), D06M (treatment technology of threads, yarns, fabrics, or fibrous goods by chemical, biochemical, or physical means), D06M (treatment, not provided for elsewhere in class D06, of fibres, threads, yarns, fabrics, feathers, or fibrous goods made from such materials), D21H (pulp compositions), D04B (knitting), D01D (mechanical methods or apparatus in the manufacture of artificial filaments, threads, fibres, bristles, or ribbons), D03D (woven fabrics, methods of weaving, looms), and D05B (sewing technology). Shaded cells indicate the significance in convergence innovation.

the frequent convergences that had taken place were between D01D (mechanical methods) and D01F (fibres technology) with 619 patents, between D03D (weaving) and D06M (treatment technology) with 158 patents, between D06M (treatment technology) and D01F (fibres technology) with 114 patents, and between D03D (weaving) and D01F (fibres technology) with 100 patents. At the four-digit level of IPCs, we can see that mechanical methods, fibre technology, and weaving technology are key components of convergence innovation in textile machinery. Mechanical methods may represent many input technologies applied for the convergence innovation. For instance, electronics technology may be included in D01D (mechanical methods) and may have greatly applied to convergence innovation of textile machinery as described in Table 1.

We found in interviews with textile firms and textile machinery suppliers that convergence innovation of textile machinery has been taking place in two ways. One is an application of textile machinery to the innovation of other machinery sectors, whereas the other is an application of other technologies to the innovation of textile machinery. An example of the former is found in Keumyong Co. that has been specialised in the manufacturing of various knitting machine such as jersey knitting machine, stripper machine, computerised jacquard machine, seamless machine, and so on. Keumyong tried to find application areas by utilising its circular-ring processing technology regarded as its core competence when domestic market for textile machinery was seriously shrinking. Keumyong's effort is equivalent to the concept proposed by Nonaka (1994), the 'externalisation' of internal knowledge. Based on technological capability on circular-ring processing, the company successfully developed exhaust valves of ship engine and now more than half of its sales come from exhaust valves. We call this kind of convergence as 'inside-out convergence'.

An example of the latter is found in most specialised suppliers including Ilsin Machine Co. and the KTMRI. The most frequently applied technologies for the innovation of textile machinery are electronic control and information and communication technology. They are integrated into new textile machines such as digital textile printing, automatic sewing thread winder, water jet, and air jet rapier looms, and so on, by R&D work of specialised suppliers or by simply combining parts and components embedding them and manufactured by related suppliers. We call this kind of convergence as 'outside-in convergence'.

Outside-in convergence is likely to be active when the textile machinery industry is in booming period because the increasing demand for textile machinery leads to an increase in its output and technical problems, which in turn generate more innovations to solve problems together with innovation of related suppliers. However, inside-out convergence is likely to be active during the recession period because specialised suppliers seek to maintain employees and operate existing production facilities by entering into technologically possible markets that require inside-out convergence innovation.

## 4. The role of textile firms in the innovation of textile machinery

### 4.1. *General perception on the role of user firms*

It has been generally accepted among innovation studies that user firms play important roles in the innovation of specialised suppliers. It is the user who generates ideas for a new product and makes, evaluates, and implements a prototype in house, particularly in such capital goods as machine tools, scientific instruments, and many industrial goods (Lee 1998). A study on a Korean case revealed that the important sources of technological innovation are customers (35.0%), followed by competing firms (20.0%), machinery suppliers (14.2%), part suppliers (13.9%), universities (12.3%), and others.

User firms of textile machines are dominantly textile firms that are likely to play a vital role in their innovation (Von Hippel 1988; Lee 1997, 1998). Innovation of textile machines has been traditionally the results of technological convergence between textile firms and specialised suppliers of textile machinery. The complexity of innovation in textile manufacturing machines varies depending upon what textiles they produce. For example, user firms have played a vital role in innovating new spinning machines (Sugiura 1994). Superior spinning machine needs a superior concept story so that user firms have moved from simple development works to concept formation and finding problems. It has been reported that machines such as peg-tray transfer and one-to-one connection between spinning and winding actually came from spinning firms.

Processing chemical fibres requires a complex machinery system that is often called as a plant. Making cloths and garments by using material fibres requires various weaving machines. The innovations of weaving machines need not only machinery technology but also some degree of textile technologies. Thus, user firms have a room to contribute to the innovation of new weaving machines. Engineers from specialised suppliers often stay at a customer factory for an extended period. If they find problems of the new machinery, they return to their factory and do R&D work in order to solve problems and improve the new machines. New textile machines therefore emerged and are completed while suppliers and users exchange and integrate their expertise through frequent interactions. We can identify such innovation taking place in textile machinery as typical convergence innovation.

The term 'convergence' here indicates technological convergence and can be defined as a horizontal integration of diverse technologies.[1] Horizontal integration means absorption of diverse fields of technological knowledge for the purpose of creating new functions and products, which often broadens the scope of their technological specialisation that can interact with user firms.[2] This phenomenon of technological convergence similarly occurred between machinery industries and electronic industries in 1970, and among variety of industries including chemicals, foods, and machine tools, and pharmaceutical industries (Lee and Hwang 2005).

### 4.2. *Decline and limited role played by textile firms*

Like the textile machinery industry of Korea, its user sector, the textile industry has continued to decline over the last decade. The number of employees in the textile industry reached the peak level of 327,000 in 2000. It afterwards continued to decline down to almost half the level employing

168,000 in 2009 as shown in Figure 6. The industry has actually lost employees at the annual rate of 7.1% for the period 2000–2009. A general expectation was that the Korean textile industry may have lost its competitive advantage, but people never imagined of this level of employment loss (Korea Federation of Textile Industries 2012). Since the economic activities of the textile industry are closely linked to the textile machinery industry (Song and Hong 1996), the decline of the textile industry must have been associated with the decline of the textile machinery industry.

Gyeongbuk and Daegu regions, the most famous two regions for the textile industry in Korea, showed similar trends to the national trends. The former lost 22,477 employees from 1999 to 2009 while its share decreased from 11.2% in 1999 to 8.0% in 2009. The latter is even worse as its number of employees became less than half for the same period, form 45,206 in 1999 to 20,024 in 2009 as shown in Figure 6. Therefore, its share also declined from 14.3% in 1999 to 11.9% in 2009. Losing their competitive advantage, CEOs of textile firms in the Daegu and Gyeongbuk regions may have sought to escape from the textile business or made foreign direct investment in developing countries with cheaper wages (Korea Textile Development Institute 2012). Many textile firms shut down their factories in Korea, and hence, their employees lost their jobs. This industrial adjustment eventually exerted serious impact not only on the local economy but also on the national economy.

The decline of the textile industry gave immediate impacts on the textile machinery industry over the recent decade. As mentioned in the front part of this paper, the number of specialised textile machinery suppliers, the number of employees, and sales of the textile machinery industry drastically decreased for the same period. Overall, economic activities of the textile industry and the textile machinery industry have remarkably shrunk in Korea as well as in Daegu and Gyeongbuk region which have to a great extent specialised in these industries. Daegu region has shown the highest level of shrinking in per capita gross regional domestic production (GRDP) among 16

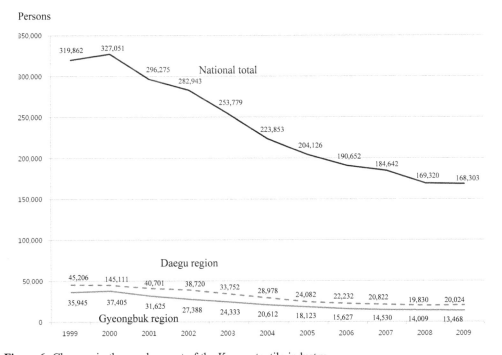

**Figure 6:** Changes in the employment of the Korean textile industry.
Source: Website of Korean Statistical Information Service (http//kosis.kr).

provincial economies over the last decade. This is why the local government of the Daegu region has struggled to survive its economy by generating diverse growth engines.

It is interesting to see what was happening in the innovation of the textile machinery industry in the stagnated situation of the textile industry. As seen in Figure 7, the number of patent applications in textile machinery tends to increase from 795 in 2000 to 1452 in 2011. Along with national total, textile machinery patents of Daegu region have shown similar trends increasing from 74 in 2000 to 146 in 2011. However, textile machinery patents of Gyeongbuk region have rapidly grown from just 14 in 2000 to 156 in 2011, finally overpassing Daegu region in 2011. Due to different growing speeds in patenting on textile machinery, the share of Gyeongbuk region remarkably increased from 1.8% in 2000 to 10.5% in 2011. The share of Daegu region has fluctuated every year without a clear tendency between 9.3% in 2000 and 10.1% in 2011. We can see that the Korean textile industry casts a gloomy vision in its growth and competence building in the future. Daegu region's textile machinery industry has similar features too.

Nevertheless, user firms exerted considerable effort to the innovation of specialised suppliers. Ms Lee, Hwa Sun, CEO of Hwa Sun Co. has recognised the importance of specialised suppliers from the early development stage of the textile machinery industry. She said that textile firms resultantly benefited from the introduction of productive textile machines by specialised suppliers. Whenever she travelled advanced countries for exhibitions of textile and machines, she collected information about new machines and ideas, and tossed them to specialised suppliers. This behaviour was motivated from her will to develop new textile materials. In order to develop new textiles, new, innovative textile machinery is necessary and hence she tried to find new machines whenever she began to develop new textiles. For instance, Hwa Sun initiated the local development of circular-ring knitting machines by a specialised supplier as it brought sample machines

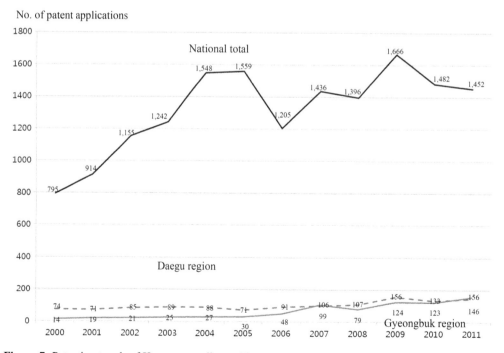

**Figure 7:** Patenting trends of Korea on textile machinery.
Source: Website of Korea Intellectual Property Rights Information Service (http//kipris.or.kr).

from German firms. Hwa Sun Co. has especially played the role of lead users mentioned by Von Hippel (1988).

### 4.3. *What was lacking in the convergence innovation?*

Textile firms that played the role of lead users like Hwa Sun were not many in Daegu region. Many textile firms may have not known that there are large scales of textile markets, e.g. medical textiles for the medical service sector and industrial textiles for the automotive industry. Only a few firms took a risk of entering into high value-added textiles because it requires burdensome investment on R&D work. This situation ultimately caused specialised suppliers to suffer from less domestic demand and less pressure to the development of new textile machinery, which further contracted the real demand size for domestic textile machines. Therefore, many specialised suppliers lying at a marginal profit line quitted the textile machinery business.

In summary, R&D work not only for the innovation of textiles but also for the innovation of new textile machines has been lacking in Korea over the last decade. It was already pointed out even in the 1980s by a policy study (Ha 1987). Even after decades have passed, neither user firms nor specialised suppliers put much resources into R&D activities or integrate market characteristics into R&D as the fourth-generation R&D suggests (Miller and Morris 1999). They could not succeed in recruiting good researchers and electronics engineers who supplement their development work. They did not take R&D work into account seriously during the time when Chinese suppliers accumulated capability to manufacture cheap textile machines and dominated global textile machinery market. Convergence innovation of specialised suppliers may as well be minimal as user–supplier interactions reduced and learning opportunities to innovate likely to be little.

The result was disastrous since many relatively large companies operating in the 1980s, such as Lucky Goldstar, Sungri Machinery, Kukje machinery, and so on, disappeared during the last decade. Many small and medium-sized enterprises running textile machine business too have disappeared. Resultantly, the number of specialised suppliers remarkably reduced from 521 in 2000 to 129 in 2010 in Korea. The surviving specialised suppliers have mostly sought other profitable businesses by utilising their core competence accumulated in textile machinery manufacturing as in the case of Keumyong. Automobile parts, electronic and industrial machinery components are prospective areas for specialised textile machinery suppliers to enter.

## 5. Major findings and conclusions

We analysed economic and patenting activities of both the textile machinery industry and the textile industry in Korea from 2000 to 2011. The employment data were analysed as representative index of economic indicators, while domestic patent applications were analysed as representative index of convergence innovation activities. They are certainly not sufficient enough to answer our research questions and understand complex industrial dynamics. Nonetheless, we have obtained some meaningful findings with respect to theoretical understanding of convergence innovation and policy implications to rehabilitate the textile industry and the textile machinery industry in Korea. Major findings are summarised as follows.

First, convergence pattern of the textile machinery industry in innovation is similar to that of other industrial machinery like intelligent robots. We also discovered that there are two types of convergence in the textile machinery industry: outside-in convergence and inside-out convergence. Inside-out convergence is an innovation generated by converging textile machinery technology and other technology areas and outside-in convergence is vice versa. The former is active in current Korean textile machinery suppliers because they struggle to survive in the market situation of recession and over supply from Chinese suppliers with cheap prices by utilising their core competence for exploiting business opportunities in other machines.

Second, we found that the most distinctive convergence within textile machinery technologies has been taking place between mechanical methods (D01D) and fibres technology (D01F). The IPC term of 'mechanical methods' is too broad to capture a distinctive trend in convergence since it includes a variety of technological class for related suppliers. Nevertheless, the two technologies indicate representative components of the textile industry and the textile machinery industry. It implies how company strategies or government policies to innovate both industries can be formed. That is, mechanical methods and fibres technology should be promoted together, not separately.

Third, patenting of both the textile firms and specialised suppliers appeared to be weak compared with other machinery industries in Korea. Only 19.9% out of total domestic textile machinery patents came from user firms (15.5%) and specialised suppliers (3.4%) from 2000 to 2011. Low portion of patenting implies that R&D activities are not active and that inside-out convergence innovation mainly took place in specialised suppliers due to entries into other industries because of contracting domestic sales of textile machinery. Decreasing domestic sales of textile machinery may also have caused decline of patenting in related suppliers of textile machinery like electronics, chemicals, metal products, and so on.

Fifth, probably as a result of non-active innovation performance in both textile firms and specialised suppliers, the economic activities of the textile industry as well as the textile machinery industry concurrently downturned over the last decade. Especially, the number of employees in both industries was remarkably reduced by almost half during the last decade. Other economic indicators such as sales, the number of firms, value added, and so on, all showed more or less the same trends. We can see how an industry and related sectors lose dynamism and their competence in a short period of time, although some industries are flourishing within a national economy.

In conclusion, convergence innovation especially in closely linked industries is very important for their competence building and maintaining employment. User firms and specialised suppliers pull together convergence innovation, strengthening their competitive positions. We found that the textile industry and the textile machinery industry of Korea did not seriously carry out R&D activities and, as a result, failed in generating convergence innovation and building up their competence. The result was the loss of employment and the stagnation of regional economies which are specialised in the textile industry and the textile machinery industry.

## Notes

1. The term 'horizontal integration' in this paper is not same as that explained by Teece (1976) who indicated the term as an organisational integration over value chains.
2. Iansiti (1998) stated that technology integration is made up of the set of problem-solving activities that are performed to match a new element of technical knowledge to the complex architecture of established competences.

## References

Ha, Jae-Young. (1987), *Technology Development System and Market Structure of the Korean Textile Machinery Industry (in Korean)*, Seoul: KIET Research Report.

Iansiti, M. (1998), *Technology Integration*, Boston, MA: Harvard Business School Press.

Kim, Euiseok. (2014), 'Evolutionary Patterns and Dynamics of Technological Convergence: The Case of Printed Electronics', Ph.D. dissertation, KAIST, Daejeon.

Kodama, F. (1986), 'Inter-disciplinary research: Japanese innovation in mechatronics technology', *Science and Public Policy*, 13(1), 44–51.

Kodama, F. (1991), *Analyzing Japanese High Technologies: The Techno Paradigm Shift*, London: Pinter Publishers.

Kodama, F. (1994), *Emerging Patterns of Innovation*, Boston, MA: Harvard University Press.

Korea Federation of Textile Industries. (2012), *Textile Industry Statistics* (Vol. 26, no. 223).

Korea Textile Development Institute. (2012), *Market Trends of Daegu-Gyeongbuk Regions*.

Kumaresan, N. (2001), 'Dynamics of Technology Accumulation and Evolution of Distributed Industries: The Case of Robotics Industry', Ph.D. thesis, Tokyo Institute of Technology, Tokyo.

Lee, Kong-Rae. (1981), 'A Study on the International Competitiveness of the Korean Heavy and Chemical Industry (in Korean)', Thesis for Master of Economics, Pusan National University, Busan.

Lee, Kong-Rae (1996), 'The role of user firms in the innovation of machine tools: The Japanese case', *Research Policy*, 25, 491–507.

Lee, Kong-Rae. (1998), *The Sources of Capital Goods Innovation – The Roles of User Firms in Japan and Korea*, Amsterdam: Harwood Academic Publishers.

Lee, Kong-Rae. (2007), 'Patterns and processes of contemporary technology fusion: the case of intelligent robots', *Asian Journal of Technology Innovation*, 15(2), 45–65.

Lee, Kong-Rae, and Hwang, Jung-Tae. (2005), *A Study on Innovation System with Multi-technology Fusion (in Korean)*, Seoul: STEPI Policy Study 2005–17.

Lee, Kong-Rae, and Seong, Tae-Gyeong. (2009), *University-Industry Collaboration for Activating Convergence Innovation (in Korean)*, Seoul: STEPI Policy Report.

Lee, Kong-Rae, Kang, Hee-Jong, Hwang, Jung-Tae, and Lee, Junhyup. (2010), *Technology Integration and Job Creation: Innovation Policies for Expanding Employment*, Seoul: STEPI Policy Report.

Miller, W.L., and Morris, L. (1999), *4th Generation R&D – Managing Knowledge, Technology and Innovation*, New York: John Wiley & Sons, Inc.

Nonaka, I. (1994), 'A dynamic theory of organizational knowledge creation', *Organizational Science*, 5(1), 14–37.

OECD. (1993), *Technology Fusion: A Path to Innovation, the Case of Optoelectronics*, Paris: OECD.

Rafols, I., and Meyer, M. (2006), 'Knowledge-Sourcing Strategies for Cross-disciplinarity in Bionanotechnology', SPRU Electronic Working Paper Series, no. 152, Brighton.

Roco, M.C., and Bainbridge, W.S. (2002), *Converging Technologies for Improving Human Performance*, Arlington, VA: NSF.

Rosenberg, N. (1963), 'Technological change in the machine tool industry, 1840–1910', *Journal of Economic History*, 23(4), 414–446.

Rosenberg, N. (1982), *Inside the Black Box – Technology and Economics*, Cambridge: Cambridge University Press.

Song, Byeong-Jun, and Hong, Seong-In. (1996), 'Strategy for the Changes in Market Demand for Textile Machinery (in Korean)', KIET Research Report no. 380, Seoul.

Sugiura, Keishi. (1994), 'Technological Role of Machinery Users in Economic Development: The Case of the Textile Machinery Industry in Japan and Korea', Ph.D. dissertation, University of Sussex, Brighton.

Teece, D.J. (1976), *Vertical Integration and Vertical Divestiture in the US Petroleum Industry*, Stanford: Stanford Institute for Energy Studies.

Von Hippel, E. (1988), *The Source of Innovation*, New York: Oxford University Press.

Website of Korea Intellectual Property Rights Information Service. (2013) http//kipris.or.kr.

Website of Korean Statistical Information Service. (2013), http//kosis.kr.

# Innovation strategy and technological competence building to provide next generation network and services through convergence – the case of NTT in Japan

Kumiko Miyazaki and Evelyn Giraldo

*Graduate School of Innovation Management, Tokyo Institute of Technology, Tokyo, Japan*

Telecommunications industry has been through major structural changes in recent years due to the Internet. Technological, economic, and social drivers have caused the telecommunications market to converge, with boundaries between diverging technologies, industries, and services becoming blurred. In this paper, an analysis is made of the impact of the paradigm shift of next generation network services on the R&D and technology strategies of Nippon telegraph and telephone (NTT) in its transition to become a leader in the provision of services, integrating technological competences in application technologies with competences in the underlying network technologies. Changes in the R&D organisation and strategy were identified to enable NTT to shift its focus to the upper-layer businesses.

## 1. Introduction

The environment in which firms compete is subject to changes that may be caused by socio-economic or political factors, changes in consumer preferences, or the advent of a new technology or technique. Therefore, firms have to react and evolve according to the changes in their environment in order to sustain their competitiveness. In high-tech sectors such as electronics, IT, and telecommunications, the clear sectoral boundaries have become fuzzy in recent years. In this paper, we use the definition of the term convergence, as the blurring of boundaries between two or more industries. As pointed out by Curran, Broring and Leker (2010), triggers and drivers exist behind the trend of convergence. These triggers include scientific findings, technological development, as well as changes in customer demands.

The telecommunications industry has been undergoing major paradigm changes in recent years due to technological, market, and socio-economic factors. Capabilities in bandwidth and processing have grown exponentially, and the digitalisation and interactivity of multimedia content and introduction of new devices have enabled the emergence of sophisticated networks and services. Users have also changed with the technologies and have become more sophisticated and demanding. These technological, economic, and social drivers have caused the telecommunication market to become convergent, with boundaries between diverging technologies, industries, and services becoming blurred as seen in the case of telecommunications and broadcasting services and between fixed and mobile networks (fixed–mobile convergence). As saturation of fixed and mobile telephony markets and the obsolescence of legacy networks have reduced the

| Layer | Activity |
|---|---|
| VI | **Customers** |
| V | **Applications**<br>(web-design, information services) |
| IV | **Navigation & Middleware**<br>(browsers, portals) |
| III | **Connectivity**<br>(internet access, web hosting) |
| IP interface | |
| II | **Network Layer**<br>(optical fibre, DSL, radio access network,<br>Ethernet, frame relay) |
| I | **Equipment and software layer**<br>(switches, transmission equipment,<br>routers, servers, billing software) |

**Figure 1:** The layer model of the info-communications industry.)
Source: 'Telecoms in the Internet Age' Martin Fransman (2002).

rents and limited the businesses growth, telecommunications firms have been prompted to build new competences in the rapidly expanding Internet-based market. As service and transport layers are taken apart, allowing applications to be defined directly at the service level and provided over different platforms, the competitive environment of the ICT industry changes dramatically as players compete across traditional boundaries to provide integrated services and solutions in a global scale. Figure 1 shows the layer model introduced by Fransman (2002) which gives a representation of what he defined as the info-communication industry, which is the telecommunications industry after the introduction of the Internet.

Next generation networks (NGNs) are 'packet based networks able to provide services including telecommunication services and able to make use of multiple broadband, QoS[1]-enabled transport technologies and in which service related functions are independent from underlying transport-related technologies'. NGN offers access by users to different service providers, and supports 'generalized mobility which will allow consistent and ubiquitous provision of services to users'.[2]

The impact of NGN resides in providing an open platform for developing services, which allows multiple players to enter and specialise in different sub-modules without providing the whole system. It also lowers the technical and financial barriers to enter the market, putting incumbent network suppliers and operators at the risk of becoming pipeline operators and pushing them to move to the upper layer of the ICT industry, by the creation of new services and applications.

Due to the technological evolution of telecommunication networks and services, firms need to reshape their strategy and organisations in order to adapt to the dynamic environment and to integrate existing technological competencies in order to achieve sustained advantage in the provision of NGN services.

Nippon Telegraph and Telephone (NTT) Corporation is the largest telecommunication carrier in Japan and one of the largest in the world. It was established in 1952 as a public telecommunications operator, and major business lines are the provision of regional, long distance, and international communication services regionally, mobile communications, and data communications services. In this study, an empirical analysis is made of how NTT has built competencies in different technological fields which are critical to its innovation strategy to create value-added services over NGNs.

We try to address the following research questions:

(1) How have the technological competences in applications and networks changed over time in order to provide value-added services over NGN, leading to convergence?

(2) How is the knowledge network of application-related technologies structured?

(3) How has the structure of R&D organisation evolved to enable the transition?

The paper is organised as follows: after the above-mentioned introduction, Section 2 briefly reviews the related literature and theoretical background. Section 3 provides an overview of NGN and the main features of services over NGN. Section 4 presents the methodology and the data used in this study. In Section 5, the findings obtained from bibliometric analyses are shown, highlighting the technological competence building and topical emphasis as well as collaborations with external actors. This is followed by Section 6 which discusses how the R&D organisation was transformed over time to enable the transition for NTT to become an integrated player. Finally, Section 7 sums up the main findings and offers some concluding remarks and implications.

## 2.  Theoretical background

Throughout their existence, firms in the ICT sector have carried out research in multiple technical fields and accumulated a large amount of knowledge on different scientific areas, production processes, markets, customers, and organisational processes, and most of this knowledge has been 'stored' in its routines, codes, procedures, and the mind of their employees. The ability to exploit the accumulated knowledge in any of those aspects gives a firm a unique advantage which becomes a core competence of the firm, and the ability to combine such competences provides the firm with the dynamic capability to adapt to the changing environment and take advantage of a technological opportunity.

Therefore, understanding the organisation as a portfolio of competences is crucial in strategic management. Iansiti and Clark (1994) explain that the dynamic capability 'will be linked to consistency in a firm's response to environmental turbulence, and effective management of problem-solving activities will lead to timely reaction to external changes through readjustments in the capability base of the organization'. Teece et al. (1997) defined it as 'the capacity of an organization to consistently nurture, adapt and regenerate its knowledge base and to develop and retain the organizational capabilities that translate the knowledge into useful actions'. Therefore, dynamic capability is the ability of the firm to react and adapt to the turbulent competitive environment.

In the search for the right combination of competences, a firm may explore different research paths or programmes in diverse technological fields to improve their knowledge base. Tidd et al. (1992) explains that technological trajectory is an exploratory path of a firm in its research and is the base for the firms to develop distinctive core competencies in order to gain competitive advantage in long-term technological and product development. Hence, the trajectories or research paths that a firm has followed are important determinants of where the firm is positioned in the present and the direction to follow in the future.

Miyazaki (1995) focused on the emergence of optoelectronics in selected Japanese and European firms in the sectors of communications, computers, and consumer electronics. By using data gathered from publications, patents, and interviews, she studied the trajectories, learning, and competence building processes at the firm level. The study places the dynamics of competence building at the centre of the technology strategy, and explains how it allows a firm to explore new areas and shift its trajectories as part of the search and learning process.

## 3. Shifting innovation strategies towards NGN

### 3.1. *Overview of NGNs*

There are many factors encouraging the need of migration towards NGN, mainly because of declining Average Revenue per User of fixed-line telecommunication services due to increased competition from mobile and broadband services. Telecommunication carriers have been forced to decrease the cost and the complexity of handling several legacy networks.

With the advances in optoelectronics, optical wires have replaced copper in the local loop, as optical fibres provide a drastic increase in data transfer speed and capacity, and decrease the cost of the service.

The Open System Interconnections (OSI) reference model has been used as the basis for tele-communications. The OSI model is made of seven-layer architecture in which each layer represents conceptually similar functions of a communication system.[3] Although the general principles apply, NGN is made up of only two functional layers. Figure 2 shows in a generalised way the functional layers of NGN, a transport layer which is made up of routers and which uses the Internet protocol to transfer packets and a service layer. The transport layer facilitates user to user connectivity, user to services platform connectivity, and services platform to services platform connectivity. The service layer provides the user services such as telephone services, data services, video services and gaming and manages sessions, quality of service, and security.

Because of the separation of the functional layers, service-related functions become independent from the transport-related technologies or networks. This means that the choice of technology in infrastructure will not affect the type of services that can be provided over it. This feature of NGN allows multiple service providers to enter markets, boundaries of which used to be defined by a platform, causing a convergence of services and industry players.

Another key feature of NGN is that all data are divided into packets, or blocks, which are sent through available communication channels. Traditionally, Public Switched Telephone Network (PSTN) have been circuit-switched networks in which a channel is dedicated during the duration

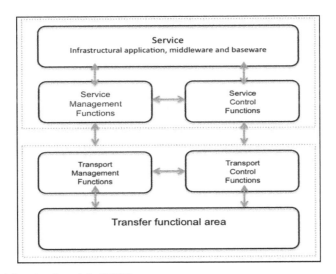

**Figure 2:** General functional model of NGN[3].

of the communication between two nodes, meaning that the electric circuit can only be used by those nodes for a certain time, and the fee is calculated according to the time the channel is kept open for connection. Because there is no need to dedicate a single channel, the fees for packet-switched networks are calculated according to the amount of data transmitted. This makes services provided over packet-switched networks much more affordable.

### 3.2. *Main distinctive features of services over NGN*

The technological paradigms of the NGN combine the advantages of the old telecommunication model with the Internet-based model, blurring the limits between formerly unrelated industries, platforms, and services. The Internet commercial model is much more deregulated than the telecommunication commercial model. Therefore, NGN has brought about significant increase in competition as different players emerge, providing service bundles in all kind of combination across the value chain. The following sections provide examples of services which represent major paradigm shifts occurring in the ICT industry.

#### 3.2.1. *Services based on convergence*

A typical example is the convergence between the broadcasting and telecommunication industry. On the one hand, due to the increase in high-speed broadband Internet access and the introduction of several capable multimedia devices such as smartphones, tablets, and video gaming consoles, the distribution of multimedia content over the Internet has become more common and has allowed many traditional broadcasting companies to transmit their content on the Internet through ad-supported services such as Youtube or online stores such as iTunes. On the other hand, telecommunication carriers have launched their own Internet Protocol TV (IPTV) service, which is expected to become a killer-application of NGN services. Video content is provided on demand by commercial subscription channels.

IPTV services may be provided in three different ways:

- Live: similar to traditional TV programming.
- Time-shifted: replays of previously broadcast programmes.
- Video on Demand (VOD): browse and choose from a catalogue.

This causes a change not only in the distribution of content and players involved but have also changed the way services are provided. TV services may become user-centric, personalised, and fragmented. Increasing media consumption and demand will allow many players to enter the market and create value at different levels.

#### 3.2.2. *Shift from ownership to use*

Another social-driven feature of future NGN services is the ownership and federation of products and services. A clear example of this is Google apps. While Microsoft's vision was a desktop in every house running Windows operating systems and Office tools, Google's vision is to run all data, applications, and utility tools over the Internet. Software resides in Google's servers on which data are processed and stored, but should be accessible anytime only if an Internet connection is provided. Users do not need to go to the store and purchase an expensive license to literally own the software and 'manage' or maintain it, but instead can open a Google account and use the software. Users can save the significant amount of money but instead have to allow for the fact that the data are being stored outside their normal geographical boundaries. In this case, reliability of the service and security of the data are the key values for users to switch to such kind of applications.

In the corporate sector, cloud computing services are key to add value to the network infrastructure of telecommunication carriers, as it provides business with a cost-efficient opportunity to offload the maintenance of IT infrastructure and increase productivity. As a result, cloud computing represents an attractive revenue potential for technology players and telecommunication carriers.

## 4. Methodology

### 4.1. *The main procedure*

At first, information from newspapers, press releases, and technical journals was collected in order to gain a deeper understanding of NTT's research on NGN-related services such as IPTV and cloud computing and the underlying technologies that support them. In the next phase, data related to the company's publications during the last 15 years, focusing on the accumulation of knowledge in the technological areas that are the foundation for IPTV and cloud computing were collected, observing changes in technological trajectories of the firm in order to adapt to the new paradigm. Through co-authorship analysis, the structure of knowledge networks has been studied. Topical emphasis through keyword co-occurrence analysis was also identified.

In order to validate the observations from the publication data and to get qualitative information of the company's strategy and organisational aspects, interviews with R&D project managers, and R&D planning who were involved in the development of NGN services were carried out. (Prof. Kitawaki at Tsukuba University who used to be at NTT's Multimedia Systems laboratory and Mr T. Nikkuni, the Manager of NTT R&D Planning Group at the time when the interview was carried out.)

### 4.2. *Overview of NTT*

As most telecommunication carriers, NTT was established as a natural monopoly, subjected to limited competition and whose innovation forces were of political nature, mainly to catch up with the technology level of western countries.

From the legal and market perspective, a major event in NTT's history was its privatisation in 1985 as a first step towards the deregulation of the Japanese telecommunication market in order to promote competition-driven innovation. As a result, NTT was reborn as an innovation-driven organisation, switching its R&D expenditure from 2.7% of its operating revenue in 1986 to 4.6% in 1992 (Fransman 1995). NTT is deeply involved in the research and design of telecommunication equipment with a family of suppliers. In collaborative R&D activities, NTT has been taking a commanding lead, as the company requires its development partners to build the prototypes of network elements according to their own specification.

In 1992, NTT DoCoMo was formed as the mobile carrier of NTT. In order to reduce the oligopolistic control, NTT was divested into a Holding Group, two local phone providers – NTT East and NTT West – and NTT Communications, which is a long distance and international carrier. As of 2009, the NTT group is made of 479 subsidiaries.

NTT's road to the deployment of NGN started in 1999, with the introduction of dial-up, always-on access to the Internet at a flat rate, resulting in a rapid increase in the number of Internet users and a rise in demand for broadband access. A bundled Internet and phone services were introduced later in December 2000 through the Asymmetric Digital Subscriber Line (ADSL) access technology.

In 1999, the Japanese government forced NTT to open and lease its copper line infrastructure. Competitors began providing ADSL services at a much more competitive price, bundling Internet access and Internet Service Provider services. NTT had to counter the effect by lowering the price of the PSTN service, making it difficult to generate sustained revenue. Consequently, NTT adopted a new strategy in 2001 in order to shift its market to the optical access market to end the disadvantageous speed competition in the PSTN market. To create value over the optical infrastructure, the company bundled optical access with its Internet Protocol (IP) telephony service.

Due to the rapid increase of subscribers to optical access and the demand for more sophisticated services such as VOD, the company announced a new medium-term strategy in November 2004, with the main goals of establishing a broadband access infrastructure and full migration of the IP network to the NGN. Field trials for NGN were carried out in 2007, and the first commercial service started in 2008. In the same year, the company established a new mid-term strategy called 'Road to a Service Creation Business Group' with the aim of developing and offering new services compatible with full IP networks that cover both fixed-line and mobile communications. The company set a goal of shifting its business infrastructure from the legacy telephone businesses to upper-layer businesses, expecting IP solutions and services such as IPTV and cloud computing to account for three quarters of its net sales over a four-year period.

### 4.3. *Data analyses*

#### 4.3.1. *Source of the data*

COMPuterized ENgineering inDEX (Compendex) is an online version of the Engineering Index, a compilation of over nine million records and references of over 5000 international sources which include journals, conferences, and trade publications. It is managed by Elsevier, a company which publishes medical and scientific literature.

Engineering Village website was used in order to collect information about NTT publications during the last 15 years. The query included the search parameters for all technical journals that have 'NTT' OR 'Nippon telegraph and Telephone' as the author affiliation within the years 1995–2009. The Engineering Village database provided a total result of 9810 records of 'documents' (journals and technical papers) published by NTT Group during the period of time specified. A verification process by author affiliation field was carried out in order to discard sources with the same name as NTT from the data set.

#### 4.3.2. *Classification of the data*

The first step is to understand the areas of research that are relevant for the company, and how their importance has been changing over time. For this purpose, the two examples of the creation of services were used since IPTV and Cloud Computing are clear examples of the paradigm shifts caused by NGN services in the ICT industry. Through the collection and investigation of NTT's R&D brochures and technical magazines, a list of keywords referring to core technologies that are critical to develop these services was identified. Table 1 provides the list of keywords which are categorised in three layers:

- Technologies related to contents and application.
- Technologies related to the information sharing platforms.
- Technologies related to networks.

**Table 1:** List of selected keywords of core technologies for NGN services

| Level | Broad category | Specific category |
|---|---|---|
| Content and applications | Speech, acoustics, and natural language | Speech recognition, speech analysis, speech synthesis, speech coding, reverberation, hidden Markov models, and speech quality |
| | Video and image | Video coding, video signal processing, video compression, VOD systems, MPEG, H.264/AVC, Video distribution, and HDTV |
| | Media computing | Cognitive systems, learning systems, decision-making, machine learning, web mining, user support systems, knowledge acquisition, and user profiling |
| Information platforms | Security | Encryption algorithms, authentication, single sign-on, data storage, and public key cryptography |
| | Service platform | IMS (IP multimedia subsystems), Internet protocols, operating systems, virtualization platform, VPN, SOA, SaaS, file sharing systems, virtual servers, Metadata, Ipv6, and Open Source Sofware (OS) |
| Networks | Core networks | IP technologies, network architecture, network operation, and network quality control. High-speed and large-volume optical IP technologies |
| | Access networks | *Fixed*: Phone line, digital subscriber line – DSL, GE-PON (gigabit ethernet-passive optical network), fibre to the home (FTTH), TDM (time-division multiplexing), and wavelength-division multiplexing – WDM. *Mobile*: GPRS, W-CDMA, long-term evolution – LTE, and high-speed downlink packet access – HSDPA. *Wireless*: Multiple input multiple output – MIMO and wireless access systems (IEEE 802.11 and IEEE 802.16) |
| Basic research | Physics and material science | Quantum computers, photonic crystals, and wide bandgap semiconductors |
| | Electronics | LSI, millimeter wave applied technology, and MEMS |
| | Photonics | PLC (planar lightwave circuits), optical semiconductors, and photonics signal processing |

The list of keywords was shown to different researchers at the Service Integration Laboratories at NTT who gave their opinion about the suitability of the keywords to describe the core technologies of which services such as IPTV or cloud computing are made up. Their comments were that the technologies are numerous and the most general keywords need to be used as technical names might be too specific and misleading since they change over time. Therefore, it was decided to use the most generic keywords as much as possible.

### 4.3.3. *Examining and assessing the data*

In order to explore and organise the data set obtained from Compendex, we used the software VantagePoint[4] which is a useful tool for tech mining, as it helps to clean up collections of text records to visualise and analyse them properly.

The data set contains valuable information about the documents published by NTT, which are key for this analysis. These are displayed as fields:

- *Author*: the author of the document.
- *Year*: the year in which the document was published.

- *Author affiliation*: institutions related to the author or sponsor.
- *Controlled terms*: the keywords related to the subject of the document which are assigned by the database.
- *Abstract*: a summary of the contents of the document.

The right combination of these fields through basic analyses gives useful information on the research activity of the company. Firstly, by combining the *keywords* and *year* fields it is possible to track the main topics the company has been working on during the last 15 years, which areas have increased and which have decreased. It is also important to identify who the top publishing *authors* are in order to observe the concentration of research competences at the level of teams and key individuals. Profiling the collaborations within NTT's laboratories and with external institutions and universities can help ascertain the development of a knowledge network. Using the *keywords* field and the year, it is possible to observe the research activity of the company in a certain topic over time, and what topics the company has been focusing on.

These basic analyses from the data on the publication activity of the company were carried out and discussed through interviews with NTT'S R&D planning group.

### 4.3.4. *Knowledge networks and topical emphasis*

For the purpose of understanding how research is concentrated and to identify collaborating partners of research and observe topical emphases over time, socio-metric and topical emphasis maps were made for the categories of interest of this study, which are the ones related to application services that contribute to add value to NTT's network infrastructure.

Socio-metric maps were made by using auto-correlation analysis in authorship at the laboratory level. The highest level of aggregation for the author affiliation was used, which means the laboratory name. The purpose is to understand in which laboratories research is concentrated and how they are linked as analysed through co-authorship of papers. A link between the nodes represents at least one member of each laboratory working together in a paper. Collaboration with external sources in the government, industry, or academia sector can also be identified from these maps.

Additionally, topical emphases maps were constructed from the analyses of co-occurrence of keywords, which are the descriptors of the publication contents. By using principal components analysis, the most frequently occurring keywords are clustered. These maps help us understand the emphasis and specialisation in certain topics. The nodes indicate principal components, in a basic form of factor analysis, showing the sets of keywords co-occurring with each other for each of the selected categories. The node size is a relative number of records containing the high-loading keywords represented by the statistical component.

## 5. Main findings

We have discussed so far on how the technological evolution of telecommunication networks and the paradigm shifts in the ICT industry have forced incumbent network operators such as NTT to move towards the upper layers of the industry and create value-added services in order to differentiate from other market players in the IP business. In this section, we present the results obtained from the analyses of the publication data of NTT to get an insight of the R&D activity of the company and observe how the process of building competencies in application services that can be combined with NTT's strong competence in network infrastructure accumulated through decades of operation and management.

## 5.1. *Technological competences for NGN*

Through a basic analysis of the absolute numbers of published papers in each area by year, it is possible to grasp a trend on the innovative activity in the development of NGN services and identify which areas are becoming more dominant and which have decreased their impact through the time.

Figure 3 shows the average number of publications in each area for five different periods of time. Publication activity in areas such as speech and acoustics, video, and image has been dominant during the first three period of time, but has slowed down since 2004. A reduction in publication activity does not imply a change of focus in an area as, taking as example research on video and image technologies, the active publication activity observed from the year 2000–2004 is related to NTT's effort to the standardisation of the Motion Picture Expert Group (MPEG)-4/H.264 codec which was released in 2003.[5] Hence, a reduction in publication activity in the area suggests that the company has achieved a satisfactory level and the technology is moving towards application stages.

Emerging areas in the application technologies are media computing and information platforms, which are the foundations for the development of portals, web services, and platforms. The emergence of these two areas shows the company's learning effort towards becoming a cloud computing solutions provider, as virtualisation is one of the major trends driving the convergence of technologies, industries, and providers of NGN services.

Information platforms are an emerging area as the converging paradigms have triggered the strategic building of competences for the provision of services such as SaaS (Software as service), PaaS (Platform as service), and IaaS (Infrastructure as service). These technologies are key to allow dedication of different physical infrastructures in a virtualised environment for full utilisation of IT resources. Competences of the company in this area were limited due to the specialisation in network operation and design in cooperation with different customers and suppliers within a controlled competition environment. Therefore, areas related to the network as platforms that will boost the creation of value-added, user-centric services are paramount. A recent increase in research topics such as service-oriented architectures (SOAs), security, software-defined networks, utility computing, virtualisation, and among others is observed. These efforts are driven by a need to serve increased demand from customers to strengthen their communications and IT services.

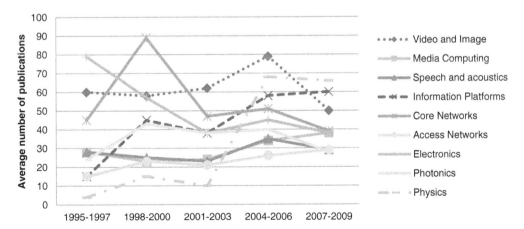

**Figure 3:** Average number of publications in each area by year.

In the network-related technologies, we observe the area of physics and material science as the most emergent area, which is consistent with the effort of improving the cutting-edge optical fibre infrastructure, seeking to move the competence of the company in the control of optics and electricity to the control of quantum effect.

The increased research in access networks is related to the fixed–mobile convergence paradigm in which research effort focused on seamlessly integrating optical access networks with wireless access networks in order to provide ubiquitous services. A decline is observed for most network-related technologies which include core networks, photonics, and electronics.

## 5.2. Knowledge networks and topical emphasis

### 5.2.1. Speech, acoustics, and language

According to the interview carried out with an expert in speech recognition and former Project Manager at NTT laboratories, the company engaged in research of digital speech coding technology in 1990 for the introduction of cellular phones. By that time, NTT contested against Motorola in the development of a new speech codec, which became the standard for Japan during the introduction of MOVA, NTT's brand name for second-generation (2G) cellular technology. Speech quality is the foundation for any media service, because even video service cannot be accepted by users unless speech quality is good. Since NTT is originally a telephone company, they allocated significant resources to ensure speech quality towards its multimedia strategy. Research has evolved into more sophisticated applications which include speech recognition and analysis. Research on speech is currently focused on new wideband speech coding algorithms designed with emphasis on factors such as wider audio frequency bandwidth, lower delay and lower complexity, and bitrate efficiency. NTT is engaged in the development of the new codec ITU-T G.711, which is a core technology for VoIP (Voice over IP) and multimedia services.[6]

Figure 4 shows the representation of a knowledge network of research on Speech. As the node size indicates, most of publications concentrate around Communication science laboratory. The links with a group of nodes in the right-upper area show possible collaborations with the Acoustic Society of Japan, the Information Processing Society of Japan (ISJ), and the Institute of Electrical and Electronics Engineers (IEEE). Major collaborating players are University of Tokyo, Nagoya University, Hokkaido University, Waseda University, and the Tokyo Institute of Technology. This shows a significant amount of knowledge exchange between NTT Labs, academic societies, and universities, indicating strong Industry–University linkages. The map also shows other NTT laboratories moderately scattered and linked to each other as in the case of Basic research laboratory and Service integration laboratory. This suggests that co-authorship among laboratories appears to be very limited in this area.

Figure 5 shows the topical specialisation within research on Speech. The higher loaded cluster is speech analysis, which includes co-occurrence of keywords such as parameter estimation, frequency domain analysis, and signal processing. The relationship to other clusters of keywords such as microphones, mathematical models, algorithms, and voice/data communication systems indicates relationship in the application layer.

### 5.2.2. Video and image

NTT built on its capabilities in speech compression technologies as the foundation for the development of a multimedia era in the early 1990s, which includes the transmission of audio, video, and data over communication networks. Since then, the company has been actively engaged in the standardisation of video compression technologies with the International Organization for

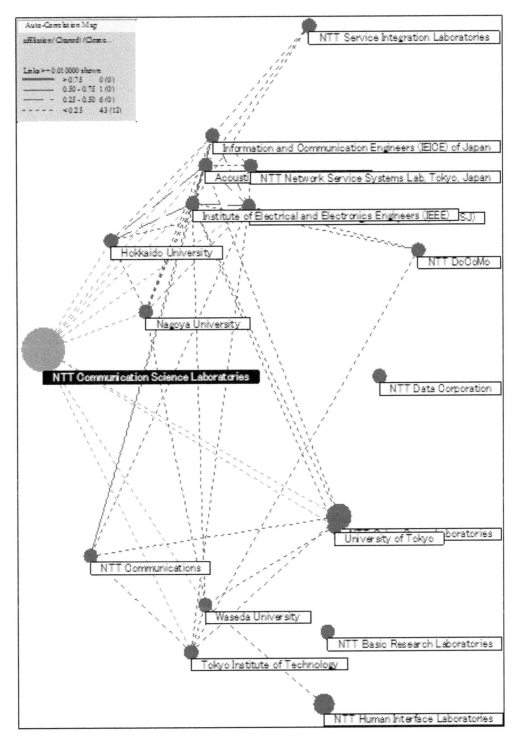

**Figure 4:** Socio-metric map on research on speech, audio, and languages

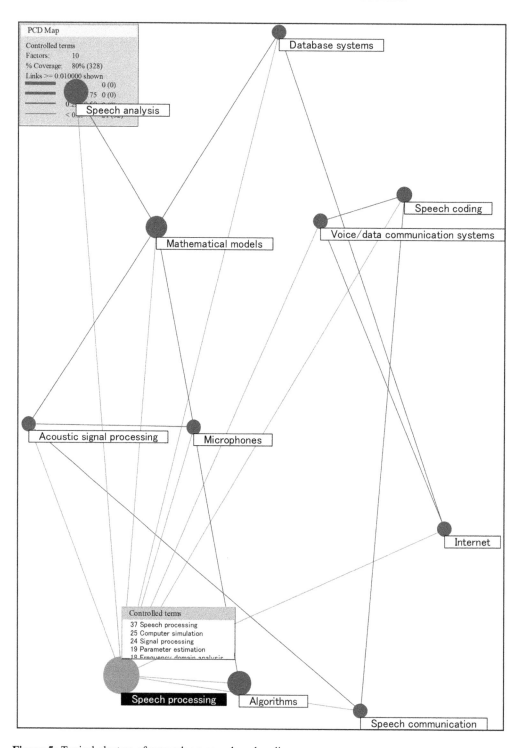

**Figure 5:** Topical clusters of research on speech and audio

Standardization for the development of the MPEG-1 formats for the compression of pictures and the MPEG-2 standard for the compression of video and movies. NTT was also involved in the development of the MPEG-4/H.264 or advanced video coding (AVC), the latest standard for video compression for the distribution of high definition television (HDTV). Research competences in this area are currently used for the development of high-quality, efficient encoding of video for use in DVDs and digital broadcasts, digital watermarking technology for adding invisible ID (identification) information to video, video monitoring technology for recognising the video output from monitoring cameras, and 3D model-construction technology.[7] These are the core technologies for the development of video delivery services such as IPTV, digital signage, and video conferencing.

The knowledge network of research on video and image technologies shows that the most active laboratories are communication science, network innovation, network service systems, service integration, and microsystems integration laboratories. Major partners in this area are the ISJ, the IEEE and the Institute for Information and Communication Engineers (IEICE). Major collaborators in the academia are University of Tokyo and Tokyo Institute of Technology. The map also shows a moderate level of collaboration with subsidiary business corporations such as NTT DoCoMo and NTT Data Corporation.

In Figure 6, the topical specialisation map reveals that the high loaded clusters are observed in the lower area of the map for the topics including image quality, image coding, feature extraction, high definition television, and Large Scale Integration (LSI) circuits. Topics on the right-hand side of the map seem to be clustered around applications of video and image technologies such as multimedia and real-time systems.

### 5.2.3. *Other areas of focus*

Research has been focusing on the development of virtual private networks (VPN) which are designed to provide virtual environments that appear to the user as a dedicated line. The main design consists of overlay model networks in which user nodes are connected by asynchronous transfer mode or frame relay technologies. Due to privacy and compliance concerns in the enterprise sector, security is the key value to provide to customers. NTT is currently undertaking R&D on security of data as well as next generation cryptography, such as ID-based encryption. Security and management of virtual resources constitute a core competence to develop open clouds required by businesses and government.[8]

The socio-economic map shows that research is concentrated around the information sharing laboratory. In this area, top collaborators are the International Association for Cryptological Research, the National Institute of Informatics, the ISJ, the IEEE, and the IEICE. Collaborators within the academia include the University of Tokyo, Tokyo Institute of Technology, and Kyoto University. The map also shows a moderate level of collaboration with subsidiary business corporations such as NTT DoCoMo and NTT Data Corporation.

Analyses of topical emphasis show the high loaded cluster on security of data and cryptography. There are no specific topical clusters on open source software and virtualisation technologies, which might indicate that the company has focused more on information and network security which are important areas of competence to migrate towards the upper layer.

The bibliometric analysis provides understanding of the development of in-house technical capabilities in the areas related to the creation of value in the services.

In the pursuit of creation of new value-added services, NTT intends to synchronise and combine its long-term competences on network infrastructure with application and services that fully exploit the network capacity. The socio-metric maps have shown to some extent the level of cross-collaboration within the NTT laboratories, subsidiaries, and external academic institutions.

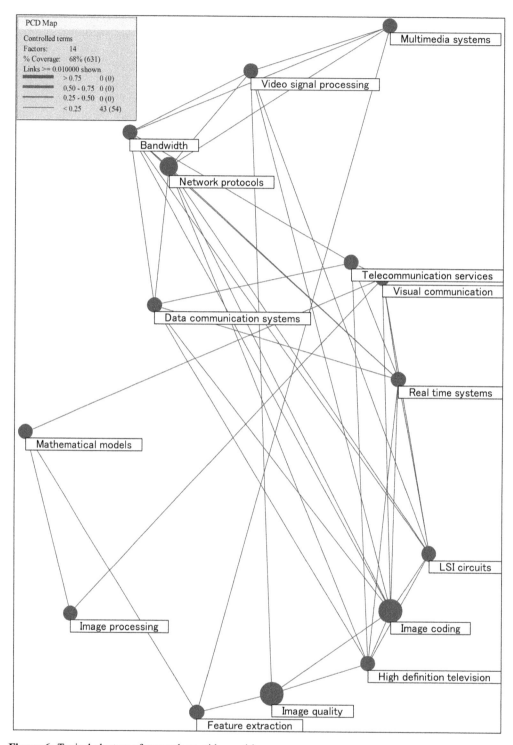

**Figure 6:** Topical clusters of research on video and image.

## 6. Management of R&D

### 6.1. *In-house R&D*

A key for service creation is to ensure early business application of the technologies through faster time-to-market and increased collaboration. Hence, the structure of NTT has changed over time to become more flexible and open. In the 1990s, the laboratories were divided by technologies such as transmission systems, radio communications systems, LSI, optoelectronics, and communications switching laboratories, as the company was very infrastructure oriented.

The R&D organisation was transformed to have three different layers of laboratories: the cyber communications lab group and information sharing lab group which focus on the application technologies and the science core technology lab group which is more focused on the cutting-edge network technologies. Therefore, there is a clear separation of research on technologies for improving services and technologies for improving the network infrastructure (See Figure 7). Integration efforts between the laboratory groups also include the creation of a Service integration laboratory, which

develops architectures from both network and service perspectives; strategically selects and plan R&D topics which adapt to global trends of technology and markets; study communication traffic and quality in the characteristics of these design, control, management and operation in the face of growing varieties of networks and services; and promote cross-laboratory commercialization activities to turn the technologies developed by NTT laboratories into business promptly and certainly.[9]

### 6.2. *Open innovation*

As part of a comprehensive commercialisation activity, collaboration within the NTT Group and other relevant parties is important. For this reason, the company also promotes an 'Open Collaboration' policy in which research themes are open to other laboratories, for cases in which

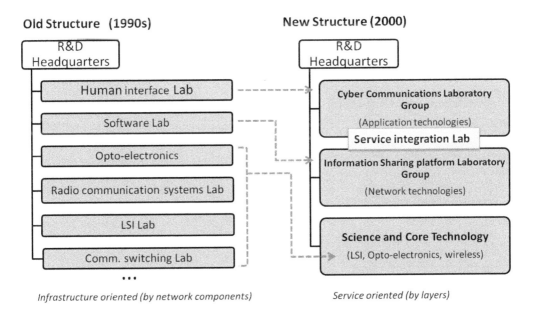

**Figure 7:** Changes in organisational structure of NTT.

research on the same subjects leads to new findings. Information exchange is also facilitated through exhibitions and the publication of two technical magazines in both English and Japanese to promote R&D results inside and outside the company.

Regular meetings and conference or committee are set up for information sharing and planning between the laboratory groups. Individual researchers may also form ad hoc study group to discuss what to do in a certain period of time. Collaborations with universities are encouraged through a flexible process of application and allocation of resources.

Through the creation of open innovation networks such as the IPTV Forum Japan, NTT collaborates with broadcasters and appliance manufacturers to exchange knowledge and achieve standardisation of IPTV services. In the area of cloud computing, the creation of a Global Inter Cloud Technology Forum[10] promotes the collaboration between academia, government, and industry. Members of the forum include NEC, Hitachi, IBM, Oracle, Cisco, BIGLOBE, Microsoft, NICT, and university professors. The forum is supervised by the Ministry of Internal Affairs and Communications of Japan.

### 6.3. *Opportunities and challenges*

In the offering of the services, NTT's major strengths rely on the company's long-term experience in network infrastructure and a wide-range of technologies, strong customer base, and reputation in the market. However, the complexity and high cost of keeping legacy systems affect the company's service innovation capacity.

Regulations place a major challenge to be overcome. In the particular case of video services, the Japanese laws for broadcasting are rigid and vertically oriented. As NTT is still regarded as a telephone company, legal issues such as the 'broadcasting law', 'telecommunications business law', 'the law concerning NTT', and 'NHK Law' restrain the company from creating contents or charging royalties over the broadcasting of NHK's contents. Therefore, NTT's service value resides in promoting the cutting-edge quality of video.

In the case of cloud computing, the opportunities of vertical extension are plenty due to the increasing interest from SMEs[11] in the cost-effective benefits of cloud computing and NTT's ability to provide a safer infrastructure than other entrants. Regulations regarding the storage of private data are a major concern to be overcome. Another issue is the complexity in the migration of the legacy systems in the client companies to cloud computing, which would require a higher level of expertise by NTT as a solutions integrator.

### 7. Conclusions and implications

In this paper, analysis was made of the impact of the paradigm shift of NGN services on the R&D and technological strategies of NTT in the transition to become an leading integrated market player, by capitalising on the opportunities offered by convergence, integrating technological competences in the upper layer of application and services with their accumulated technological competences in the underlying networks.

Through a bibliometric analysis of the company's publication activity in the last 15 years, long-term accumulation of technological competence in both network and application technologies was observed. A dominant share of competence in speech and video was observed due to the evolution of the company from telephone operator to a multimedia business corporation and its engagement in developing codecs. Building on this, the company has been shifting emphasis towards more sophisticated applications such as speech recognition and video analysis to create highly competitive NGN services. Video services are at the top of the service creation strategy, because of the large amount of data transfer and network utilisation they imply. Hence, for the development of a killer-application such as IPTV, NTT relies on their long-time accumulation of know-how in speech and video compression technologies which has been achieved through active participation in the development of international standardisation of speech, video, and image compression technologies.

Emerging areas of competence include media navigation and information integration platform technologies. Media computing is used to exploit the rich amount of information and social capital of the web. Such competence is fundamental for the creation of more user-centric, context-aware services. A significant increase in publications of information sharing platforms indicates sustained competence building process for cloud computing solutions. As security is a key issue, a special emphasis in security of data and cryptography has also been observed.

Through co-authorship analysis of the publication data, the structure of the knowledge network was identified. A strong presence of universities and academic societies indicates the company's evolution from a closed-innovation environment with a family of vendors and special-ised suppliers towards an open innovation environment. Collaboration with subsidiary businesses such as NTT DoCoMo, NTT data, and NTT communications indicates more market-oriented R&D and increased integration capability with market inputs. To complement the competence building process in these areas, the company has started using mechanism such as forums and alliances with key technological players for the exchange of knowledge.

NTT's major changes in R&D organisation include the clear-cut separation of research on network-related technologies and application technologies by adopting a three-layer laboratory structure and the introduction of a service integration functional unit in the middle layer of its R&D organisational chart. Therefore, it was possible to see how strategically the R&D organis-ation was re-structured to enable NTT to pursue strategies to become a more integrated operator by shifting its focus towards the upper layer of applications and services, in line with the previous findings by Miyazaki (1995) who pointed out that top management strategy affects the evolution of R&D organisation which in turn affects the competence building process.

This study has some limitations that also offer opportunities for future research. First, our study focused on only one case within an industry and therefore the findings should be interpreted with caution. Major players in the ICT industry such as IBM, Microsoft, and Cisco as well as network operators are also challenged to build competences that will allow them to innovate and create services in the upper layer of the value chain, in which new trends such as big data, cloud services, and Internet of Things are disrupting the way the market has been defined and segmented. Hence, the way such companies are re-designing their strategy and structure to compete in the new environment caused by convergence could be a topic for future research. Second, this study has covered the technological competence building process by NTT in appli-cation technologies related to NGN services that will enable them to move forward in the service creation strategy. However, there are other technologies related to NGN that might fall out of the scope of the analysis as we have focused mainly on two types of NGN services. Third, while the findings revealed the numerous collaborative relationships between NTT and other institutions through the knowledge network analyses, we have not been able to explore the linkages at the individual level, only at the inter-organisational level. As it has been pointed out by Oliver and Liebeskind (1998), understanding how the two levels of collaboration, the organisational and individual levels, interact may be a topic for future research.

**Notes**

1. Quality of service.
2. ITU-T terms of reference of NGN-GSI July 2009 version. http://www.itu.int/dms_pub/itu-t/oth/2C/04/T2C040000030003PDFE.pdf.

3. The OSI model is extensively explained by the Cisco Internetworking technology handbook http://docwiki.cisco.com/wiki/Open_System_Interconnection_Protocols.
4. VantagePoint is software developed by the Georgia Institute of Technology and licensed by Search Technology Inc.
5. MPEG-4 is a collection of standards for compression of visual data used in High Definition Video systems. Standardisation is supervised by the International Organization for Standardization ISO.
6. Source: NTT Technical Review. https://www.ntt-review.jp/archive/ntttechnical.php?contents=ntr2008 08le1.pdf&mode=show_pdf.
7. For more information see: 'Toward Next-generation High-quality, High-reality Video Surpassing HDTV' NTT Technical Review, Vol. 5, No. 11, November. 2007.
8. Source: NTT Information Sharing laboratories. http://www.ntt.co.jp/islab/e/org/pf.html#1.
9. Source: http://www.ntt.co.jp/islab/e/org/si.html.
10. Official site: http://www.gictf.jp/.
11. Small and Medium Enterprises.

## References

Curran, C-S., Broring, S., and Leker, J. (2010), 'Anticipating converging industries using publicly available data', *Technological Forecasting & Social Change*, 77, 385–395.

Fransman, M. (1995), *Japan's Computer and Communications Industry*, Oxford: Oxford University Press.

Fransman, M. (2002), *Telecoms in the Internet Age: From Boom to Bust to … ?*, Oxford: Oxford University Press.

Iansiti, M., and Clark, K. B. (1994), 'Integration and dynamic capability: evidence from product development in automobiles and mainframe computers', *Industrial and Corporate Change*, 5(3), 509–533.

Miyazaki, K. (1995), *Building Competencies in the Firm: Lessons from Japanese and European Optoelectronics*, Basingstoke: Macmillan.

Oliver, A. L., and Liebeskind, J. P. (1997–1998), 'Three levels of networking for sourcing intellectual capital in biotechnology', *International Studies of Management and Organization*, 27(4), 76–103.

Teece, D., Pisano, G., and Shuen, A. (1997), 'Dynamic capabilities and strategic management', *Strategic Management Journal*, 18(7), 509–533.

Tidd, J., Bessant, J., and Pavitt, K. (1992), 'Paths: exploiting technological trajectories managing innovation', in *Managing Innovation*, eds. J. Tidd, J. Bessant, and K. Pavitt, New York: Wiley, pp. 105–132.

# Convergence innovation in railway technology: how ERL of Malaysia attained its co-evolution structure for systemic development

Mazmiha Mohamed, Hon-Ngen Fung and Chan-Yuan Wong

*Department of Science and Technology Studies, Faculty of Science, University of Malaya, Kuala Lumpur, Malaysia*

By examining the co-evolution structure between two processes – accumulation and assimilation – of Express Rail Link Sdn Bhd's (ERL) system over the past decade, this paper explores the transformation of ERL of Malaysia; from a mere user of Siemens's technology, to Siemens's technology partner capable of attaining state-of-the-art operating systems for a high-speed rail (HSR) technological system. Both accumulation and assimilation processes of ERL are examined in detail to elucidate the dynamic process of the 'multilateral model' of a HSR system. The approaches have led ERL to witness convergence innovation between Siemens's technology and ERL's knowledge in operating systems. The convergence innovation between the two processes has enabled ERL to venture into engineering consulting services, exporting innovative operating solutions to other firms abroad. The strategic approaches discussed in this paper may thus provide policy lessons for other firms in developing countries aspiring to emulate the upgrading process of rail technology.

## 1. Introduction

With recent plans unveiled for an ambitious Southeast Asian rail link that would connect China and Singapore, the rail industry in Asia is set for a boom that could see an increasing demand for rail systems, parts, and services globally. However, the rail industry is one of the least studied elements in the transportation discourse (Janelle and Beuthe 1997). Although some are of the view that railway growth is slow (Couto and Graham 2008), many anticipated the rise of the railway industry, especially in the light of globalisation and rising oil prices (Lacôte 2005; World Bank 2007).

Most railway industries around the world started as a necessary means of transporting freight (agricultural or mining products) from the point of production or harvest to ports and major cities. The transportation of passengers via railways was secondary to the aforementioned natural products (Basri 1985). However, rail transport is rather common in urban and rural settings of today. It provides connections between cities and suburban areas as well as poorly connected cities or towns. Today, many developing economies have increased their investment in railway networks to facilitate transit and alleviate traffic congestion. This is particularly evident in Malaysia and Indonesia. Malaysia, for example, is expanding its urban transit network with a new transit line being constructed, while Indonesia has rolled out a railway master plan to address poor connectivity in their existing railway system (Dikon 2010). The critical role played by urban rail network systems is exemplified by the success of the Mass Rapid Transit (MRT) (Singapore) and Mass Transit Railway (MTR) (Hong Kong), and so on in terms of timeliness, dependability, and safety.[1]

Developing countries like Malaysia have recognised the importance of an advanced, integrated rail system that would spur urban and industrial development in rural areas while alleviating congestion. With a specific aim of attaining operational and maintenance capability for HSR, Malaysia planned to develop its railway knowledge in anticipation of future railway growth. The motivation to attain this capability came from the awareness of the importance of railways as a future transport of choice, not only in the Asian region but also worldwide.

However, in order to catch up with the railway standards and connectivity status of the developed countries, it is necessary for developing countries to upgrade their railway systems using imported technology. The case in point would be the import of HSR technology from Siemens for the airport rail link between Kuala Lumpur International Airport (KLIA) and Kuala Lumpur (KL) city, which will be discussed in this paper. For technology developments in a complex system, such as the railway network system, developing countries often opt for technology transfer (Chen 1994; Kim 1997; Cohen 2004) as they lack the technological knowhow and proprietary technology that are used in state-of-the-art systems. However, the onus is on the recipients of the technology transfer to adapt and innovate the processes, ultimately 'melding existing knowledge with new knowledge from external sources', (Cohen 2004) in order to reduce their reliance on imports and drive down costs.

The melding of existing knowledge (from the technology proprietor) with new knowledge from external sources (from the local service provider), or rather the convergence of knowledge that occurred in a technology transfer, is the central theme of this paper and has been studied at length by Kim (1980). The model refers to the development stages of industrial technology in developing countries, which are acquisition of technology, assimilation of technology, and improvement for competitiveness. Kim's model presents strong evidence for the importance of assimilation of knowledge for capability building (Kim 1980). The significance of capability building in this case is that – with the right strategy – capability building at the firm and sectoral level contributes to national development through the identification and exploitation of strategic niches (Lall 1992, p. 169).

'Convergence includes bringing together all relevant areas of human, machine, and natural resource capabilities that enable society to answer questions and solve problems that isolated capabilities cannot' (Roco and Bainbridge 2013, p. 2). Apart from convergence of the older and the newer knowledge, convergence also occurred between all the interrelated systems of the major components of a railway system. The components of a railway system may differ over time according to technology changes of each component (see Suzuki and Kodama 2004).

Nonetheless, the complexity of our case study – HSR systems – complicates the capability-building process due to the technicality and specificity of the technology. For countries that already have conventional railway systems, a progress into a more advanced railway system may mean the advancement from an older knowledge stock to the newer knowledge stock of a modern railway through convergence.

To understand the railway system, one needs to understand the concept of 'system'. Bunge (2003, p. 35) defined a system as 'a complex object every component of which is related to at least one other component'. Bunge's definition is based on four basics of (1) system composition, (2) environment, (3) structure, and (4) mechanism. Lee (2011) observed that there are six core technologies of a HSR system. These technologies – which are the components of a railway system – are civil and track works, traction power supply, train control and communication systems, high-speed train (rolling stock), information system, and the operation and maintenance (O&M) system.

Our study of the HSR system requires us to adapt Carlsson's (1997) definition of technological system (Carlsson 1997), which characterises technological systems as 'knowledge and competence networks supporting the development, diffusion and utilization of technology in established or emerging fields of economic activity'. By looking at the overall system rather than each component, the relationship and dynamic interaction between each component is scrutinised. Because our study is concentrated on a single railway company, the systemic development studied can be considered as a firm-level railway development. Hence, our study attempts to identify the path-dependent elements that contribute to the development of technological capability and competence within the HSR system in Malaysia.

This paper tracks the process of convergence occurring between existing and new knowledge, and also convergence among the related components of a railway system in the technology transfer, which has ultimately lead to the export of services by the Malaysian HSR firm, Express Rail Link Sdn Bhd (ERL).

## 2. Literature review

### 2.1. *Learning and its contribution to capability building*

Lundvall and Johnson (1994) stressed the importance of having a learning organisation in order to codify knowledge. This depends on the firm's ability to learn and accumulate knowledge and its contribution to capability building. In this sense, learning plays an important role in capability building (Malerba 1992; Liu, Qian, and Chen 2006). This aspect of capability building for catching up has also been widely discussed by many scholars (Kogut and Zander1992; Kumar, Kumar, and Persaud 1999; Radosevic 1999; Liu et al. 2006; Wong and Goh 2009; Fu, Pietrobelli, and Soete 2011; Liu, Cheng, and Chen 2011).

Organisational learning in itself depends on many contributing factors; evident in literature are those focusing on existing available knowledge of the firm (Cohen and Levinthal 1990), sources of knowledge (Malerba 1992), openness in accepting new knowledge (Caloghirou, Kastelli, and Tsakanikas 2004), and learning through imitation (Kim 1997).

Cohen and Levinthal (1990) stressed the importance of absorptive capacity in learning new knowledge and further assimilation between the newly learnt knowledge and existing knowledge, implicitly referring to two separate bodies of knowledge which converge to strengthen the understanding of the overall body of knowledge. This explanation is evident in the case of the technology transfer of HSR to ERL, whereby the newer body of knowledge refers to the HSR system brought into the country by Siemens of Germany (transferor). The importance of existing knowledge was also mentioned by Kim (1998) who stressed that the two important elements in effective organisational learning are the intensity of effort and the existing knowledge.

Even though various studies have been conducted on learning and capability building, most of the literature focused on learning and capability building of the manufacturing industry, such as the automotive industry (Kim 1998; Lee 2005, Kodama 2014) and semiconductor industry (Lee 2005). There is a lack of studies exploring the railway system which has its own unique attributes that warrant further investigation. Despite it being classified as medium technology (Lall 2000), the railway system – and in particular the HSR – presents an interesting case for study due to the complexity of its components. The shift from diesel power to electrified rails means that components are constantly being improved and innovated at different rates. Nonetheless, even in modern-day railway systems, not all railways run on electricity and some railways still operate using diesel engines. In contrast, railway signalling components existed even before the twentieth century and remain a requisite part of a railway system until today.

## 2.2. *Knowledge in the railway sector*

As in most other sectors, the adoption of a HSR system requires a firm to have a working knowledge (existing knowledge) of operating rail systems and common understanding of its various components. However, the challenge with implementing a HSR system in this case study is the need to adapt new knowledge which has yet to be implemented locally. A pivotal factor which ensures proper adaptation hinges on the absorptive capacity of the existing stock of knowledge available in the country's human capital (Cohen and Levinthal 1990; Kim 2001; Liao, Fei, and Chen 2007). For developing countries, it is important that the new knowledge being transferred can be absorbed and learnt due to the high cost of building and operating these railway systems (Gaabucayan, Doi, and Takada 1999; Campos and de Rus 2009; Cheng 2010). Campos and de Rus (2009) calculated the average cost per kilometre for the construction of a HSR system to be around €9–39 million.

The cost of operating railway systems can fluctuate based on how efficiently the system is managed by the railway firm. However, according to Oum and Yu (1994), the efficiency of a rail system, including HSR, also depends on government policy and regulation, which are beyond firm management. They found that highly subsidised railway lines, which are the financial tendency for developing countries, prove to be more inefficient than less subsidised railways.

## 3. Conceptual framework

### 3.1. *Vertical and horizontal convergence in the railway system*

The multilateral model as shown in Figure 1 is a combination of the systems approach adopted from Carlsson (1997). We integrate the concept of assimilation and accumulation in narrating the systems approach of knowledge defined by Wei (1995). The system approach is reflective of and aptly describes the railway system due to its composition of various components within the system. The assimilation and accumulation of knowledge, according to Wei, provide a transition between the two separate bodies of knowledge which are the existing technology and the imported technology. Wei's explanation on assimilation and accumulation of knowledge is specific to technology transfer, which is why his views are taken into consideration for the multilateral model.

Knowledge in this study refers to both the formal knowledge or codified knowledge and tacit knowledge (Kogut and Zander 1992). The flow of knowledge, in contrast to the flow of goods and services in a technological system (Carlsson and Stankiewicz 1991), indicates a progression of accumulated knowledge. To demonstrate the flow of knowledge of the ERL technology transfer, a model showing convergence of knowledge in a generic railway system is illustrated in Figure 1. While Carlsson's (1997) view covered a rather comprehensive aspect of technological system – with an intention to elucidate a network of firms and R&D infrastructures with policies and academic institutions as part of the linkages – this study focuses on the integration between components and core technological systems present in a railway system.

With reference to Figure 1, the model showing the railway system is illustrated by a single horizontal plane where the smaller boxes on the horizontal plane marked as C1, C2, and so forth represent the components of the system. For this case study, the basic component for a railway system is based on the core technologies of a railway system. Again, we refer to Lee (2011) for the core technologies of the railway system – civil and track works, traction power supply, train control and communication systems, rolling stock, information system, and O&M system. For instance, C1 and C2 could represent traction power and track works, respectively. In this model, O&M system is represented by the outer border of the horizontal plane on which each individual component (C1, C2 ... ) is embedded. The reason for this is that O&M

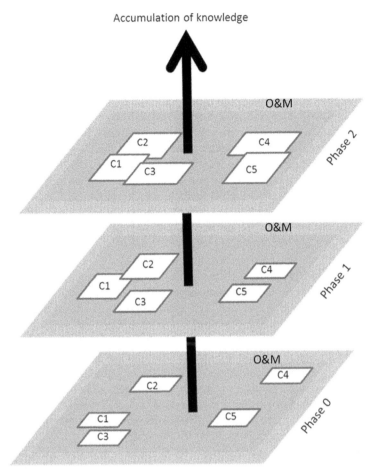

**Figure 1:** Diagram showing the accumulation of knowledge (vertical plane) and assimilation of core components (horizontal plane) in the technology transfer of a railway system.

does not reflect a particular technology per se; instead, it serves as the organisational management that binds and provides the setting for each core component of the railway system.

Each horizontal plane in the model represents a different time phase of the railway system in a technology transfer. A different horizontal plane (or a different O&M system) at one point of time can consist of different components. For example, the O&M of a railway system at an earlier time such as in the late 1800s may consist of only rolling stock, civil and track work, traction power (in this case, steam), and train communication system (signalling). In such case, the horizontal plane would be represented by a fewer number of components, representing fewer core technologies that make up the railway system.

The upward arrow indicates accumulation of new knowledge over time. Hence, the horizontal plane shifts upwards, accumulating and converging with new knowledge over time. The components on the horizontal plane (C1, C2 ... ) may move to converge with other components (indicating assimilation of technologies) or increase in size (accumulation of knowledge) along with the advancement of technology in that particular component.

The multilateral model helps to illustrate the dynamics undergone by a railway system in a technology transfer environment, and shows how its components assimilate with other components within different time frames. The model also visually explains the technological and knowledge growth of the components over time. This is shown by the increasing size of the components C1, C2, and so forth.

### 3.2. *The technology transfer of ERL*

The HSR technology adopted by ERL was done via concession agreement to finance, design, construct, operate, and maintain the daily HSR service between KL's central railway station and the KLIA. Concession holder ERL is a company partly owned by YTL Corporation Bhd (50%), Lembaga Tabung Haji Bhd (40%), and Trisilco Equity Sdn Bhd (10%). Lembaga Tabung Haji is a government-linked company while the remaining shareholders are private companies.

There were early setbacks to the ERL HSR project due to the Asian Financial Crisis of 1997. The crisis had disrupted the procurement process for key components including the procurement of the rolling stock. Nevertheless, because the project was a national interest, construction works for the tracks continued and ERL was able to resume the project in 1999 after the crisis ended. The rolling stocks arrived in 2001, and operations began in 2002.

Soon after the project resumed, ERL established a wholly owned subsidiary to manage the train O&M of the HSR system. The subsidiary, ERL Maintenance Support Sdn Bhd or E-MAS, was formed as a joint venture (JV) between Siemens (51%) and ERL (49%) and became the technology recipient for the project. The contractual JV ended in June 2005, after which ERL took over the Siemens shares, 3 years after the ERL operation started.

With a presence in over 40 countries, Siemens's expertise in rail technology offered the ERL project a full spectrum of services ranging from rolling stocks, automation, and power, as well as electrification and signalling systems (Siemens 2013). Siemens provided the technology, expertise, manpower, and training for the construction and installation of the HSR technology. E-MAS used to rely heavily on the expertise of Siemens in the initial stages, as well as in the training of local talent for the ongoing maintenance of the system.

After the JV between ERL and Siemens ended, E-MAS took over the O&M of the ERL system independently while constantly communicating with Siemens technical personnel for guidance on technical issues or problems. Any process innovations and improvements to the system were made with the approval of Siemens and within the safety parameters defined by Siemens.

In order to investigate the horizontal convergence and accumulation of knowledge in ERL, we conducted several primary interviews with key technical personnel in electrification, rolling stock, and signalling as well as management personnel overseeing these departments. Our interviews were semi-structured, focusing on learning, convergence, and process innovation. The framework illustrated in Figure 1 is used as a guide in this study to narrate the convergence process of rail systems of ERL.

### 4. Convergence of knowledge

### 4.1. *Phase 0: pre-conditions to the ERL project*

The diffusion of technological capability in the Malaysian railway industry is relatively slow, as the Malaysian railway industry took about a century to progress from diesel-powered, conventional type rail to the more modern types of railway system which operate on electricity.

Rail in Peninsular Malaysia was a crucial form of transportation for both freight and passengers since the British colonial period, serving as an efficient method for the transport of agricultural and mining commodities from inland plantations and mines to key transport hubs such as Port Klang and Butterworth (Basri 1985). The rail industry began to decline with the improvement of the road infrastructure linking the towns in Peninsular Malaysia in the 1980s and early 1990s, culminating in the opening of the PLUS North South Expressway that stretches from the Malaysia–Thailand border at Bukit Kayu Hitam in the north to the Malaysia–Singapore border at Johor Bahru in the south.

The Malaysian Railway Company (Keretapi Tanah Melayu, KTM) has been endowed to operate and maintain the railway line system, primarily the one powered by diesel fuel. KTM was started as the railway association of several state-run railways during the British colonial era.

As for urban transport, in contrast to other countries, Malaysia was a late adopter of electrified railway technology. The first electrified system was launched in 1993 by KTM Komuter, linking KL city with the suburbs of Rawang, Sentul, Seremban, and Port Klang. This electrified system ran along existing train tracks, powered by electricity supplied from overhead catenary lines.

In 1996, the STAR LRT was launched to serve a number of stops connecting the areas in the northern and eastern sides of Selangor state. The track was mainly built overhead or on the surface with no underground tracks, and drew power from a third rail running alongside the track on the underside of the carriage. The rolling stock consisted of a fleet of 90 Adtranz standard-gauge trains manufactured by Walkers Limited, an Australian engineering company. In 2001, Adtranz was bought over by Bombardier, the manufacturer for the next LRT system, PUTRA LRT.

In 1998, the above-mentioned PUTRA LRT was launched and served the areas in the northeast to the southwest of KL. Notably, the STAR LRT system does not intersect with the KTM Sentral Station, but does intersect with the Putra LRT line at other points in the rail system. The PUTRA LRT is mostly elevated, but goes underground after the KL Sentral station, providing better access to key locations in the KL city centre. The PUTRA LRT was also the first driverless rail system to be implemented in Malaysia. Serving inner city urban areas, the difference in size of the rolling stock or passenger capacity was the major differing factor between light rail transit and conventional rail.

In the 1990s Malaysia witnessed a boom in transport infrastructure development, and rail transport was considered a crucial element to relieve traffic congestion in KL which would in turn improve productivity and efficiency. By the time the ERL project was commissioned, several players were already operating rail lines in Malaysia; however, each achieved only limited success. The initial batch of trainees recruited by E-MAS, under guidance from Siemens recruitment experts, came from two major technical backgrounds – rail engineering and rail-related engineering such as from aviation and military system backgrounds.

It is clear that the presence of electrified systems served as the pre-condition setting for E-MAS to recruit experienced technical professionals. This reduced the learning curve needed for the adoption of the ERL HSR system. This is important as it serves as the basis of Phase 1, which is the technology transfer period.

Towards the end of Phase 0, the main components (or the core technologies) have grown in number compared to conditions in the earlier part of Phase 0. The core technologies as per Table 1

**Table 1:** Railway system core technologies and the E-MAS departments responsible.

| Core technology | Department |
| --- | --- |
| (1) Traction power supply | Electrification |
| (2) Train control and communications | Telecommunications |
| (3) Information system | Telecommunications |
| (4) High-speed train | Rolling stock |
| (5) O&M system | Telecommunications and Operations |
| (6) Civil and track works | Outsourced |

Source: E-MAS (2014).

are easily accessible in the Malaysian market. For instance, information system has materialised as a component which contributes to the railway system. The biggest leap in the upgrade of technologies within Phase 0 occurred with the advancement and use of a type of remote industrial control system called SCADA.[2] SCADA is also used to monitor and control electrification, for example, in remotely controlling the switchgears for the traction power substation that supplies electricity to the rail system.

In terms of track work, the common use of standard gauge in the LRT systems has served as another pre-condition setting for the introduction of HSR systems. The standard gauge track is a pre-requirement for the establishment of the HSR infrastructures. The metre gauge for the KTM tracks (track width of 1000 mm) has been substituted by the standard gauge with track width of 1435 mm.

Additionally, there is also assimilation between the communication network and O&M components of the railway system. For example, train movement and data can be collected via the Open Transport Network, a network of fibre optic cables along the track which enables trains to be controlled at a centralised remote location such as at an operation control centre (OCC) for operations purposes. This is an example of assimilation between the core components of communication and electrification.

Nevertheless, at this point, the components of the electrified rail systems vary from case to case in terms of electrification, signalling, and rolling stock, which means a strong reliance on installers and their ability to train and transfer the technology to local staff.

We argue that at this phase (0) of the railway industry in Malaysia, the accumulation of new knowledge is at its starting point, where the core knowledge from the innovators is being transferred to local human capital for the O&M of the railway systems. At this point, convergence is limited as the key activity is training and adherence to the Standard Operating Procedures (SOPs) outlined by the technology transferors.

### 4.2. *Phase 1: introduction of HSR*

We define Phase 1 in this case study as the commencement of the technology transfer of the HSR until the end of the JV period between ERL and Siemens.

The primary challenges at the beginning of this phase include the upgrading of capability for rolling stock, namely from conventional electric trains to high-speed trains, which required assimilation between track works technologies and rolling stock technologies. In civil and track works, the introduction of axle counters[3] increased the safety level of modern railway systems, as the systems are now able to track trains on particular sections of the railway line. In assimilation with communication technology, axle counters also provide train location information to the Train Management System (TMS) which operates using fibre optic cables (Optical Transport Network) throughout the track length. This way, trains are centrally controlled not to enter a track section that is already occupied by another train, thus preventing train collisions.

Assimilation of knowledge also occurred in other instances of the ERL railway system, such as the merging of the rolling stock component with track work technology to enable higher speed trains on the tracks; as well as in train control and communications using SCADA, merging electrification and information systems to provide better safety features and on-time information to operators and also to the paying passengers. This horizontal convergence of knowledge occurred in the industry through the upgrading of human capital that was familiar with systems brought into the country via other rail projects.

The knowledge from the railway projects cited in Phase 0 (such as STAR and PUTRA LRT) spilled over to E-MAS via human capital mobility. Paired with guidance from Siemens, the knowledge gained by human capital from previous railway projects in Phase 0 helped E-MAS to populate and structure its organisation. As such, the technical organisation of E-MAS addresses all the core technologies of a modern railway system. The information of the technical organisation of E-MAS was obtained via interviews with relevant technical heads of departments. The three main technical departments at E-MAS are the telecommunications (TEL) department, electrification (ELT) department, and rolling stock department (RST). For operation of the system, the Operations (OPS) department works closely with TEL, since OPS relies on the information fed by the TEL team to operate the trains on the main line.

During the set-up of E-MAS, the early batches of technical personnel were hand-picked by Siemens recruitment experts based at E-MAS in accordance with the technology transfer process. Subsequent recruitment after these early intakes was handled directly by E-MAS Human Resources. Based on interviews with senior technical officers at E-MAS, the important criteria during the earliest selection of personnel were: English language literacy, technical aptitude, and mathematical concentration level. These were ascertained via examinations held during the first interview. Only those who passed the examination went on to the second stage to be personally interviewed. Quite a number of the early 'management trainees' came from rail-related backgrounds; however, there were also many who had no prior rail experience but who had attained industrial mechanical or electrical technical knowledge. This batch of employees formed the existing knowledge for E-MAS.

At Phase 1, assimilation of knowledge at the firm level occurs in the merging of old knowledge stock of new recruits at E-MAS with the new knowledge from Siemens.

The transfer of knowledge, both tacit and codified, forms the technology transfer process. Codified knowledge was done through formal classroom training, while tacit knowledge was mostly gained through on-the-job training. Part of the transfer process was done via reading and understanding reports and manual documents supplied by Siemen. These documented papers imparted local technical officers with the codified knowledge in operating the ERL system. A senior technical officer at E-MAS claimed that 'anyone who could read and has a technical background would be able to understand the SOP required in operating the ERL system'. For on-the-job training, assimilation between new HSR knowledge and existing railway knowledge at the firm level was done by rotating new recruits between all the main technical departments (TEL, ELT and RST) in order to familiarise the employees with the various core technologies of a HSR system. To diffuse tacit knowledge, Siemens used a pairing method for on-the-job training, where an expert would be paired with a small group of employees when troubleshooting train repair problems.

Towards the end of Phase 1, long-term employees of E-MAS were now able to link the core technologies that make up the railway system. This is shown in Figure 1 by the closing distance between the components as they move towards each other. An important transfer of tacit knowledge during the phase was the adoption of best practices in managing a railway O&M company, which was the ultimate aim of the technology transfer in ensuring O&M capability. E-MAS also adopted much of Siemens's organisation methods during the technology transfer, for instance, the set-up and assimilation of the maintenance system, the choice of enterprise software (SAP) and also in its referencing and documentation of the management system.

### 4.3. *Phase 2: export of services*

We define Phase 2 as the period from the time when the JV between Siemens and ERL ended in 2005. By now, the ERL HSR system had been in joint operation for 3 years. The major observation in this phase is the degree of technical knowledge accumulated by E-MAS over that period in partnership with Siemens personnel on the ground.

The accumulated knowledge is depicted in the multilateral model (Figure 1) as the enlarging of the size of components C1, C2, and so forth. The components get bigger as the model moves upwards from Phase 0 to Phase 2.

One impetus which propelled the knowledge accumulation was the high usage of trains, which affected the operation of the rail system. For the ERL project, a total of 12 train sets were purchased – 4 sets to operate on the KLIA Transit commuter service and 8 sets to operate on the KLIA Express direct fast rail link between KL Sentral in the city centre and KLIA. Both services use the 57-km track length with only the transit service making stops at intermediate stations. The whole system has a total of six stations – KL Sentral, Bandar Tasik Selatan, Putrajaya, Salak Tinggi, KLIA and KLIA2 (the newly opened low-cost carrier terminal extension to KLIA). Operating hours are long, with only 4 or 5 hours of non-operation each day. With that in mind, each train set accumulated mileage very rapidly. The mileage gained was so rapid, that the ERL project's Siemens trains were the first in the world to reach a critical point in the scheduled maintenance, a complete overhaul upon reaching 1.5 million kilometres in mileage (T6).

Since ERL trains reached T6 mileage earlier than other counterparts anywhere else, the overhaul was the first of its series and was handled by the E-MAS staff with close monitoring by Siemens. The ability to carry out T6 maintenance signifies a high level of technical capability for any railway maintenance firm, and thus the ability of E-MAS to carry out T6 was a notable achievement.

Apart from accumulation of knowledge at Phase 2, assimilation of knowledge was also observed; specifically, the assimilation is between the HSR knowledge and other alternative knowledge outside the Siemens SOPs. The new alternative knowledge was gained as an innovative step initiated by E-MAS maintenance management – to explore other maintenance procedures that could complement the existing maintenance procedures handed down by the technology transferor, Siemens. In Phase 2, Siemens knowledge has become the existing knowledge or the base knowledge.

These changes are most reflected in the training structure of E-MAS technical personnel. Assimilation with other technologies could be seen in the choice of training taken up by maintenance personnel as seen in Figure 2.

In deviating somewhat from the original maintenance procedure provided by Siemens, the technical personnel have incorporated other forms of maintenance activities to preserve the operational condition of the system. One example presented was the checking of electricity leaks at overhead catenary poles, where the management incorporated the use of thermal photography to quickly eliminate overhead poles that are 'safe', concentrating instead on poles with potential leaks.

From the above, it can be surmised that assimilation of knowledge at E-MAS involved other core technologies which could be outside the core technologies normally used in railways. In an interview with the E-MAS maintenance department, it was noted that the innovative steps taken are not high technology, rather they are in the form of small incremental innovations in the maintenance procedure or in the daily tasks. This is in line with the observation by Hobday (2005) that catching up in developing countries occurs in small medium enterprises where the 'substantial innovation occurs based on minor improvements'.

With the addition of using other forms of technology that are not conventional to railway maintenance, E-MAS maintenance departments were now not restricted to costly OEM conditions for maintenance. This can occur due to the accumulation of knowledge by E-MAS technicians over the length of time that they have been operating the HSR system. By this phase, the technical experience prepares E-MAS to explore alternative maintenance options.

For example, in Phase 2, E-MAS embarked on condition-based monitoring for maintaining its railway system. This is an indicator that the E-MAS technical department now has sufficient

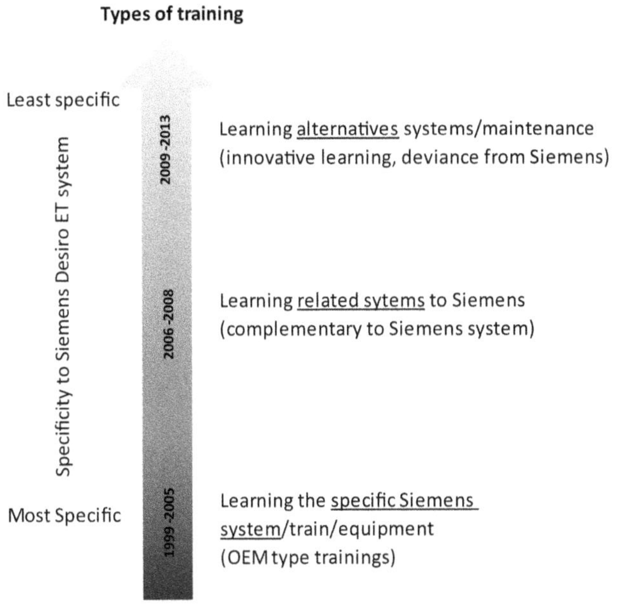

**Types of training**

**Figure 2:** Dynamics of training specificity at E-MAS.

knowledge in maintenance activities that do not strictly go by the book of Siemens. At Phase 2, it has the capability to reduce costs by implementing alternative forms of maintenance, and this allows them to offer railway maintenance services to other countries by exporting services.

The exports of services completed by E-MAS were in the form of technical and also operational maintenance. An example of technical maintenance service would be the procurement of E-MAS expertise by Thailand for installation of overhead catenary poles for its air rail link (also a Siemens project).

In addition, the E-MAS ELT department took the opportunity to work with KTM in its upgrading and extension of KTM's Sentul–Batu Caves railway extension, which included installation of overhead catenary poles. Apart from that, the Makkah–Madinah rail link has procured the services of E-MAS operations department personnel to strengthen its operations during the pilgrimage season for the past two years. And recently, the extension of the ERL railway system to the newly built KLIA airport extension was done solely by E-MAS.

## 5. Discussion

Technology transfer of a railway system in a developing country such as Malaysia requires a more complex acquisition of knowledge exemplified by the case study of ERL. This is due to the various technical core technology contained in a railway system, whereby each core technology may advance or accumulate knowledge independently. Having existing knowledge of each core technology would assist in understanding the assimilation between the core technologies as well.

Table 2 provides a summary of the available railway capability in Malaysia over the various phases discussed earlier. The major difference after the technology transfer is the availability of a new type of rolling stock, which is the high-speed train. In addition, the adoption of a HSR system introduced the use of axle counters and TMS. Both of these core technologies were not available in the country prior to the technology transfer.

**Table 2:** Brief description of the core technologies over the various phases.

Core technology availability in different phases

| | Phase 0 – Pre-conditions (prior to 1999) | Phase 1 – Introduction of HSR (1999–2005) | Phase 2 – Export of services (2005–present) |
|---|---|---|---|
| Traction power supply | Diesel, Electric | Diesel, Electric | Diesel, Electric |
| Train control and communications | SCADA | SCADA<br>Axle counters<br>Train management system | SCADA<br>Axle counters<br>Train management system |
| Civil and track works | Standard gauge | Standard gauge | Standard gauge |
| O&M system | OCC | OCC | OCC<br>Innovation in maintenance |
| High-speed train | N/A | Available | Available |
| Information system | Computerised system | Computerised system | Computerised system |

By using a dynamic multilateral model presented in this paper, the complex process of learning can be illustrated more clearly. The learning process requires both vertical and horizontal convergence, which Siemens and E-MAS understood and incorporated into their technology transfer process. The horizontal convergence relates to the assimilation of the Siemens knowledge with the existing railway knowledge available in Malaysia at the beginning of Phase 1, while the vertical convergence relates to the accumulation of knowledge gained by E-MAS in operating and maintaining a HSR system seen at Phase 2.

Both types of convergence contribute to substantial gain of knowledge for E-MAS since they enabled the company to rapidly gain technological capability within a short time frame, such that it is able to provide technical maintenance and operation services to other railway providers in the region. We deduced that there are two determinant factors that allowed ERL to rapidly catch up with Siemens and shortened the learning curve. The first determinant factor is the presence of prior railway knowledge and human capital already existing in Malaysia such as the experience from KTM, PUTRA, and STAR. The second determinant factor is the repetitive or heavy usage of the newly received HSR technology. In ERL's case, the rapid accumulation of train mileage prompted the ERL maintenance team to service the trains within a shorter time span than it would have normally taken for similar trains in Europe.

Apart from being a determinant factor that hastens the catching up process, the heavy train usage in the ERL system aided in shaping the coevolution structure of the Siemens–ERL JV. The rapid mileage accumulation of the ERL trains eventually surpassed the mileage of other similar train models in Europe, and ERL now has maintenance information not yet possessed by Siemens. Another factor that helped to shape the coevolution structure is the fact that the ERL trains are operating in a tropical climate that is very different from the climate conditions in Europe. What this means is that there are operating challenges encountered by ERL which were never experienced by Siemens before, such as frequent lightning strikes to the main lines.

In solving these challenges, the JV between Siemens and ERL (E-MAS) provided a technical platform where both parties coevolved through mutual learning and close interaction. This resulted in a reinforced understanding of the ERL system by technology owner, Siemens. Eventually, the reinforced understanding gained during the evolution sequence of the ERL operation contributes to the evolution sequence of Siemens technology.

For instance, the knowledge gained in solving the lightning problems now can be used by Siemens in solving similar problems for their trains operating in tropical climates such as in

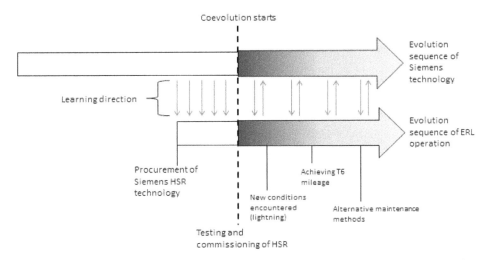

**Figure 3:** Comparison of evolution sequence of Siemens technology (top arrow) and ERL operation (bottom arrow).

Thailand, where Siemens trains are also used. In addition, alternative maintenance methods adopted by E-MAS which were not originally part of Siemens maintenance procedure now add to the maintenance options for Siemens trains that operate in tropical conditions similar to the ERL system. Figure 3 illustrates the coevolution between Siemens technology and ERL operation.

Table 3 provides a summarised view of the overall process of the HSR system's adoption of ERL. It states the objective, the plan, and the execution in gaining this capability according to the different phases. The main focus of the transferor at Phase 1 is the process of assimilation of knowledge whereby the core activities are *learning* and *imitation*. At Phase 2, after having gained an overall knowledge of the system, the transferee begins accumulating knowledge via *experience* and also by differing *operation circumstances*.

**Table 3:** Summarised view of the technology transfer objective, plan and execution according to the phases.

| Phase 0 |
| --- |
| Diesel-powered trains and electrified light rail transit in KL |
| Urgent demand to link KLIA to KL |
| Pool of available human capital from existing train systems |

| | Phase 1<br>Successful integration of ERL<br>systems (assimilation) | Phase 2<br>Co-evolution between ERL operations and Siemens<br>technology (accumulation) |
| --- | --- | --- |
| Objective | To adopt HSR technology | Export of services<br>New market niche |
| Tactical plan | Learning of new system<br>Assimilating knowledge (Phase 0 and Siemens) | Accumulating expertise<br>Assimilating knowledge (Phase 1 and newer) |
| Execution | Training (classroom and on-the-job) | Training (external courses)<br>Marketing of services |

## 6. Conclusion

From the analysis of the convergence that occurred in this case, there are clearly two types of convergence that can be observed in the railway system. The horizontal convergence, which involves the convergence of knowledge between Siemens and ERL, benefited both parties whereby each party learned from each other's knowledge. Hence, the horizontal convergence can be categorised as complementary convergence.

On the other hand, the vertical convergence of rail technology demonstrated that there are instances where newer technology evolves and replaces older technology. Thus, for vertical convergence in a railway system, the convergence can be categorised as substitutive convergence.

Apart from the above conclusions, the following observations can also be derived from the case study:

(1) Appropriating the pre-condition settings and creating an organisational structure that would respond to the path-dependent market opportunities (the order of events).
(2) Assimilating foreign technology and exploring an institutional routine that would lead to the development of niche markets.
(3) The assimilation processes would witness a convergence path leading to accumulation process, after which
(4) accumulation of capabilities (knowledge) can lead to new niches.

While this study contributes to the literature by using the anecdotal experience between Malaysia's ERL and Siemens's rail technology system to document the convergence process, it is important to recognise that the principles extracted from the processes are subject to the limits of anecdotal evidence. Nonetheless, the framing of the convergence process in this study would provide useful guides for the rail industrial stakeholders who aspire to emulate ERL's convergence path for upgrading and development.

### Acknowledgments

The authors wish to acknowledge the 2014 Asialics conference travel fellowship support. Thanks are extended to Prof. Kong-Rae Lee and Prof. Fumio Kodama for their insights on technology convergence.

### Funding

The authors are grateful for the research support [FL025-2012] of the Equitable Society Research Cluster of University Malaya.

### Notes

1. Probably, the most aggressive adaptor of rail technology in Asia is China, as demonstrated by the committed improvement of its railway network since the turn of the twenty-first century (Luger, 2008). In Europe, Germany and Great Britain have restructured their railway industries to allow non-state-owned operators to govern their rail networks (Link, 2009; Shaw, 2000). This points to a paradigm shift where the railway is no longer viewed as a public service, but instead has developed as a private enterprise. Cheng (2010) studied the impact of high-speed rail (HSR) in the development of interregional areas in Taiwan, providing easier access to new labour markets and leading to the establishment of new economic corridors.
2. SCADA stands for supervisory control and data acquisition. Using telecommunication networks to relay and acquire data regarding the trains, the use of SCADA has expanded the core technology of communication.

3.  An axle counter is a device used to detect train presence on particular sections of a track. It operates by counting the number of train axles that enter and depart a particular track section. The information is passed to the operation control centre to notify when a track is occupied or vacant.

## References

Basri, M.A. Fawzi. (1985), *Sejarah Keretapi di Malaysia*, Kuala Lumpur: KTM.

Bunge, M. (2003), *Emergence and Convergence: Qualitative Novelty and the Unity of Knowledge*, Toronto: University of Toronto Press.

Caloghirou, Y., Kastelli, I., and Tsakanikas, A. (2004), 'Internal capabilities and external knowledge sources: complements or substitutes for innovative performance?', *Technovation*, 24(1), 29–39.

Campos, J., and de Rus, G. (2009), 'Some stylized facts about high-speed rail: a review of HSR experiences around the world', *Transport Policy*, 16(1), 19–28.

Carlsson, B. (ed.) (1997), *Technological Systems and Industrial Dynamics*, Dordrecht: Kluwer Academic Publishers.

Carlsson, B., and Stankiewicz, R. (1991), 'On the nature, function and composition of technological systems', *Journal of Evolutionary Economics*, 1(2), 93–118.

Chen, E.K.Y. (ed.) (1994), *Transnational Corporations and Technology Transfer to Developing Countries* (Vol. 18), London: Routledge.

Cheng, n (2010), 'High-speed rail in Taiwan: new experience and issues for future development', *Transport Policy*, 17(2), 51–63.

Cohen, G. (2004), *Technology Transfer: Strategic Management in Developing Countries*, New Delhi: Sage Publications.

Cohen, W.M., and Levinthal, D.A. (1990), 'Absorptive capacity: a new perspective on learning and inno-vation', *Administrative Science Quarterly*, 35(1), 128–152.

Couto, A., & Graham, D.J. (2008), 'The impact of high-speed technology on railway demand', *Transportation*, 35(1), 111–128.

Dikon, S. (2010), *Future Indonesian Railways: An Interface Report Towards the National Railway Master Plan*, Jakarta: Indonesia Infrastructure Initiative.

Fu, X., Pietrobelli, C., and Soete, L. (2011), 'The role of foreign technology and indigenous innovation in the emerging economies: technological change and catching up', *World Development*, 39(7), 1204–1212.

Gaabucayan, M.S.A., Doi, K., and Takada, K. (1999), *A Comparative Study of the Effectiveness of Private Financing Initiatives in Urban Transport Infrastructure Development in Metro Manila and Kuala Lumpur*. Proceedings of Infrastructure Planning, Vol. 22, pp. 63–66.

Hobday, M. (2005), 'Firm-level innovation models: perspectives on research in developed and developing countries', *Technology Analysis & Strategic Management*, 17(2), 121–146.

Janelle, D. G., and Beuthe, M. (1997), 'Globalization and research issues in transportation', *Journal of Transport Geography*, 5(3), 199–206.

Kim, L. (1980), 'Stages of development of industrial technology in a developing country: a model', *Research policy*, 9(3), 254–277.

Kim, L. (1997), *Imitation to Innovation: The Dynamics of Korea's Technological Learning*, Boston, MA: Harvard Business Press.

Kim, L. (1998), 'Crisis construction and organizational learning: capability building in catching-up at Hyundai motor', *Organization Science*, 9(4), 506–521.

Kim, L. (2001), 'The dynamics of technological learning in industrialisation', *International Social Science Journal*, 53(168), 297–308.

Kodama, F. (2014), 'MOT in transition: from technology fusion to technology-service convergence', *Technovation*, 34(9), 505–512.

Kogut, B., and Zander, U. (1992), 'Knowledge of the firm, combinative capabilities, and the replication of technology', *Organization Science*, 3(3), 383–397.

Kumar, V., Kumar, U., and Persaud, A. (1999), 'Building technological capability through importing technology: the case of Indonesian manufacturing industry', *The Journal of Technology Transfer*, 24(1), 81–96.

Lacôte, F. (2005), 'Alstom – future trends in railway transportation', *Japan Railway and Transport Review*, 42, 4–9.

Lall, S. (1992), 'Technological capabilities and industrialization', *World Development*, 20(2), 165–186.

Lall, S. (2000), 'The technological structure and performance of developing country manufactured exports, 1985–98', *Oxford Development Studies*, 28(3), 337–369.

Lee, K. (2005), 'Making a technological catch-up: barriers and opportunities', *Asian Journal of Technology and Innovation*, 13(2), 97–131.

Lee, K.K. (2011), *The Evolution and Outlook of Core Technologies for High Speed Railway in China.* Paper presented at the 1st International Workshop on High-Speed and Intercity Railways, Shenzen and Hong Kong.

Liao, S., Fei, W., and Chen, C. (2007), 'Knowledge sharing, absorptive capacity, and innovation capability: an empirical study of Taiwan's knowledge-intensive industries', *Journal of Information Science*, 33(3), 340–359.

Link, H. (2009), 'Regional rail companies in Germany', *Japan Railway and Transport Review*, 52, 38–45.

Liu, J., Qian, J., and Chen, J. (2006), 'Technological learning and firm-level technological capability building: analytical framework and evidence from Chinese manufacturing firms', *International Journal of Technology Management*, 36(1), 190–208.

Liu, X., Cheng, P., and Chen, A. (2011), 'Basic research and catch-up in china's high-speed rail industry', *Journal of Chinese Economic and Business Studies*, 9(4), 349–367.

Luger, K. (2008), *Chinese Railways: Reform and Efficiency Improvement Opportunities*, Heidelberg: Physica-Verlag.

Lundvall, B., and Johnson, B. (1994), 'The learning economy', *Journal of Industry Studies*, 1(2), 23–42.

Malerba, F. (1992), 'Learning by firms and incremental technical change', *The Economic Journal*, 102, 845–859.

Oum, T. H., and Yu, C. (1994), 'Economic efficiency of railways and implications for public policy: a comparative study of the OECD countries' railways', in *Railways*, ed. C. Nash, Cheltenham: Edward Elgar Publishing Limited, pp. 121–138.

Radosevic, S. (1999), *International Technology Transfer and Catch-up in Economic Development*, Cheltenham: Edward Elgar.

Roco, M.C., and Bainbridge, W.S. (2013), 'The new world of discovery, invention, and innovation: convergence of knowledge, technology, and society', *Journal of Nanoparticle Research*, 15(9), 1–17.

Shaw, J. (2000), *Competition, Regulation and the Privatisation of British Rail*, Aldershot: Ashgate Publishing.

Suzuki, J., and Kodama, F. (2004), 'Technological diversity of persistent innovators in Japan: two case studies of large Japanese firms', *Research Policy*, 33, 531–549.

Wei, L. (1995), 'International technology transfer and development of technological capabilities: a theoretical framework', *Technology in Society*, 17(1), 103–120.

Wong, C.Y., and Goh, K.L. (2009), 'Modeling the dynamics of science and technology diffusion of selected Asian countries using a logistic growth function', *Asian Journal of Technology Innovation*, 17(1), 75–100.

World Bank. (2007), *Decade of Action in Transport: An Evaluation of World Bank Assistance to the Transport Sector, 1995–2005* (P. N. Freeman, ed.), Herndon, VA: World Bank Publications.

# Is the technological capability gap between Hyundai and Mitsubishi converging or diverging? Findings from patent data analysis

Chul Oh[a] and Si Hyung Joo[b]

[a]Department of International Trade & Business, Sangmyung University, Jongno – gu, Seoul, Republic of Korea
[b]Department of Industrial Engineering, Chonnam National University, Buk-gu, Gwangju, Republic of Korea

With few capabilities in automobile production or development, Hyundai Motors began its automobile business in 1967. Hyundai had to surrender a 10% equity stake to receive technology transfer from Mitsubishi Motors in 1982. Surprisingly, this situation reversed 20 years later, in 2004, when Mitsubishi came to license Hyundai's engine technology. As of 2013, Hyundai is the 5th largest automobile manufacturer in the world, while Mitsubishi is the 14th. To explain this reversal, this study investigates the technological capability gap between Hyundai and Mitsubishi by analysing patents data (and related citations) for Hyundai and Mitsubishi to assess their technological capabilities. The study finds that Hyundai not only narrowed the technological capability gap with Mitsubishi, but also recently overtook Mitsubishi. The results suggest that Hyundai's success in the market would not be possible without its ceaseless accumulation of technological capabilities.

## 1. Introduction

The history of the Korean automobile industry dates back to 1955, when the first Korean automobile, Sibal, or 'New Start' in English, was produced based on Willy's Jeep. Korean automobile production multiplied very rapidly from 7000 in 1955 up to 115,000 in 1979.[1] However, its share in the world's automobile production was rather small until the early 1980s. In 1980, automobile production in Korea was only one-tenth of that in Brazil, the 10th largest automobile-producing country in the world (Kim 1997, p. 141). Since then, the Korean automobile industry has made great strides. Its production continued to expand, and Korea became the world's 9th largest automobile-producing country in 1991 and 5th in 1996.[2]

The outstanding achievements of the Korean automobile industry were led by the Hyundai Motor Company (hereafter Hyundai), which has been the largest automobile manufacturer in Korea since the mid-1970s. Hyundai was merely a small assembler focusing on the domestic market at this time, but has multiplied its production tenfold every decade to become the world's 16th largest automobile manufacturer in 1991 and the 8th largest in 2001. Hyundai has been the 5th largest automobile manufacturer in the world since 2010.

Compared to the automobile industries and manufacturers of the BRIC and ASEAN countries, the success of the Korean automobile industry, and Hyundai in particular, contains some unique features. Domestic automobile firms have led the growth of the Korean automobile industry, especially Hyundai, not by the multi-national automobile corporations. In addition, the Korean indigenous automobile firms have succeeded in the international automobile market, in both developing and advanced economies, such as the USA and Western European countries. Furthermore, their exports are not limited to sub-compact and compact cars, but encompasses the luxury car segments.

It is of great interest how the Korean automobile industry, and Hyundai in particular, has caught up with the world's leading automobile manufacturers in such a short period. Research has identified the accumulation of technological capability as a crucial factor for the successful growth of the Korean automobile industry in general, and the success of Hyundai more specifically (Green 1992; Jo 1993).

With in-depth analysis of Hyundai's technological learning and innovation process up to the mid- or late 1990s, Hyun (1995) and Kim (1997) highlighted the pivotal role of Hyundai's strategy and efforts to assimilate external knowledge and develop technological capability. Hyundai first focused on assimilating imported technologies, and tried to improve on them. In parallel, Hyundai swiftly and increasingly shifted its effort towards developing more sophisticated and up-to-date technologies. Hyundai accelerated its pace of technological catch-up by skipping some stages of the technological trajectory (Lee and Lim 2001). Hyundai's development of self-reliant technological capability was identified as a key enabling factor of its success.

Compared to Hyundai's successful launch, which has been extensively studied, its unremitting growth that followed has not attracted enough scholarly attention, especially from the technological capability perspective. Some research attempted to explain Hyundai's recent growth from various perspectives, including quality, product architecture, globalisation, and marketing (Hyun 2008, 2014; Chung 2009; Hyun and Lee 2013). However, there is a lack of attention towards its technological capability, considering its paramount importance in the automobile industry. An automobile manufacturer cannot expect to survive in the market without accelerating its technological innovation, as governments' safety and environmental regulations have tightened, and customers' needs have diversified and grown more sophisticated (Talay, Calantone, and Voorhees 2014). Although Hyundai's recent continuing growth cannot be easily explained by its technological capabilities in the 1990s, research on its recent development is rare. In addition, Hyundai's technological capability has often been investigated using partial and anecdotal evidence, and rarely through a systematic and comprehensive investigation. Hyundai's technological self-reliance in the 1990s may be an important indicator of its development of technological capability; however, it does not mean that Hyundai came to have competitive technological capabilities.

To fill the research gap, this study investigates Hyundai's recent technological capability development by analysing patent data. Though not perfect, patent data have long been accepted as a reliable source of information to measure firms' technological capabilities (Narin, Noma, and Perry 1987; Patel and Pavitt 1997). To reflect competitive conditions, we investigated Hyundai's technological capability using Mitsubishi Motors (hereafter Mitsubishi) as a reference firm since Hyundai has long relied on and learned from Mitsubishi's technology.

The rest of the paper is structured as follows. Section 2 reviews the theoretical and empirical literature related to Hyundai's success in the automobile industry, and describes the research methodology. Section 3 provides a brief history of Hyundai and Mitsubishi, and the progress of Hyundai's technological development. Section 4 investigates Hyundai's technological capability compared to Mitsubishi by analysing patent data. Finally, Section 5 summarises the findings and offers concluding remarks.

## 2. Theoretical review and research methodology

### 2.1. *Theoretical review*

Changes in the economic and technological leadership between countries (and firms) were traditionally explained using product life cycle theory (Posner 1961; Vernon 1966) and its variant, the flying geese model (Kojima 2000). Product life cycle theory suggests that the production of goods moves from developed countries to developing countries, which have lower labour and production costs, as industries mature through the product life cycle. It also predicts that the migration of production begins in the late stage of the product life cycle when production technologies have matured, and firms in developed countries will exit the market.

The growth of the Korean automobile industry cannot be easily explained using the traditional product lifecycle theory. Firms in developed countries, such as the USA and Japan, did not exit the market. On the contrary, they are increasingly competing against Korean firms.

Fröbel, Heinrichs, and Kreye (1980) explained the shift of production from developed to developing countries as a process of integrating the developing countries into the 'new international division of labour' system that has emerged through modern production technologies. This theory predicts that production in developing countries would mostly be carried out by multi-national corporations, and its growth would be limited by the persistent reliance on technologies and major components from developed countries. However, the Korean industry has been led by domestic firms, and their technological reliance on developed countries has constantly decreased.

Contrary to both the product lifecycle and new international division of labour theories, the neo-Schumpeterian approach focuses on learning and technological capability building in developing countries as the factors enabling them to catch up (Nelson and Winter 1982). Moreover, it emphasises developing countries' local technological capabilities because developed countries are increasingly reluctant to transfer their technologies to developing countries.

In addition, it also finds that seizing windows of opportunities contributes towards their catch-up (Perez and Soete 1988; Lee 2005). Windows of opportunity to catch up are not always opened, though they do occasionally open when a sectoral innovation system (Malerba 2002, 2004) undergoes a process of change and transformation.

The take-off and success of Hyundai and the Korean automobile industry must be understood within the automobile sector's innovation system. There have been significant changes in the global automobile sector's innovation system since the 1970s, such as changes in technological paradigms, market conditions, and the surrounding institutions (Figueiredoa 2007; Freyssenet 2009; Fujimoto 2013; Townsend and Calantone 2014).

In the 1970s, most automobile manufacturers in developed countries rapidly expanded their overseas production to realise economies of scale in pursuit of a global strategy. Their competition for internationalisation gave the automobile manufacturers in developing countries far more bargaining power. The increased international automobile production also brought internationalisation to automobile part and component suppliers (Lall 1980).

Japanese automobile manufacturers, who were renowned for producing small, fuel-efficient cars, successfully expanded their exports exploiting the opportunity created by the oil crises in the 1970s. However, the decline of USA and European automobile industries, coupled with the rise of Japanese automobile exports, raised governments' restrictions on the automobile industry in the 1980s, such as the Voluntary Export Restraints (VERs) that set a quota for Japanese automobiles exported to the USA.

The successful growth of the Korean automobile industry can be explained by Korean automobile manufacturers' technological progress and a window of opportunity. Green (1992) and Jo (1993) identified the opening of a window of opportunity for the Korean automobile industry with the changes in the international automobile industry in the 1980s, including VERs limiting the export of Japanese automobiles to the USA, the competitive structure of developed countries' automobile manufacturers that enabled Korean manufacturers to access advanced technology via technology transfer, and changes in regulations on international trade that allowed Korean manufacturers to easily import major parts and components. However, they suggested that Korean automobile manufacturers' technological competitiveness, which was strongly supported by the government's industrial policy, was a major driver of this success.

With a comprehensive review of the early history of Hyundai, Kim (1997) found that Hyundai first focused on assimilating and improving the mature stages of foreign technologies to build absorptive capacity, then shifted its focus to developing more sophisticated and updated technologies. The history of Hyundai's new product development studied by Kim (1994), Hyun (1995), and Park (2001) provided evidence that Hyundai accumulated indigenous technological capabilities, from production technologies to more sophisticated technologies, including body design and styling to chassis layout and power train, simultaneously across its product range, from sub-compact cars to large luxury cars. Hyundai also accelerated the pace of technological catch-up by skipping some stages of the technological trajectory (Lee and Lim 2001). When Hyundai began developing its first engine, the dominant design was a carburettor-type, while an electronic injection-type engine with better fuel economy and performance was an emerging technological paradigm. Considering Hyundai's technological capability at that time, developing an electronic injection-type engine was quite challenging and risky; however, the company decided to develop an electronic injection-type engine for fear of being locked in an old technological paradigm. The successful development of an electronic injection-type engine in 1990 narrowed Hyundai's technological capability gap with multi-national manufacturers and allowed it to successfully enter developed countries' markets.

In the 1990s and 2000s, the global automobile industry underwent major changes (Freyssenet 2009; Fujimoto 2013; Townsend and Calantone 2014), which might be more unfavourable to developing countries' automobile manufacturers, like Hyundai. The recessions in this period damaged automobile demand in developed countries, and manufacturers worked towards cost reduction. While there was increasing opportunity in newly emerging countries, it was hard to meet the needs of local customers with a one-size-fits-all type of car. Governments raised safety and environmental standards through regulation, and consumer needs diversified and grew in sophistication. Manufacturers therefore had to accelerate innovation, while it became more difficult to easily realise economies of scale. To cope with the challenges, automobile manufactures increasingly adopted modular architecture and electronic components, and tried to increase platform sharing between models. To differentiate their products, they accelerated innovations in cutting-edge technologies, such as alternative powertrains and unmanned autonomous driving.

The intensified competition quickly eroded profitability, especially in the low-end segment. The price competitiveness of automobile manufacturers from developing countries eroded through increasing labour costs and exchange rates. Without diversifying into higher-end segments, they could not stay in the market.

In the 1990s, automobile manufacturers responded by increasing productivity and efficiency. However, intensified competition quickly levelled these gains. Hence, the automobile manufacturers have shifted their strategic focus from productivity and efficiency to new product development and innovation in the 2000s.

The automotive sector greatly increased their patent activities, by as much as 35% per year (Thomson Reuters 2014). A series of KPMG (2014) surveys showed top management's increasing recognition of innovation as a source of sustainable competitive advantage. The automotive industry now considers technological leadership as the key to survival, and developing new products and technologies as the single most effective strategy for growth.

The global automobile industry severely suffered from such changes, with several company bankruptcies and mergers. However, Hyundai and the Korean automobile industry not only successfully overcame the difficulties, but also continued their growth. In addition, automobile industry executives bet big on Hyundai's future growth (KPMG 2014).

The unremitting growth of Hyundai and the industries' expectations of its future growth suggest that Hyundai successfully responded to the challenges by flexibly adjusting its strategies, accumulated technological capabilities, and building innovative capacity for future innovation.

Considering the volatility of competitive advantage from sources other than technological capability, Hyundai's success must be explained from the perspective of technological capability. However, the recent growth of Hyundai has attracted scant scholarly attention (Hyun 2008, 2014; Chung 2009; Hyun and Lee 2013), and in-depth investigations into Hyundai's success from the technological capability perspective are rare.

Recently, Hyun (2008, 2014) and Hyun and Lee (2013) investigated Hyundai's strategies and capabilities from wider perspectives, including quality, product architecture, and marketing innovation. In comparison with Hyundai's successful expansion, which has been extensively studied, its unremitting growth has not attracted enough scholarly attention.

## 2.2. *Research methodology*

This study analyses patent data to systematically investigate Hyundai's technological capability and quantitatively identify Hyundai's innovation strategy. Patent data offer methodological and technical advantages compared with other sources of information like new product introduction data or innovation surveys, and provide detailed information about inventions over a long period of time in an objective and consistent manner (Griliches 1990). In addition, patent citation data offer an opportunity to measure the quality of inventions and various characteristics of knowledge bases related to inventions (Jaffe and Trajtenberg 2002).

Additionally, we investigated Hyundai's technological capability and innovation strategy using Mitsubishi as a reference firm. The accumulation of technological capability can be assessed in either absolute or relative terms; however, a relative analysis may provide additional insights considering the highly competitive nature of the international automobile industry. Mitsubishi is taken as the reference firm because Hyundai had long relied on and learned from Mitsubishi's technology, as most of Hyundai's indigenous models were based on Mitsubishi's chassis and power train. Joo and Lee (2010) took a similar approach by adopting Sony as a reference firm in an investigation into Samsung Electronics' technological capability and innovation strategy.

We used the two firms' patent applications since 1989[3] and those registered by 2012 at the United States Patent and Trademark Office (USPTO).[4] The patents were reorganised according to their application year to properly reflect the timing of the invention. Various citation-based indices were constructed by using related citation data from the 2013 April Edition of EPO Worldwide Patent Statistical Database.

Number of patents, claims per patent, received citations per patent, and the share of citations directed to the counterpart firm's patents were analysed to investigate the technological capabilities of both companies. Additionally, we analysed backward citation lag, self-citation ratio, and citations directed to non-patent literature (NPL) to investigate Hyundai's innovation strategy to accelerate technological innovation and business performance.

## 3. Technological capability gap between Hyundai and Mitsubishi

### 3.1. *Introduction to Hyundai and Mitsubishi*

Hyundai comes from humble beginnings. Hyundai started in 1967 as a Semi-Knock-Down assembler producing Ford's Cortina, without any capabilities in automobile production, let alone development. Initially, Hyundai acquired automobile production technologies from Ford.

Hyundai was eager to acquire more advanced technology, but was also reluctant to sacrifice its controlling share of ownership, which most the multi-national manufacturers, including Ford, demanded in return for the technology transfer. Hyundai instead decided to adopt technology from Mitsubishi, who asked for only a 10% ownership stake.[5]

With constant efforts to build technological capabilities, Hyundai introduced its first indigenous model, Pony, in 1975; its first indigenous engine, Alpha, in 1991; and its first independently developed model, Accent, in 1994.

Notwithstanding, Hyundai's technological progress in its early development was largely based on Mitsubishi's technologies. Mitsubishi had been major source of technology for Hyundai since 1973. In 1975, when Hyundai was introducing its first indigenous model, Hyundai almost fully relied on Mitsubishi for its engine, transmission, and exhaust systems. Only in the mid-1990s did Hyundai become fully independent of Mitsubishi's technologies. Hence, Hyundai's early technological progress can be described as a process of independence from Mitsubishi's technologies.

Mitsubishi's technological capabilities can be interpreted from its corporate history, which dates back to 1917, when it began production of the Mitsubishi Model A, Japan's first mass produced car. In 1970, Mitsubishi was spun off as an independent firm from Mitsubishi Heavy Industries, which had built the legendary A6M Zero fighter plane and Musashi battleship during WWII. Mitsubishi established its authority as an innovator in automotive technology, developing Japan's first diesel engine in 1931, Japan's first four-wheel drive passenger car in 1934, and the world's first 'Silent Shaft' technology in 1975.

Figure 1 illustrates Hyundai's product development history, clearly showing its long and deeply embedded technological dependence on Mitsubishi, as well as Hyundai's accumulation of technological capability.

Hyundai, with its own body design and styling based on Mitsubishi's chassis and engine, introduced its first indigenous model, Pony, in 1975, and extended its indigenous product line to include mid-sized cars in 1983 and large cars in 1986. Finally, in 1994, Hyundai, introduced its first independently developed model, Accent, based on its own body design, styling,

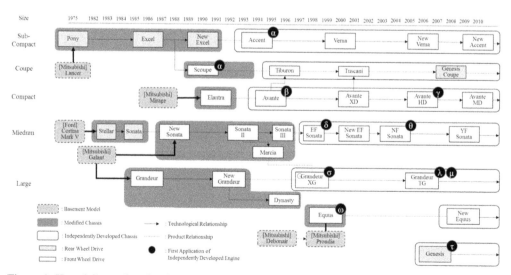

**Figure 1:** Hyundai's product development history.

chassis, and engine. Again, it extended its independently developed product line into larger vehicles. By 1998, Hyundai offered a full line of independently developed models.

In 1991, Hyundai developed its first independent engine, the Alpha engine (1300–1500 cc), which outperformed comparable Japanese engines in acceleration and fuel efficiency (Kim 1998). By developing the Alpha engine, Hyundai could save royalty payments to Mitsubishi, which were 90 USD per engine (Hyun 1995). With development of the Beta engine (1600– 2000 cc) in 1995, Hyundai became completely free from royalty payments for engines for mid-size, compact, and sub-compact cars. In 1998, Hyundai developed its first V6 engine, the Delta (2500 ~2700 cc), and Sigma Engines (3000–3500 cc).

From 2000, Hyundai spurred its engine development with aggressive investment and consolidated its research units into the Powertrain Center in the Namyang R&D Center. Hyundai also strengthened its research collaboration by establishing the Next Generation Vehicle centre, which coordinates all collaborative R&D at Hyundai. Hyundai expanded its research collaboration to specialised automobile component suppliers, such as Bosch, Delphi, and Siemens. In addition, Hyundai intensified its research on convergence technologies by collaborating with a wide variety of firms in industries ranging from electric/electronics to chemical/materials.

In collaboration with various R&D partners, Hyundai realised its efforts and finally developed the Theta engine in 2004. With the Theta engine, Hyundai transformed itself from a licensor to a licensee of engine technology, licensing the Theta engine to Mitsubishi and Daimler-Chrysler and earning 57 million dollars in royalty payments.

Hyundai continued developing large engines and introduced the V6 Lambda (3000–3800 cc) engine in 2005, and its first V8 engine, the Tau engine (4,600 ~5,000cc) in 2008. The Tau engine was selected as one of the world's 10 best engines by Ward's Auto World magazine from 2009 to 2011.

The history of Hyundai's product development shows that its innovation focus shifted from assimilating and improving mature imported technologies to developing and innovating more sophisticated and updated technologies, from body design and styling to chassis layout and power train, for car sizes from sub-compact to large luxury cars, and from small to large engines.

Mitsubishi also continued its technological innovation. Mitsubishi developed the world's first Traction Control System in 1990 and Multi-mode Anti-lock Breaking System in 1991. In 1992, Mitsubishi introduced its Intelligent & Innovative Electronic Control System, an electronic automatic transmission that learns and adapts to a driver's driving habits. The world's first mass-produced Gasoline Direct Injection engine was introduced in 1995.

### 3.2. *Hyundai's catch-up with Mitsubishi in the market*

Hyundai was merely a small automobile assembler focusing on its domestic market until the mid-1970s, when it first entered the international automobile market with the Pony in 1976. In the 1980s, Hyundai consolidated its dominant position in the domestic market by introducing mid- and large-sized indigenous models. At the same time, Hyundai rapidly expanded its exports to Latin American, Middle Eastern, South Asian, and European markets by the mid-1980s. Finally in 1986, Hyundai successfully entered the US market with Excel.

Meanwhile, during the 1980s, Mitsubishi expanded its global production by taking over Chrysler Australia, and launching a joint venture, Diamond-Star Motors, with Chrysler in the USA. By ending the captive import agreement with Chrysler, Mitsubishi also entered the US market under its own brand for the first time in 1982. In addition, Mitsubishi pioneered the emerging sport utility vehicle segment from the late 1980s.

In 1991, Hyundai became the 16th largest automobile manufacturer in the world; however, its revenue was no more than a half of Mitsubishi's revenue. As of 2013, Hyundai is the 5th largest automobile manufacturer in the world, leaving Mitsubishi far behind at 14th place.

As depicted in Figure 2, both companies' revenues doubled from 1990 to the mid-1990s. Hyundai's exports increased, but at lower rates. Hyundai had difficulty in the US market during the 1990s because of its low quality and poor brand image. Growing domestic demand contributed much to Hyundai's growth. Mitsubishi's growth in this period was based on the SUV boom in the USA and increasing demand from Asian markets, where it had solid positions. However, in the late 1990s, both firms' revenues drastically decreased due to the Asian financial crisis.

In addition, Hyundai rapidly improved productivity during the 1990s. Figure 3 provides the total factor productivity for Hyundai and Mitsubishi, and shows that Hyundai's productivity was less than 50% of Mitsubishi's until the late 1980s. With rapid improvements in productivity, Hyundai almost caught up to Mitsubishi by the late 1990s.

In the 2000s, Hyundai recouped its position and growth momentum quickly with quality improvements and aggressive marketing, such as through its 10-year/100,000-mile warranty programme. In contrast, it was hard for Mitsubishi to recover its growth momentum.

The results of J.D. Power's Initial Quality Study (IQS), which measures the number of defect/malfunctions and design problems per 100 new vehicles[6] during the first three months, shows that Hyundai had improved its product quality in the early 2000s (see Figure 4). Hyundai caught up to Mitsubishi in terms of IQS score in 2003.

In the late 2000s, automobile manufacturers experienced a dramatic drop in sales caused by the global financial downturn. Once again, Hyundai rebounded quickly with its 'Assurance' buy-back programme, which allows consumers to return their car within a year of purchase if they lose their job. Hyundai improved its brand image by marketing high-end luxury sedans. It also expanded its production capacity in emerging markets, including China, India, and Brazil.

The results of J.D. Power's Automotive Performance, Execution, and Layout Study (APEAL), which measures new vehicle owners' overall satisfaction with performance and design in the first three months, showed that Hyundai had greatly enhanced product performance and design from the late 2000s, while Mitsubishi fell behind (see Figure 5).

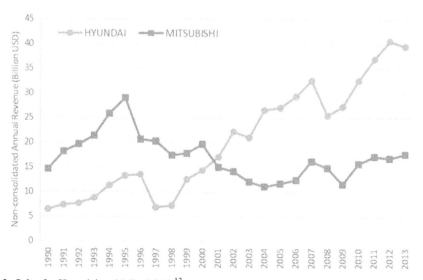

**Figure 2:** Sales for Hyundai and Mitsubishi.[13]

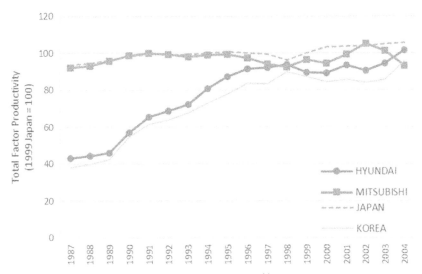

**Figure 3:** Total factor productivity at Hyundai and Mitsubishi.[14]

## 4. Patent data analysis measuring converging trends at Hyundai and Mitsubishi

### 4.1. Trend in the quantity of patents

The number of US patents forms the starting point to compare the technological capabilities of Hyundai and Mitsubishi, which are illustrated in Figure 6.[7] While Mitsubishi showed an overall stagnating or decreasing trend, Hyundai showed an overall increasing trend starting from its first two patents in 1989. Hyundai, by tripling its patents, came to file more patents than Mitsubishi in 1995, when it established its Namyang R&D Center. In 2008, Hyundai held 4.5 times more patents than Mitsubishi. This divergent tendency was found in the quantity of patents.

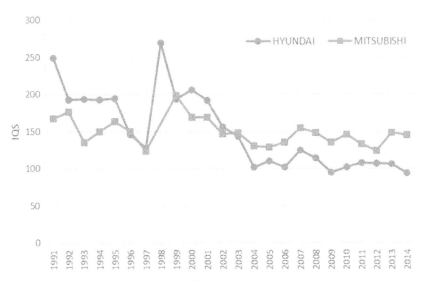

**Figure 4:** IQS scores for Hyundai and Mitsubishi.

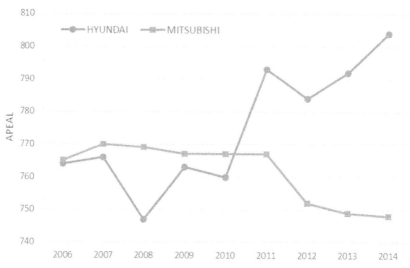

**Figure 5:** APEAL scores for Hyundai and Mitsubishi.

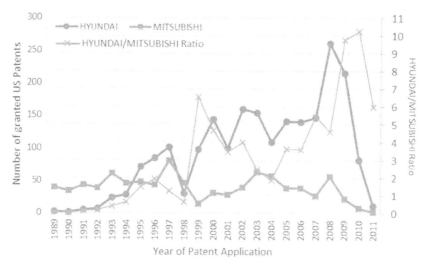

**Figure 6:** Number of patents held by Hyundai and Mitsubishi.

By comparing Figure 2 with Figure 6 it can be seen that Hyundai's catch-up with Mitsubishi in patent count precedes its catch-up in the market, as measured by sales revenue, product quality, and customer satisfaction.

### 4.2. *Trend in the quality of patents*

Patent quality was investigated based on the number of received citations. More frequently cited patents are considered more valuable or worthy of use (Albert, Avery, Narin, and McAllister 1991; Hall, Jaffe, and Trajtenberg 2005).

Figure 7 provides the average citations received by the patents held by Hyundai and Mitsu-bishi.[8] In the early 1990s, Hyundai narrowed its gap with Mitsubishi in the average citations

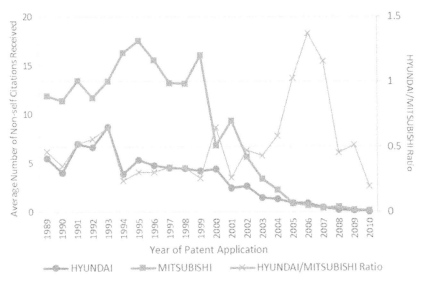

**Figure 7:** Average citations received by Hyundai and Mitsubishi's patents.

received; however, the gap widened again and Mitsubishi received significantly more citations on average than Hyundai by 2004.

However, the average number of received citations does not mean that Hyundai failed to generate as many high-quality patents as Mitsubishi, considering the large discrepancy between Hyundai and Mitsubishi in the quantity of patents.

Figure 8 provides number of patents by number of citations received. Figure 8(c) shows that Mitsubishi had more top-quality patents (patents with more than 15 citations) than Hyundai, though Hyundai came to have more high-quality patents (patents with 5–14 citations) than

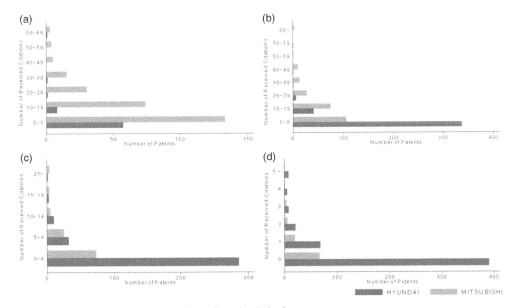

**Figure 8:** Number of patents by number of received citations.

Mitsubishi in the early 2000s. Although the result is less reliable because of the truncation problem, Figure 8(d) shows that Hyundai generated more top- and high-quality patents than Mitsubishi in the late 2000s.

The received citation results show that Hyundai failed to raise its overall patent quality, though it successfully generated more patents than Mitsubishi in the 2000s.

### 4.3.  *Trends in the breadth of patents*

The number of patent claims is taken as a metric to analyse patent breadth, another qualitative aspect of patents. Patent claims determine the boundaries of exclusive rights, and only the technological aspects covered in the patent claims can be legally protected and enforced. Thus, the number of patent claims reflects the breadth of the rights from the patent (Lanjouw and Schankerman 2001; Gambardella, Harhoff, and Verspagen 2008).

Figure 9 illustrates the average claims of patents held by Hyundai and Mitsubishi. While Mitsubishi showed a decreasing average number of claims from the mid-1990s, Hyundai almost doubled its number of claims on average from the early 1990s to the late 2000s. For average patent claims, there is a converging trend between Hyundai and Mitsubishi. The results imply that the overall gap in the breadth of patents has narrowed.

Figure 10, which shows the number of patents by number of claims, demonstrates that Hyundai exceeded Mitsubishi in terms of patent breadth from the early 2000s (see Figure 10(c) and Figure 10(d)).

The results from the analysis of patent quality and breadth provide clear evidence that Hyundai has not merely generated numerous incremental innovations, but has reinforced the quality of innovations and expanded the scope of innovation. Hyundai's rapid product quality improvement in the early 2000s can be taken as an outcome of its qualitative advances in technological innovations.

### 4.4.  *Trends in technological dependence*

Latecomers usually begin catching up technologically by acquiring and assimilating knowledge from existing firms, and making improvements or innovations afterward (Kim 1997). Without

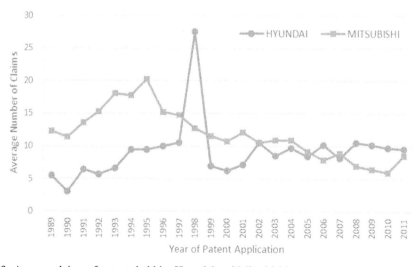

**Figure 9:** Average claims of patents held by Hyundai and Mitsubishi.

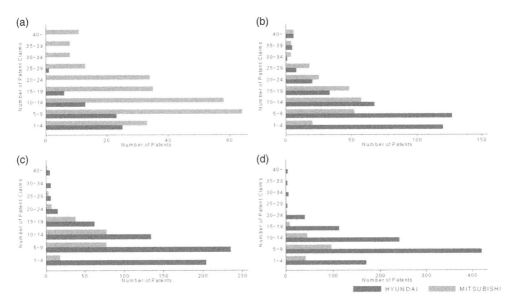

**Figure 10:** Number of patents by number of claims.

their own innovation, latecomers are unlikely to sever their reliance on existing knowledge, and hence this break can be a good signal that the latecomer has its own innovation. If latecomers' technological dependence on older firms persists or deepens, the latecomer's patents would cite more of those from the existing company. However, the existing company's patents would cite the latecomer's patents once the latecomer develops superior technology. Thus, the level of technological dependence between the new and the leading firms can be analysed based on the degree of mutual citations (Joo and Lee 2010).

The degree of mutual citations between Hyundai and Mitsubishi is investigated to analyse technological dependence between the two firms (see Figure 11).

With firm $i$'s patent $p$, the technological dependence of firm $i$ on firm $j$ can be measured as follows:

$$\text{Technological dependence}_{ij}^{P} = \frac{\text{Number of citations directed to patents held by firm } j}{\text{Total number of citations made by patent } p}.$$

Figure 11 shows that Hyundai's patents eventually cited fewer of Mitsubishi's patents, and Mitsubishi's patents began to cite more of Hyundai's. In the early 2000s, Hyundai and Mitsubishi come to cite each other's patents almost equally. In 2004, when Hyundai first licensed its Theta engine to Mitsubishi, Mitsubishi's citation ratio of Hyundai's patents reached its peak. The results can be interpreted as a decreasing technological dependence of Hyundai on Mitsubishi, whereas Mitsubishi has grown more reliant on Hyundai's technologies.

### 4.5. *Trends in appropriability and cumulativeness*

Appropriability is the ability to protect one's innovations from being copied by others, thus monopolising any profits from the innovations. A lower appropriability increases the designs' vulnerability to infringements, so the innovation yields less profit. A higher appropriability results in fewer subsequent innovations that can be drawn from the previous innovation by others.

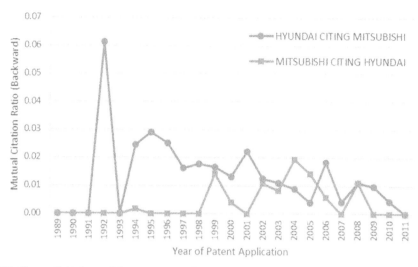

**Figure 11:** Share of citations of the counterpart firm's patents.

Hence, appropriability can be measured by the proportion of forward self-citations (Trajtenberg, Jaffe, and Henderson 1997). A higher appropriability results in a higher forward self-citation ratio.

Cumulativeness is the extent to which one's technological innovation today depends on its own past innovation. An innovation may generate new opportunities for subsequent innovations and opportunities to improve and/or apply the previous innovation. High levels of cumulativeness may generate positive feedback in innovative activities (Breschi, Malerba, and Orsenigo 2000). The higher the cumulativeness, the more innovations are based on the firm's previous innovations. Cumulativeness is therefore measured by the proportion of backward self-citations. A higher cumulativeness results in a higher backward self-citation ratio.

With firm $i$'s patent $p$, the forward (backward) self-citation ratio be measured as follows:

$$\text{Forward (backward)self-citation ratio}_i^p$$
$$= \frac{\text{Number of citations received (directed)to patents held by } i}{\text{Total number of citations received (made)by patent } p}.$$

Figure 12 shows that Hyundai's forward self-citation ratio has been higher than that of Mitsubishi, except for the year 1990.[9] It implies that Hyundai has been more successful than Mitsubishi in protecting and reaping benefits from its innovations. Hyundai's high forward self-citation ratio in the early 1990s can be interpreted as an indication that Hyundai's innovations in the early 1990s, which contributed to its early development of independent models and indigenous engines, formed the basis of its future developments.

Figure 13 shows that Hyundai's backward self-citation ratio increased rapidly in the late 1990s, but dropped abruptly in the 2000s.[10] The trend in Hyundai's backward self-citation ratio can be interpreted as an indication that Hyundai accelerated its innovation in the 1990s based on its own previous innovations, but changed its innovation strategy to use various external sources of ideas, such as collaborative R&D partners, in the 2000s.

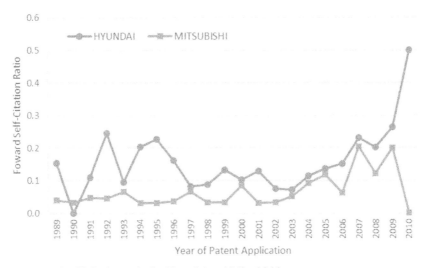

**Figure 12:** Forward self-citation ratio for Hyundai and Mitsubishi.

### 4.6. *Trends in the backward citation lag*

The backward citation lag of a patent measures how recent or up-to-date the technologies a patent is based on Narin (1994). It shows a firm's technological capability to quickly acquire and recreate recent technologies for its innovation. The backward citation lag of a patent $p$ is measured as follows:

$$\text{Backward citation lag}_p = \sum_{q=1}^{\text{NCITINC}_p} \frac{\text{LAG}_q}{\text{NCITING}_p}.$$

NCITINC$_p$ is the total citations made by patent $p$, LAG$_q$ is the difference in the filing date between patent $p$ and patent $q$ cited by patent $p$.

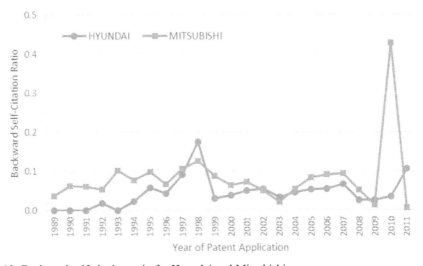

**Figure 13:** Backward self-citation ratio for Hyundai and Mitsubishi.

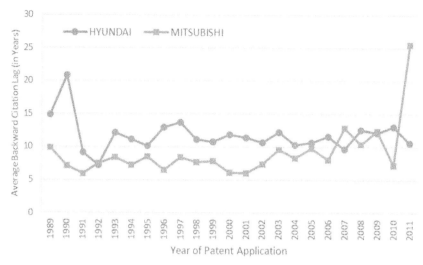

**Figure 14:** Average backward citation lag of Hyundai and Mitsubishi's patents.[15]

Figure 14 provides the average backward citation lag of both firms' patents, and shows that Hyundai used to cite older patents on average than Mitsubishi in the 1990s; however, the gap almost disappeared in the late 2000s.[11] The result implies that Hyundai has improved its technological capability to assimilate and improve new technologies.

Figure 15 provides the number of patents by backward citation lag. Figure 15(b) shows that Hyundai was able to keep abreast of contemporary technologies as much as Mitsubishi as early as the late 1990s. Figure 15(c) and Figure 15(d) show that Hyundai has been more vigorously adopting newly emergent technologies than Mitsubishi in the 2000s.

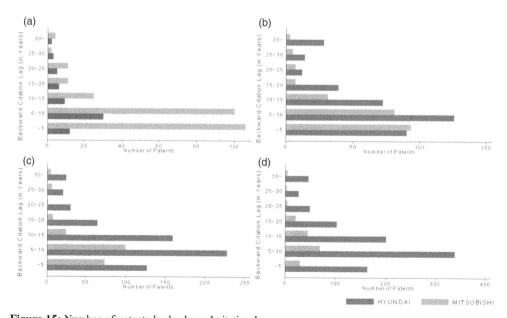

**Figure 15:** Number of patents by backward citation lag.

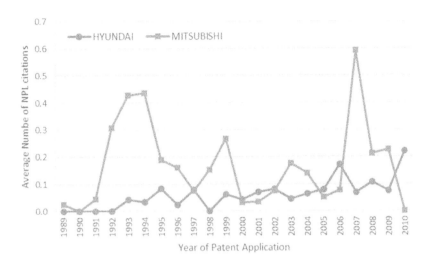

**Figure 16:** Average number of citations of NPL by Hyundai and Mitsubishi.

The results of the backward citation lag analysis shows that Hyundai has not shifted its overall research focus on new technologies; however, Hyundai has been more successful than Mitsubishi in exploring the opportunities created by cutting-edge technologies in the 2000s.

### 4.7. *Trend in the basicness*

The extent to which a firm draws ideas from basic research can be investigated by the number of citations of NPL, most of which are scientific articles in academic journals. This reflects the proximity to basic research – the more ideas are taken from basic research, the more NPL it cites (Trajtenberg et al. 1997).

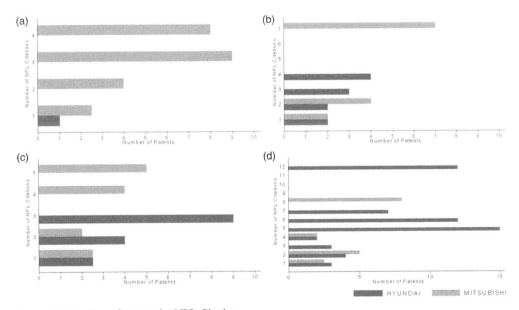

**Figure 17:** Number of patents by NPL Citations.

Figure 16 shows the average number of NPL citations. Hyundai's average NPL citations show an overall increasing trend, implying that Hyundai has shifted its innovation to more basic areas. Mitsubishi's average NPL citations show an overall decreasing trend to the mid-2000s, but have recently rebounded,[12] suggesting that Mitsubishi had reduced its focus on basic technologies until the mid-2000s.

Figure 17, which provides the number of patents by NPL citations, shows that Hyundai came to have more patents with more NPL citations. Compared with Mitsubishi, Hyundai had more patents with NPL citations from the early 2000s, and patents with increasing NPL citations in the late 2000s. The results show that Hyundai was more successful than Mitsubishi in generating basic technologies in the late 2000s.

## 5. Summary and Concluding remarks

This study investigated the technological capabilities of Hyundai and Mitsubishi by analysing various patent-based indexes, and found that Hyundai has successfully accumulated technological capability based on patents quantity, quantity, breadth, and mutual citations. The results provide evidence that Hyundai not only narrowed the technological capability gap with Mitsubishi, but also recently came out ahead. In addition, the patent citation lag and NPL citation results suggest that Hyundai also overtook Mitsubishi in new technologies and adopting ideas from basic research.

From the results of backward/forward self-citation ratios, citation lag, and NPL citations, it is possible to identify the innovation strategy that enabled Hyundai to successfully and rapidly build technological capability. In the 1990s, Hyundai focused on reaping the full benefits of its early innovations by strongly protecting and continuously drawing innovation from its past innovation. In the 2000s, Hyundai adopted an open innovation strategy to combine its accumulated technological capabilities with external technological capabilities. Simultaneously, Hyundai intensified its innovation in newly emergent technologies and basic research areas.

The results suggest that the accumulation of technological capabilities could be a source of competitive advantage for catching up and ultimately succeeding in the automobile industry when the competitive advantage from other sources, such as low labour costs, productivity, marketing, or globalisation are all temporary.

## Funding

The second author acknowledges financial support received from Chonnam National University, 2011–0683 and 2012–1575.

## Notes

1. Korean Automobile Manufacturers Association (www.kama.or.kr). The figure only includes passenger cars.
2. U.S. Department of Transportation (2014), National Transportation Statistics 2014.
3. Hyundai applied for its first US patent in 1989.
4. It is highly challenging to correctly identify a firm's patent because a firm may use company names different from its legal name when they apply for patents. To overcome this difficulty, this study used the 'representative firm name' from the WINTELIPS system (www.wintelips.com), which is carefully constructed by patent information experts to mitigate the problem.
5. Mitsubishi was motivated to make a favourable offer to Hyundai by its alliance with Chrysler to enable it to enter the US market. Mitsubishi granted Chrysler exclusive rights to sell Mitsubishi cars in the USA in 1971. Because of the agreement with Chrysler, Mitsubishi lost its chance to independently sell in North America, and sought opportunities in the Asian markets of Korea, Taiwan, China, and ASEAN countries.
6. A low IQS score means better quality because IQS scores count defects.
7. Because of the truncation problem, the time lag between patent applications and grants, the results after 2008 must be interpreted more carefully.

8.  An overall decreasing trend in average citations received shows that citation-based quality measures reflect not only the quality of the patents but also the opportunity for patent citations. Older patents have more such opportunities than newer patents. In addition, received citations data have a more severe truncation problem than patent counts because it takes more time for a patent to be cited than granted. The absolute number of received citations tends to decrease significantly for recent patents. In spite of this limitation, considering that both firms' patents had the same opportunities to be cited, the truncation problem can be partly mitigated by analysing the ratio (Joo and Lee 2009). Nevertheless, the results after 2005 must be interpreted more carefully.
9.  As with received citations, forward self-citation has a truncation problem. The increasing trend in recent years can be partly explained by the time lag in knowledge diffusion.
10. In contrast to the forward self-citation ratio, backward self-citation does not have a truncation problem.
11. Backward citation lags do not have a truncation problem.
12. Mitsubishi's average NPL citations index is more sensitive and less reliable than that of Hyundai, especially for recent years, considering Mitsubishi's small number of patents.
13. Annual revenue data were collected from each firm's financial statements. The original annual revenues in KRW (Hyundai) and JPY (Mitsubishi) were converted to USD using the exchange rate on the audit date of each firm. To control the revenues from subsidiaries of Hyundai and Mitsubishi, non-consolidated annual revenues were used. Consolidated annual revenue also showed a similar pattern.
14. The authors would like to express their deepest gratitude to Professor Moosup Jung for providing the total factor productivity data in Jung (2008).
15. The backward citation lags were measured by days and converted into years.

# References

Albert, M.B., Avery, D., Narin, F., and McAllister, P. (1991), 'Direct validation of citation counts as indicators of industrially important patents', *Research Policy*, 20, 251–259.

Breschi, S., Malerba, F., and Orsenigo, L. (2000), 'Technological regimes and schumpeterian patterns of innovation', *Economic Journal*, 110(463), 388–410.

Chung, M. (2009), 'Hyundai: is it possible to realise the dream of becoming a top five global automaker by 2010?', in *The Second Automobile Revolution. Trajectories of the World Carmakers in the 21$^{st}$ century*, eds. M. Freyssenet, Basingstoke, NY: Palgrave Macmillan, pp. 7–37.

Figueiredoa, P.N. (2007), 'What recent research does and doesn't tell us about rates of latecomer firms' capability accumulation', *Asian Journal of Technology Innovation*, 15(2), 161–195.

Freyssenet, M. (2009), 'Wrong forecasts and unexpected changes: the world that changed the machine', in *The Second Automobile Revolution. Trajectories of the World Carmakers in the 21$^{st}$ century*, eds. M. Freyssenet, Basingstoke, NY: Palgrave Macmillan, pp. 7–37.

Frobel, F., Heinrichs, J., and Kreye, O. (1980), The New International Division Of Labour: Structural Unemployment In Industrialised Countries and Industrialization in Developing Countries, Cambridge, MA: Cambridge University Press.

Fujimoto, T. (2013), 'The long tail of the auto industry life cycle', *Journal of Product Innovation Management*, 31(1), 8–16.

Gambardella, A., Harhoff, D., and Verspagen, B. (2008), 'The value of European patents', *European Management Review*, 5, 69–84.

Green, A.E. (1992), 'South Korea's automobile industry: development and prospects', *Asian Survey*, 32(5), 411–428.

Griliches, Z. (1990), 'Patent statistics as economic indicators: a survey', *Journal of Economic Literature*, 28(4), 1661–1707.

Hall, B.H., Jaffe, A., and Trajtenberg, M. (2005), 'Market value and patent citations', *Rand Journal of Economics*, 36(1), 16–38.

Hyun, Y. (1995), 'The Road to the Self-Reliance: New Product Development of Hyundai Motor Company', in *The IMVP Annual Sponsor Meeting*, June.

Hyun, Y. (2008), 'The quality triumph of Hyundai motor', *Journal of the Korean Production and Operations Management Society*, 19(1), 125–151. (in Korean)

Hyun, Y. (2014), *Hyundai Speed Management*, Daejun: Lean Enterprise Institute Korea. (in Korean)

Hyun, Y., and Lee, J. (2013), 'Dynamic innovation as a major source of competitive advantage of Hyundai motor company', *Journal of the Korean Production and Operations Management Society*, 24(1), 111–132. (in Korean)

Jaffe, A.B., and Trajtenberg, M. (2002), *Patents*, Citations, and Innovations: A Window on the Knowledge Economy, Cambridge, MA: MIT Press.

Jo, H. (1993), 'Strategic options for the Korean auto industry in response to the emerging new production system, 1980–1992', *Korea Journal of Population and Development*, 22(1), 43–67.

Joo, S.H., and Lee, K. (2010), 'Samsung's catch-up with Sony: an analysis using US patent data', *Journal of the Asia Pacific Economy*, 15(3), 271–287.

Jung, M. (2008), 'Productivity(TFP) and Catching up of Korean Firms with the Japanese Firms', unpublished Ph.D. dissertation, Seoul National University.

Kim, G. (1994), 'Growth structure of Korean automobile industry from the perspective of technological capability building – focusing on Hyundai motor case', *Review of Political Economy*, 7, 316–350. (in Korean)

Kim, L. (1997), *Imitation to Innovation: The Dynamics of Korea's Technological Learning*, Boston, MA: Harvard Business School Press.

Kim, L. (1998), 'Crisis construction and organizational learning: capability building in catching-up at Hyundai Motor', *Organization Science*, 9(4), 506–521.

Kojima, K. (2000), 'The "flying geese" model of Asian economic development: origin, theoretical extensions, and regional policy implications', *Journal of Asian Economics*, 11, 375–401.

KPMG (2014), KPMG's Global Automotive Executive Survey 2014.

Lall, S. (1980), 'The international automotive industry and the developing world', *World Development*, 8, 789–812.

Lanjouw, J., and Schankerman, M. (2001), 'Characteristics of patent litigation: a window on competition', *RAND Journal of Economics*, 32, 129–151.

Lee, K. (2005), 'Making a technological catch-up: barriers and opportunities', *Asian Journal of Technology Innovation*, 13(2), 97–131.

Lee, K. (2013), Schumpeterian analysis of economic catch-up: knowledge, path-creation, and the middle-income trap, Cambridge: Cambridge University Press.

Lee, K., and Lim, C. (2001), 'Technological regimes, catching-up and leapfrogging: findings from the Korean industries', *Research Policy*, 30(3), 459–483.

Malerba, F. (2002), 'Sectoral systems of innovation and production', *Research Policy*, 31(2), 247–264.

Malerba, F. (2004), Sectoral Systems of Innovation: Concepts, Issues and Analyses of Six Major Sectors in Europe, New York, NY: Cambridge University Press.

Narin, F. (1994), 'Patent bibliometrics', *Scientometrics*, 30(1), 147–155.

Narin, F., Noma, E., and Perry, R. (1987), 'Patents as indicators of corporate technological strength', *Research Policy*, 16(2–4), 143–155.

Nelson, R., and Winter, S. (1982), *An Evolutionary Theory of Economic Change*, Cambridge, MA: Harvard University Press, Belknap Press.

Park, J.C. (2001), 'A company growth by the dynamic development process of technology – a case study on Hyundai motor company', *Journal of Korea Technology Innovation Society*, 4(1), 32–48. (in Korean)

Patel, P., and Pavitt, K. (1997), 'The technological competencies of the world's largest firms: complex and path-dependent, but not much variety', *Research Policy*, 26(2), 141–156.

Perez, C., and Soete, L. (1988), 'Catching-up in technology: entry barriers and windows of opportunity', in *Technical Change and Economic Theory*, eds. G. Dosi, C. Freeman, R. Nelson, G. Silverberg and L. Soete, London: Pinter Publishers, pp. 458–479.

Posner, M.V. (1961), 'International trade and technical change', *Oxford Economic Papers*, 13(3), 323–341.

Talay, M.B., Calantone, R.J., and Voorhees, C.M. (2014), 'Coevolutionary dynamics of automotive competition: product innovation, change, and market place survival', *Journal of Product Innovation Management*, 31(1), 61–78.

Thomson Reuters. (2014), *2014 State of Innovation*, Thomson Reuters, http://ip.thomsonreuters.com/sites/default/files/2014stateofinnovation.pdf.

Townsend, J.D., and Calantone, R.J. (2014), 'Evolution and transformation of innovation in the global automotive industry', *Journal of Product Innovation Management*, 31(1), 4–7.

Trajtenberg, M., Jaffe, A.B., and Henderson, R. (1997), 'University versus Corporate Patents: a window on the basicness of invention', *Economics of Innovation & New Technology*, 5(1), 19–50.

U.S. Department of Transportation (2014), *National Transportation Statistics 2014*, U.S. Department of Transportation, http://www.rita.dot.gov/bts/sites/rita.dot.gov.bts/files/NTS_Entire_14Q4.pdf.

Vernon, R. (1966), 'International investment and international trade in the product cycle', *The Quarterly Journal of Economics*, 80, 180–207.

# Do latecomer firms rely on 'recent' and 'scientific' knowledge more than incumbent firms do? Convergence or divergence in knowledge sourcing

Jinhyuck Park and Keun Lee

*Department of Economics, Seoul National University, Seoul, Republic of Korea*

This study deals with the convergence and divergence issue in terms of the possible difference in the knowledge-sourcing behaviour of latecomer and incumbent firms. Consequently, empirical analysis using the patent citation data shows that no significant difference exists in the knowledge-sourcing behaviour of the incumbents and latecomers in long-cycle time-based sectors, particularly in terms of whether each type of firm relies more or less on 'recent' and 'scientific' knowledge. By contrast, a significant difference is observed in the short-cycle technology-based sectors, such that the latecomer firms tend to rely more on 'recent' and 'scientific' knowledge than the incumbents. Thus, the findings suggest that the answer to the question of whether convergence or divergence exists in knowledge sourcing is that it depends on the knowledge regime of the sectors, specifically on the cycle time of the technologies of sectors. This finding is consistent with the reasoning that the latecomer firms can afford to rely only on recent technologies in short-cycle sectors in which technologies tend to change quickly or become obsolete; latecomer firms are also keen on their knowledge sourcing to broadly search not only into technological knowledge (patents) but also into scientific knowledge (articles) in short-cycle sectors with rapid change of technologies.

## 1. Introduction

The cycle time of technologies has been an important concept since earlier studies, including those conducted by Narin (1994) and Jaffe and Trajtenberg (2002). Such a cycle refers to the speed of knowledge obsolescence associated with technologies and can be measured with the mean backward citation lags in patent data. This concept has gained significant implications for catch-up strategies and patterns of latecomer firms and countries since the investigation by Park and Lee (2006) and the follow-up study by Lee (2013). These studies reported that successful latecomer countries tend to specialise in sectors featured by short cycle time of technologies or sectors with lower dependence on the existing or old knowledge owned by the incumbents. In other words, in such sectors, the latecomers are more likely to achieve a certain degree of technological catch-up without significantly mastering the existing technologies. This observation is also consistent with the idea of leapfrogging introduced by Perez and Soete (1988) and Freeman and Soete (1997); shift in paradigms or generations of technologies may serve as a 'window of opportunity' for leapfrogging by the latecomer countries or firms. This argument is also verified in case studies by Lee and Lim (2001) and Lee, Lim, and Song (2005) on CDMA wireless technology and digital TV cases in Korea.

A new angle of looking at these studies is from the point of view of convergence or divergence in knowledge-sourcing behaviour of the incumbents versus the latecomers. In particular, a possible issue is whether the technologies adopted and developed by the latecomers would eventually become similar to or different from those of the incumbents. Fagerberg and Godinho (2005, p. 514) defined convergence as a trend towards a reduction in differences in productivity and income in the world as a whole, and catch-up as a narrowing of a country's productivity and income gap vis-à-vis a leading country. The current study considers this usage of the term 'convergence' in the knowledge-sourcing behaviour of firms, and aims to explore whether the two types of firms (incumbents and latecomers) become similar or remain different.

The sector-level studies by Park and Lee (2006) and Chapter 4 by Lee (2013) revealed that more successful latecomer firms and countries tend to specialise in sectors with shorter cycle time of technologies, whereas the less successful latecomers, such as Latin American firms, tend not to realise the same pattern, but to have more patents in long-cycle sectors, somewhat similar to those of the advanced countries. In the meantime, the comparison between the Korean and American firms in Chapter 5 by Lee (2013) specified that the catching-up Korean firms have more patents in short-cycle sectors, contradicting the case of the American firms, which tend to show their patent portfolio with a significantly longer cycle than that of average Korean firms. Joo and Lee (2010) also discovered that the patent portfolio of Samsung featured shorter cycle time on average than that of Sony.

In this case, a question that is yet to be answered is to what extent such findings are generalisable. In particular, does it make sense for the latecomer firms to rely always on short-cycle technologies? The answer hypothesised in this study is that the latecomer firms might depend on the knowledge regime of sectors, or more particularly that such a strategy may make sense only in short-cycle sectors, but not necessarily in other or long-cycle sectors. In long-cycle sectors, the old knowledge still matters. Even the latecomers cannot afford to ignore this considerable knowledge and have to rely on it.

One may think that the incumbents also try to apply new technologies, particularly in short-cycle technology-based sectors, given the importance of new or recent technologies in such sectors. This case must be true and applicable, but even in that context, the incumbent has a reason to minimise its reliance on recent technologies or to maximise the utilisation of existing technologies in which the firm has accumulated dominance. In other words, the incumbent has invested more in the existing technologies and therefore has a reason to try to fully recover its investment before switching to recent or emerging technologies. This situation is a kind of dilemma encountered by the incumbents, that is, the balance between the need to adopt new technologies and the need to utilise old technologies. Such a dilemma is more acute in the case of short-cycle technology sectors than in long-cycle technology sectors. In the latter sectors, the old or existing technologies tend to matter for a longer period of time so that the incumbents and latecomers have more reason to respect the existing technologies.

Accordingly, by conducting an empirical analysis with the patent citation data, this study demonstrates that no significant difference exists in the knowledge-sourcing behaviour of the incumbents and latecomers in long-cycle time-based sectors, particularly in terms of whether either of them relies more or less on 'recent' knowledge. By contrast, we will show a significant difference in the short-cycle technology-based sectors, such that the latecomer firms tend to rely more on 'recent' knowledge than the incumbents.

Another aspect of convergence or divergence in knowledge sourcing is the relative reliance on scientific knowledge represented by academic articles. In general, scientific knowledge in the form of academic articles reflects more recent knowledge and is less constrained by intellectual property right (IPR) issues. Thus, the latecomer or catching-up firms may want to rely more on scientific knowledge than technological knowledge protected by IPRs. A similar question remains to be clarified, that is, to what extent can this reasoning be generalised across sectors? In other words, the question is whether such a pattern would be true in every sector or only in some sectors such as those with a short cycle. One proposition is that such an instance may be true only in short-cycle sectors in which firms should be more keen on their knowledge sourcing to search 'broadly' not only into technological knowledge (patents), but also into scientific knowledge (articles), given that knowledge rapidly changes over time or becomes obsolete in such sectors.

In sum, this study aims to verify the convergence or divergence in the knowledge-sourcing behaviour of the latecomer and incumbent firms, with a focus on their reliance on 'recent versus old' knowledge and on 'scientific versus technological' knowledge. The aforementioned hypotheses are tested by using the US patent data compiled by the National Bureau of Economic Research (NBER) group and PATSTAT provided by European Patent Office (EPO) to conduct econometric analysis at both patent and firm levels. To this end, the latecomer firms are defined as those which 'entered late in technology race' or competition in terms of the time of their 'first registering' of US patents, compared with the average entry time of all existing inventor firms in each sector.

The rest of the paper is organised into five sections. Section 2 explains the research methods and describes data and key variables. Section 3 discusses the regression models and results, highlighting the hypothesis on whether the latecomers rely more on recent patents. Section 4 also presents the validity of the proposition, focusing on the hypothesis on whether the latecomers rely more on scientific knowledge than the incumbents. Finally, Section 5 concludes the paper.

## 2. Research methods

### 2.1. *Concept of cycle time of technologies*

The key variable of this study is the cycle time of technologies. This variable can be measured with patent citation data. In this study, the cycle time of technologies is calculated as the mean backward citation lag (Narin 1994; Jaffe and Trajtenberg 2002).

$$\text{Cycle time of technology of patent } i = \frac{\sum_{j=1}^{\text{NCITING}_i} \text{LAG}_i}{\text{NCITING}_i}, \tag{1}$$

where $\text{LAG}_j$ is the difference between the applied year of citing patent $i$ and the applied year of cited patent $j$ (this is called backward citation lag) and $\text{NCITING}_i$ is the total citations made by patent $i$.

That is, such a variable is the average of backward citation lags. The year of registration (granted year) could have been used, but the applied year is generally utilised more often, so it is used herein as well.

This concept is highly useful for explaining the technological features of patents and industries. If the cycle time of a patent is shorter than those of other patents, then this patent can be interpreted as being based on more recent technologies. Meanwhile, the industry or sector cycle times of technologies can be defined as the average of the cycle times of all the patents in the sector during a certain period. In this case, sectoral cycle times are considered as the speed of obsolescence of knowledge in a sector. This definition implies that in sectors with a shorter cycle time of technologies (so-called short-cycle sectors), older patents are not much utilised to invent new patents. By contrast, in sectors with a longer cycle time of technologies (so-called long-cycle sectors), older patents are useful in a longer period.

## 2.2. Data: US patent data

Technologically advanced states or enterprises could produce a larger number of higher quality patents; thus, patent data can serve as an appropriate proxy of technological innovation (Griliches 1998; Igami and Subrahmanyam 2013). Moreover, these data are easily quantifiable and are therefore considered appropriate for quantitative analysis.

The present study uses patent data registered with the United States Patents and Trademark Office (USPTO). Meanwhile, the data set employed for this study is provided by the NBER, with Pat76_06 and Cite76_06 being referred to the most. The two files contain detailed information on the citation of all patents registered from 1976 to 2006 in the USA.[1] The data have also been used in many other studies and are deemed appropriate for the current study because of the high reliability and the tendency of major global enterprises to apply for patents in the USA (see Hall, Jaffe, and Trajtenberg 2001 for more information on NBER patent data). The information on whether the patent cites scientific literature, which is not presented in the recent NBER data, is extracted from PATSTAT (EPO Worldwide Patent Statistical Database) and merged with the NBER data.

For this study, 1,217,178 sets of patents are collected from the data in all industries of six countries, including the USA, Japan (JP), Germany (DE), Korea (KR), Taiwan (TW), and China (CN), registered with USPTO from 1997 to 2006. The number of patents accounts for approximately 76.2% of the US-granted patents from 1997 to 2006. The five countries excluding China are top five on the list of US patent issuance and are included in the study for their large number of patents. For China, although its number of patents in the corresponding years are not significantly large, it is included for its recent emergence in the economic scene so that we can examine its technological trend. Table 1 shows the number of patents per year according to the countries sampled in this study.

Among the 959,517 sets of patents (78.8% of the entire sampled patents) with identifiable assignees, 8864 are non-enterprise patents (individual or government patents) that account for approximately 0.7% of the entire sample. Considering that the figure is small and its inclusion does not cause any significant gap in the analytical results explained later, we have included it in the analysis.

## 2.3. Sector specification: short-, middle-, and long-cycle sectors

Industrial classification is conducted according to patent class division. In other words, a single-patent class division is viewed as a single industrial sector. USPTO divides patents into 444

**Table 1:** Number of US patents registered by country.

|  | China | Germany | Japan | Korea | Taiwan | USA | Total |
|---|---|---|---|---|---|---|---|
| 1997 | 39 | 6158 | 24,230 | 1866 | 946 | 51,878 | 85,117 |
| 1998 | 50 | 8069 | 32,045 | 3213 | 1506 | 67,777 | 112,660 |
| 1999 | 64 | 8189 | 32,666 | 3534 | 2080 | 71,045 | 117,578 |
| 2000 | 78 | 9183 | 32,800 | 3243 | 3124 | 72,623 | 121,051 |
| 2001 | 74 | 10,249 | 34,881 | 3399 | 3666 | 76,220 | 128,489 |
| 2002 | 145 | 10,250 | 36,776 | 3623 | 3647 | 76,014 | 130,455 |
| 2003 | 179 | 10,528 | 37,637 | 3742 | 3666 | 77,313 | 133,065 |
| 2004 | 215 | 10,074 | 37,514 | 4324 | 4421 | 74,926 | 131,474 |
| 2005 | 249 | 8488 | 32,244 | 4234 | 3917 | 66,970 | 116,102 |
| 2006 | 381 | 9321 | 39,414 | 5787 | 5244 | 81,040 | 141,187 |
| Total | 1474 | 90,509 | 340,207 | 36,965 | 32,217 | 715,806 | 1,217,178 |

classes. All patents used in this study belong to 421 classes. We define the top 140 classes in terms of the length of cycle times as 'long-cycle sectors' and the lower 140 classes with shorter cycle times as 'short-cycle sectors'. The rest of the classes are included in middle-cycle sectors.[2] Thus, we divide all patents into three categories, namely, short-, middle-, and long-cycle sectors. NBER also provides a higher level patent classification to further categorise the USPTO classification into six large categories along with 37 subsectors, and we use these classifications to control the subsectors.

## 2.4. *Defining the latecomers: entry-year approach*

In this investigation, the latecomer firms should be identified and defined in the first place. The NBER patent data do not provide any separate enterprise information; they offer only patent-related information. Additional data (e.g. enterprise sales or market performance) should be secured from other sources and must be linked to the patent information. If separate sets of enterprise information data are used to identify the latecomers, any patent with an unidentifiable owner is likely to be excluded from the data-matching process. Moreover, linking each of the 88,491 assignees in six different countries is not realistic. For these reasons, the years of initial patent registration have been taken in this study for each sector (3 or 421) with unique assignee IDs (*pdpass*) in the data to identify the latecomers simply with the NBER data. We use two concepts, namely, the 'entry year' and 'average entry year', to identify the latecomers easily.

*Entry year* of a firm in a sector refers to the year when the patents of a firm are granted for the first time in a certain sector.

*Average entry year* of a sector is the mean of entry years of all firms in a sector weighted by the number of patents of each firm.

In this case, latecomers are defined in each sector as firms with a later *entry year* than *average entry year* as specified in the following.

If a certain firm $A$ in a specific sector $s$ meets the following conditions:

$$\text{Entry year of } A \geq \frac{\sum_{c=1}^{N} \sum_{t=1997}^{2006} P_{sct} E_{sc}}{\sum_{c=1}^{N} \sum_{t=1997}^{2006} P_{sct}} = \text{average entry year of } s \text{ sector} \qquad (2)$$

then, $A$ is a latecomer, where $P_{sct}$ is the number of total patents of company $c$ in the year $t$ in sector $s$, $E_{sc}$ is the company $c$'s entry year in sector $s$, and $N$ is the number of companies in sector $s$.

That is, the entry years of applicants in a certain sector are the weighted average with the numbers of patents of each applicant in the sector. In this event, latecomers are defined as firms with a later entry year than the average entry year. This case is consistent with the intrinsic manner of thinking (i.e. firms with earlier entry years are incumbents, whereas those with later years are latecomers). This method is also efficient for examination because it divides the data on the patents of firms into incumbent and latecomer categories at similar levels in all sectors. Long-established enterprises that register patents may probably be considered as latecomers. However, acquiring large gaps between business start and patent registration dates is relatively uncommon among enterprises. Moreover, recognising technological latecomers or incumbents mainly based on patent registration timing regardless of their business start date would not be far-fetched. Latecomers are identified according to each sector. Latecomers and incumbents are divided at both levels of the three sectors (short-, middle-, and long-cycle sectors) and 421 sub-sectors for this research analysis.

Table 2 demonstrates the descriptive statistics with a focus on the comparison between the latecomers and incumbents. In particular, the first row of the table shows the average cycle

**Table 2:** Descriptive statistics with comparison between latecomers and incumbents.

| | Latecomers' patents (a) | Incumbents' patents (b) | (a) to (b) (P-value) |
|---|---|---|---|
| Mean cycle time (standard deviation) | 7.56 (4.1) | 7.01 (4.03) | 0.55*** (.000) |
| Share of patents with citations to NPL (scientific articles) | 41% | 39% | 2%*** (.000) |
| Mean grant year (standard deviation) | 2002.11 (2.74) | 2001.45 (2.8) | 0.66*** (.000) |
| Mean impact factor (standard deviation) | 4.2 (9.7) | 4.4 (8.9) | −0.2*** (.000) |
| Share of patents without any citations | 2.7% | 3% | −0.3%*** (.000) |
| Mean of the number of patents held by an assignee (standard deviation) | 39.39 (86.34) | 315.95 (416.61) | −276.56*** (.000) |
| Mean of the impact factor of the patents held by an assignee (standard deviation) | 5.79 (6.3) | 6.55 (2.84) | −0.76*** (.000) |
| Total number of patents (share in total) | 573,589 (47%) | 643,589 (53%) | |

Notes: More detailed information on the variables in this table is provided in Table 3. The third column shows the results of statistical tests for difference in means of two groups, namely, the latecomers and incumbents.
***1% level of significance.

time of all patents. The patents of the latecomers are identified to have longer cycle times on average than those of the incumbents. This particular observation is relatively different from our expectations, but is subjected to a more rigorous econometric analysis in the next section. In the meantime, the share of non-patent literature (NPL) (scientific articles)-cited patents in the total patents of latecomers is higher than that in the total patents of incumbents. In the cases of 'impact factor' and 'impact factor of the patents held by an assignee' related to quality of patents (forward citations), the patents of incumbents exhibit higher means of these values than those of the latecomers. This condition signifies that incumbent firms generally produce patents with higher quality. In particular, in terms of the 'mean of the number of patents held by an assignee', the average number of patents granted to the incumbent firms is significantly larger than that of the latecomers.[3] The descriptive statistics in terms of sector specification (i.e. short-, middle-, and long-cycle sector) are presented in the appendix.

## 3. Convergence or divergence in terms of 'recent or old' knowledge

We conduct regression analysis at both patent and firm levels to determine whether latecomers use recent patents more than incumbents in short-cycle sectors. The detailed information on the models and regression results are presented as follows.

### 3.1. *Patent-level regression*

The subject patents are first divided into three sectors driven by the USPTO patent classification to compare the patent cycle times of technologies of latecomers with those of incumbents. The pooled ordinary least square method is employed to simultaneously analyse the patents for a decade from 1997 to 2006 in a cross-sectional manner. The regression model of this patent-level analysis is indicated as follows (Table 3).

First, the dependent variable is the cycle time of technologies of individual patents defined in Equation 1. The explanatory variable, the latecomer dummy, is endeavoured to assign 1 to an individual patent owned by a latecomer. Latecomers are defined in Equation 2. The individual patent characteristics are then controlled. In particular, 'impact' refers to the number of total citations of

**Table 3:** Explanation for model.

| Variable type | Title | Contents | Detailed variable | Explanation |
|---|---|---|---|---|
| Dependent variable | Cycletime$_i$ | Cycle time of technologies | Mean backward citation | Cycle time of patent $i$ |
| Independent variable | Latecomer_D$_{sc}$ | Latecomer dummy variable | 1 or 0 | If $i$ is a patent by a latecomer, '1' is assigned; otherwise '0' |
| Control variables | Properties of Patent$_i$ | Properties of patents | Impact | Forward citations of $i$ (number of citations a patent $i$ receives) |
| | | | Nocitation | If $i$ is a nocitation patent (patent with no record of patent citation), '1' is assigned; otherwise '0' |
| | Capability of Assignee$_{sc}$ | Capability of assignees | Assignee_PN | Total number of patents of a company possessing $i$ in sector $s$ |
| | | | Assignee_PQ | Average of citation frequencies of the patents of a company possessing $i$ in sector $s$ |
| | Country_D$_c$ | Country dummy variable | DE, KR, TW, CN, JP | National dummies of five states based on US patents |
| | Subsector_D$_{si}$ | Subsector dummy variable | Sub1 to 68 | Subcategory of sector $s$, dummy variable assigning 1 to the subsector containing patent $i$ |
| | Year_D$_i$ | Year dummy variable | D_1998 to 2006 | '1' is assigned for patent $i$'s granted year |

individual patents that the latecomers received. The frequent citation by other patents demonstrates that the corresponding patent has high quality in general (see Trajtenberg 1990; Hall, Jaffe, and Trajtenberg 2005), implying that citation data (forward citation) can be an effective measurement of patent quality and innovation. This certain citation is used to control patent quality. 'Nocitation' is a dummy variable that represents patents established without any citation, with values set as 1 for such patents.[4] 'Asignee_PN' is the number of total patents owned by a certain patent-owning firm in the same corresponding sector. The number is normalised by dividing the sector average (the average number of patents owned by a company in the sector). 'Asignee_PQ' stands for the total frequency of citation of the patents of a firm in the corresponding patent sector divided by the intrasectoral total patent number of a firm (in other words, the total forward citation of a firm divided by the total number of patents of the firm). The two indices are employed to quantitatively and qualitatively control the level of technological capability of patent owners. The country dummy assigns 1 to the country of a patent-owning firm according to its nationality. A total of 36 dummies are named subsector dummy variables driven by the sectors based on the 37 classifications under NBER. Meanwhile, the dummy variable assigns 1 to the subsectors that contain a corresponding patent to control the characteristics of the subsectors to which the patent belongs. The year dummy variables represent the year of individual patent registration (granted year) ranging from 1997 to 2006. The baseline is 1997; thus, a total of nine dummy variables are generated.

**Table 4:** Reliance on recent technologies: results with the sectors divided into three groups.

| Variables | (Short-cycle sector) Cycle time | (Middle-cycle sector) Cycle time | (Long-cycle sector) Cycle time |
|---|---|---|---|
| Latecomer_D | −0.02* (0.01) | −0.05*** (0.02) | −0.04 (0.02) |
| Impact | −0.10*** (0.00) | −0.16*** (0.01) | −0.15*** (0.01) |
| Nocitation | −7.28*** (0.01) | −8.97*** (0.02) | −9.92*** (0.02) |
| Asignee_PN | −0.00*** (0.00) | −0.00*** (0.00) | −0.00*** (0.00) |
| Asignee_PQ | −0.02*** (0.00) | −0.07*** (0.00) | −0.05*** (0.01) |
| DE | 0.23*** (0.02) | −0.35*** (0.03) | −0.23*** (0.04) |
| KR | −0.98*** (0.02) | −1.10*** (0.06) | −1.26*** (0.12) |
| TW | −1.38*** (0.02) | −1.86*** (0.06) | −1.43*** (0.11) |
| JP | −0.43*** (0.01) | −1.26*** (0.02) | −0.98*** (0.03) |
| CN | −0.31** (0.13) | −0.06 (0.21) | 0.26 (0.30) |
| Constant | 8.89*** (0.03) | 9.27*** (0.04) | 9.91*** (0.06) |
| Year dummy | Yes | Yes | Yes |
| Subsector dummy | Yes | Yes | Yes |
| Observations | 824,023 | 271,933 | 121,222 |
| R-squared | 0.19 | 0.16 | 0.15 |

Notes: Robust standard errors are in parentheses. All coefficients are rounded off to the nearest thousandth.
*10% level of significance.
**5% level of significance.
***1% level of significance.

The results of the regression analysis following the given model are presented in Table 4. In particular, the results are divided into each of the three sectors. The variables of subsector and year dummy are used in the investigation but are not reported. The white heteroskedasticity-consistent standard error (the robust standard errors) is applied, and the multicollinearity problem is checked with the variance inflation factor and turns out to be not serious.[5]

Table 4 indicates that, in the results with the short- and middle-cycle sectors, the coefficients of the latecomer dummy (Latecomer_D) are negative and significant at the 10% and 1% levels, respectively. On the contrary, the other sector, which is the long-cycle sector, has a negative coefficient of the latecomer dummy, but is not significant. This condition implies that the latecomers in the two former sectors tend to use more recent patents than the incumbents. Meanwhile, in the long-cycle sector, no significant difference can be observed between the latecomers and incumbents. Such an observation suggests that the latecomers use recent technologies comparable to that incumbents use. This finding is consistent with the hypothesis that in short-cycle sectors, including the computers and communications and electrical and electronics sectors, the latecomers tend to use more recent technologies. However, in the long-cycle sectors (e.g. biomedical industry), this trend is not as strong as in the short-cycle sectors.

Reading the results with other variable, we notice that when the capabilities of a company represented by the number of registered patents (Assignee_PN, Assignee_PQ) are stronger, the cycle time of a patent in all sectors is shorter. Such a relation indicates that a firm with greater capability tends to be better at applying short-cycle patents. Moreover, when the patent quality is higher (Impact), the cycle times in all sectors are shorter. The 'Nocitation' coefficients are negative, which is a natural phenomenon.

Another means of testing the hypothesis and determining whether a significant difference exists in the estimated coefficient of the latecomer variables between the long- and short-cycle sectors is by employing a dummy for these sectors using all observations together and by adding an interaction term of a latecomer and cycle time dummies, respectively. To this end, the top 211 sectors with the longest cycle times among the 421 sectors[6] are classified into the long-cycle sector group. Moreover, the long-cycle dummy (Long-cycle_D) is added to assign 1 to the patents belonging to this group. An interaction variable (Interaction (1)&(2)), which is the product of the long-cycle and latecomer dummies, is employed. The basic regression model specification is identical to that presented in Table 4. Meanwhile, the variables of the capacity of firms are recalculated not based on the three large groupings (short, middle, and long) but on all the 421 sectors. In other words, the latecomer firms and the level of capabilities are identified according to each of the 421 sectors.

The results are presented in Table 5. The column 2 in Table 5 represents the results when the long-cycle sector dummy is added, whereas column 3 shows the results when the long-cycle sector dummy and interaction term are simultaneously added. In column 3 of the table, the latecomer dummy coefficient is −0.04, which signifies that the latecomers rely more on recent patents. The coefficient of the interaction terms is 0.22, and the sum of the coefficients of the interaction variable and latecomer dummy coefficients is a positive number or 0.18 (−0.04 + 0.22).

**Table 5:** Reliance on recent technologies: results with a dummy for long-cycle sectors.

| Variables | (1)<br>Cycle time | (2)<br>Cycle time | (3)<br>Cycle time |
|---|---|---|---|
| Latecomer_D (a) | −0.01 | 0.00 | −0.04*** |
| | (0.01) | (0.01) | (0.01) |
| Interaction (a) and (b) | | | 0.22*** |
| | | | (0.02) |
| Long-cycle_D (b) | | 1.51*** | 1.39*** |
| | | (0.01) | (0.02) |
| Impact | −0.08*** | −0.07*** | −0.07*** |
| | (0.00) | (0.00) | (0.00) |
| Nocitation | −7.84*** | −7.82*** | −7.82*** |
| | (0.01) | (0.01) | (0.01) |
| Asignee_PN | −0.01*** | −0.01*** | −0.01*** |
| | (0.00) | (0.00) | (0.00) |
| Asignee_PQ | −0.05*** | −0.04*** | −0.04*** |
| | (0.00) | (0.00) | (0.00) |
| DE | 0.07*** | 0.06*** | 0.06*** |
| | (0.01) | (0.01) | (0.01) |
| KR | −1.23*** | −1.14*** | −1.13*** |
| | (0.02) | (0.02) | (0.02) |
| TW | −1.50*** | −1.42*** | −1.41*** |
| | (0.02) | (0.02) | (0.02) |
| JP | −0.80*** | −0.71*** | −0.72*** |
| | (0.01) | (0.01) | (0.01) |
| CN | −0.03 | −0.03 | −0.03 |
| | (0.11) | (0.11) | (0.11) |
| Constant | 9.42*** | 8.85*** | 8.87*** |
| | (0.02) | (0.02) | (0.02) |
| Year dummy | Yes | Yes | Yes |
| Subsector dummy | Yes | Yes | Yes |
| Observations | 1,217,178 | 1,217,178 | 1,217,178 |
| R-squared | 0.25 | 0.26 | 0.26 |

Notes: Robust standard errors are in parentheses. All coefficients are rounded off to the nearest thousandth.
*10% level of significance.
**5% level of significance.
***1% level of significance.

This instance implies that the average cycle time of patents of the latecomers in long-cycle sectors tend to be longer by 0.18 years than that of the incumbents.[7] When the short-cycle dummy variable is added instead of the long-cycle sector dummy, the result is consistent with the findings presented. Consequently, in short-cycle sectors, the latecomers tend to use recent patents more than the incumbents. In long-cycle sectors, however, the latecomers no longer use more recent patents compared with the incumbents. These analytical results slightly differ from those in Table 4, but both are consistent with the interpretation that the propensity of a latecomer in using recent technology more is hardly observed in long-cycle sectors. This explanation does not contradict the research hypothesis.

### 3.2.   *Firm-level regression: panel data analysis and results*

The analysis in the preceding subsection is a patent-level cross-sectional analysis, with patents classified into those owned by the latecomer or incumbent firms. Now, to verify the robustness of the findings, we now conducted a firm-level panel analysis. For this, patent information in the NBER data is aggregated to the firm levels. The analysis period is limited to the same decade (i.e. 1997–2006) where the NBER data are available. Most firms in the sample do not file their patents every year, and those firms with high patent-filing frequencies may be interpreted as those with strong technological capability. We intend to examine all types of firms, including the less capable ones, to test our hypotheses. Thus, we construct an unbalanced panel of firms which have filed patents at least once. This analysis is also conducted under the three-sector classification, including the short-, middle-, and long-cycle sectors.

The dependent variable is the cycle time of technologies of enterprise $c$ in sector $s$ in year $t$ ($Cycletime_{sct}$). Moreover, this variable is the average of cycle times of enterprise $c$'s patents registered in year $t$ in sector $s$. The latecomer dummy ($Latecomer\_D_{sc}$) is the same variable used in Section 3.1 (Patent-level regression) and does not change with time. Firm-level capabilities are represented by the number of its patents ($CompanyPN_{sct}$) and their quality ($CompanyPQ_{sct}$). The former is the total number of patents of a firm $c$ in sector $s$ in year $t$. This variable is logarithmically transformed because it has the widest range among all variables. The latter is the average of the citation frequencies of firm $c$'s patents registered in sector $s$ in year $t$. The non-citation patents of the company ($CompanyNocite_{sct}$) are also controlled. These patents are the share of non-citation patents among firm $c$'s patents registered in year $t$ in sector $s$. Moreover, country is controlled by adding dummies and year dummy variables to control the years. 'Filing frequency' variable (Filing Frequency$_{sc}$) represents the number of years a firm filed patents within the 10-year sample period, and is also added to control the capability of a firm. Given that the key explanatory variable, the latecomer firm dummy, is time invariant, a random-effect model is employed for the analysis. The results of the analysis are as follows (Table 6).

The short- and middle-cycle sectors on the left column of the table indicate that latecomer dummies are negatively significant at the 1% level. In the long-cycle sector (e.g. biochemical and mechanical sectors), the latecomer dummy coefficient is negative and significant, but the absolute value of the coefficient is smaller than that in the short-cycle sector. These results imply that, in short-cycle sectors, latecomers tend to apply patents with a 0.88-year shorter cycle time than the incumbent firms. However, in long-cycle sectors, the latecomers tend to cite patents with a 0.25-year shorter cycle time. This finding is somewhat different from those at the patent level presented in the preceding subsection, but remains consistent with the idea that latecomers use more recent technology in the short-cycle sector than in the long-cycle one.

In sum, three different quantitative analyses are performed to verify the hypothesis, which states that latecomer firms tend to use recent technologies more than incumbents in short-cycle sectors, whereas no such tendency is observed in long-cycle sectors. In Tables 4–6, all

**Table 6:** Reliance on recent technologies: results of firm-level panel analysis.

| Variables | (Short-cycle sector) Cycle time | (Middle-cycle sector) Cycle time | (Long-cycle sector) Cycle time |
|---|---|---|---|
| Latecomer_D | −0.88*** (0.05) | −0.53*** (0.04) | −0.25*** (0.05) |
| CompanyPN | −0.23*** (0.02) | −0.13*** (0.02) | −0.07** (0.04) |
| CompanyPQ | −0.03*** (0.00) | −0.05*** (0.00) | −0.05*** (0.00) |
| Filing frequency | −0.02*** (0.01) | −0.07*** (0.01) | −0.06*** (0.01) |
| CompanyNocite | −7.65*** (0.04) | −9.47*** (0.06) | −10.19*** (0.06) |
| DE | 0.62*** (0.06) | −0.13** (0.05) | −0.07 (0.06) |
| KR | −0.94*** (0.10) | −0.99*** (0.14) | −1.15*** (0.19) |
| TW | −1.30*** (0.07) | −1.54*** (0.10) | −1.09*** (0.16) |
| JP | −0.39*** (0.05) | −0.81*** (0.05) | −0.60*** (0.06) |
| CN | −0.45** (0.19) | −0.34 (0.29) | −0.10 (0.37) |
| Constant | 8.98*** (0.06) | 10.03*** (0.06) | 10.28*** (0.07) |
| Year dummy | Yes | Yes | Yes |
| Subsector dummy | No | No | No |
| Observations | 107,723 | 76,596 | 52,065 |
| Number of firms | 49,164 | 37,227 | 26,805 |
| R-squared | 0.16 | 0.16 | 0.16 |

Notes: Robust standard errors are in parentheses. All coefficients are rounded off to the nearest thousandth.
*10% level of significance.
**5% level of significance.
***1% level of significance.

coefficients of latecomer dummies of the three models are no doubt negative and significant in short-cycle sectors, whereas the coefficients of the dummies are positively significant, insignificant, or larger in long-cycle sectors. These results support the main hypothesis.

## 4.   Convergence or divergence in the reliance on 'scientific' knowledge

In this section, the hypothesis that the latecomer firms generate new knowledge (patents) by relying more on scientific literature compared with the incumbents is verified. The patent citation information is extended by merging the information from PATSTAT provided by EPO with the NBER data, because the information on whether the patent cites scientific literature is not available in the more recent NBER data. Information on all the NPL or scientific articles cited by the patent is present in the PATSTAT data.

One issue is that the citations added by the patent examiner in the USPTO and those added by the assignee may imply varied connotations, although both are identifiable in the US patent data after 2001. The problem is that the citations added by the examiner, regardless of the intention of the latecomer firms, can form a bias in analysing the behaviour of latecomers because only the behaviour intended by the latecomer firms should be analysed. In fact, Jaffe, Trajtenberg, and Fogarty (2000) already observed that the examiners greatly influence the citations. Alcacer and Gittelman (2006) even clarified that the citations added by the examiners might produce a significant bias, thereby affecting the research findings in some cases. In this event, we construct an NPL dummy variable, in which 1 is assigned if the patent cites NPL at least once regardless of who (the examiner or the assignee) added the citation in patents registered in the USA within the 10-year period from 1997 to 2006. We further generate another variable of the NPL_APP dummy variable, in which 1 is assigned if at least one NPL is cited only by the assignee when the patents are registered in the USA for six years from 2001 to 2006. This particular undertaking is intended to examine if the citation information added by the examiner forms a bias in the behaviour analysis of the latecomer and to check the robustness of the verification of the research hypothesis.

The basic empirical strategy is to examine how different the coefficients of the latecomer dummy are across the short- or long-cycle sectors, with slightly different dependent variables of NPL and NPL_APP to check the robustness of the research hypotheses. If the patents of the latecomers tend to use more NPL, then the coefficient of the latecomer dummy should be estimated as a positive number. If the mentioned research hypothesis is valid (i.e. the latecomers tend to rely significantly more on NPL in the short-cycle sector, but such a tendency is less in the long-cycle sector), then the coefficient of the latecomer dummy may be estimated to be a positive number in the short-cycle sector, whereas it is not significant in the long-cycle sector or at least the size of the coefficient would become smaller.

## 4.1. *Patent-level regression*

First, similar to the preceding section, the patents are divided into three sectors (i.e. short-, middle-, and long-cycle sectors), and a pooled probit regression is conducted for patents in each sector because the dependent variable has binary values (i.e. 1 or 0). We used the same control variables as before, and used the NPL dummy as the dependent variable. The results of the regression analysis are presented in Tables 7 and 8.

In Table 7, columns 1 and 2 show the regression results in the short-cycle sector. On the one hand, columns (3) and (4) represent the results in the long-cycle sector. In the results in (1) and (3) with the NPL dummy as the dependent variables, we do not distinguish the citations by the examiners or by the assignees. On the other hand, in the results presented in (2) and (4) with the NPL_APP, we have removed the citation information added by the examiner. In either means, the coefficients of the latecomer dummy are positive and significant in the short-cycle sector. In the long-cycle sector, contrarily, the case of NPL as the dependent variable (i.e. (3)) induces

**Table 7:** Reliance on NPL (scientific articles): results by long- or short-cycle sectors.

| Variables | (1)<br>(Short-cycle sector)<br>NPL | (2)<br>(Short-cycle sector)<br>NPL_APP | (3)<br>(Long-cycle sector)<br>NPL | (4)<br>(Long-cycle sector)<br>NPL_APP |
|---|---|---|---|---|
| Latecomer_D | 0.03*** (0.00) | 0.03*** (0.00) | −0.04*** (0.01) | −0.00 (0.01) |
| Impact | 0.04*** (0.00) | 0.07*** (0.00) | 0.03*** (0.00) | 0.07*** (0.01) |
| Nocitation | 0.14*** (0.01) | −0.10*** (0.01) | −0.03 (0.03) | −0.00 (0.05) |
| Asignee_PN | 0.00*** (0.00) | −0.00*** (0.00) | −0.00*** (0.00) | −0.00*** (0.00) |
| Asignee_PQ | 0.01*** (0.00) | 0.03*** (0.00) | 0.03*** (0.00) | 0.04*** (0.00) |
| DE | −0.12*** (0.01) | −0.09*** (0.01) | −0.24*** (0.01) | −0.25*** (0.02) |
| KR | −0.62*** (0.01) | −0.58*** (0.01) | −0.50*** (0.04) | −0.45*** (0.05) |
| TW | −1.02*** (0.01) | −1.22*** (0.01) | −1.23*** (0.06) | −1.50*** (0.09) |
| JP | −0.34*** (0.00) | −0.30*** (0.00) | −0.32*** (0.01) | −0.37*** (0.02) |
| CN | −0.46*** (0.05) | −0.53*** (0.05) | −0.30*** (0.09) | −0.39*** (0.11) |
| Constant | −0.25*** (0.01) | −0.41*** (0.01) | −0.89*** (0.02) | −0.96*** (0.03) |
| Year dummy | Yes | Yes | Yes | Yes |
| Subsector dummy | Yes | Yes | Yes | Yes |
| Observations | 824,023 | 541,960 | 121,222 | 72,833 |

Notes: Robust standard errors are in parentheses. All coefficients are rounded off to the nearest thousandth. The results are obtained from the probit models. The robustness of the findings is verified by conducting logistic regressions. However, no significant difference is observed between the results of the probit and logit regression analysis.
* 10% level of significance.
** 5% level of significance.
*** 1% level of significance.

**Table 8:** Reliance on NPL (scientific articles): results with a dummy for long-cycle sectors.

| Variables | (1)<br>NPL | (2)<br>NPL_APP |
|---|---|---|
| Latecomer_D (a) | 0.03*** (0.00) | 0.06*** (0.00) |
| Interaction (a) and (b) | −0.02*** (0.01) | −0.03*** (0.01) |
| Long-cycle_D (b) | −0.12*** (0.01) | −0.08*** (0.01) |
| Impact | 0.03*** (0.00) | 0.07*** (0.00) |
| Nocitation | 0.15*** (0.01) | −0.04*** (0.01) |
| Asignee_PN | −0.00*** (0.00) | −0.00*** (0.00) |
| Asignee_PQ | 0.01*** (0.00) | 0.02*** (0.00) |
| DE | −0.18*** (0.00) | −0.17*** (0.01) |
| KR | −0.63*** (0.01) | −0.63*** (0.01) |
| TW | −1.05*** (0.01) | −1.26*** (0.01) |
| JP | −0.35*** (0.00) | −0.34*** (0.00) |
| CN | −0.45*** (0.04) | −0.53*** (0.04) |
| Constant | −0.54*** (0.01) | −0.67*** (0.01) |
| Year dummy | Yes | Yes |
| Subsector dummy | Yes | Yes |
| Observations | 1,217,178 | 780,772 |

Notes: Robust standard errors are in parentheses. All coefficients are rounded off to the nearest thousandth.
*10% level of significance.
**5% level of significance.
***1% level of significance.

significant and negative results. Nonetheless, the more rigorous case (4) of using only the citations by the assignees (NPL_APP) as the dependent variable exhibits the expected result; that is, the coefficient of the latecomer dummy is not significant. This observation implies that latecomers produce patents by using more NPL in the short-cycle sector, but use less or insignificantly less NPL in the long-cycle sector. Overall, such finding conforms to the conclusion that the latecomers tend to use more NPL in the short-cycle sector. However, this trend is not the case in the long-cycle sector.

As an additional test whose results are reported in Table 8, we now use the interaction terms as before with all the patents together. In this case, a dummy for the long-cycle sectors is once again developed and interacted with a latecomer dummy.

The results acquired from a pooled probit regression shown in Table 8 reveal that the coefficients of the latecomer dummies are all positive and significant in either using NPP or NPP_APP. This instance suggests that the latecomers use significantly more NPL than the incumbents in the short-cycle sector; the baseline is the short-cycle sector. Meanwhile, the interaction term of the latecomer and long-cycle sector dummies is negative and significant. In the case of (1), the size of the coefficient of the latecomer dummy is 0.03 and that of the coefficient of interaction term is −0.02. The sum of these two coefficients is close to zero. In the case of (2), that is, the case in which the citations added by the examiner have been removed, the former is 0.06, the latter is −0.03, and the sum of the two measures is smaller than the size of the original coefficient.

### 4.2. Firm-level regression: panel data analysis and result

Now, a 'firm-level NPL dummy variable' is generated to serve as the dependent variable to eventually conduct the firm-level panel analysis. This variable indicates whether a firm has a granted patent that cites at least one NPL in a given year. If a certain firm in a given year has at least one NPL-based patent, we assign the value of 1; otherwise, it is set as 0.

**Table 9.** Reliance on NPL (scientific articles): firm-level panel analysis.

| Variables | (Short-cycle sector) NPL_D | (Short-cycle sector) NPLapp_D | (Long-cycle sector) NPL_D | (Long-cycle sector) NPLapp_D |
|---|---|---|---|---|
| Latecomer_D | 0.14*** (0.03) | 0.17*** (0.04) | −0.03 (0.03) | −0.01 (0.04) |
| CompanyPN | 1.27*** (0.02) | 1.24*** (0.02) | 1.15*** (0.02) | 1.16*** (0.04) |
| CompanyPQ | 0.01*** (0.00) | 0.02*** (0.00) | 0.02*** (0.00) | 0.03*** (0.01) |
| Filing frequency | 0.06*** (0.00) | 0.07*** (0.00) | 0.04*** (0.01) | 0.04*** (0.01) |
| CompanyNocite | 0.87*** (0.04) | 0.59*** (0.05) | −0.01 (0.07) | 0.05 (0.11) |
| DE | −0.38*** (0.03) | −0.33*** (0.03) | −0.37*** (0.03) | −0.42*** (0.04) |
| KR | −0.83*** (0.05) | −0.97*** (0.06) | −0.74*** (0.11) | −0.79*** (0.12) |
| TW | −2.06*** (0.05) | −2.41*** (0.07) | −1.93*** (0.12) | −2.26*** (0.17) |
| JP | −0.70*** (0.02) | −0.77*** (0.03) | −0.57*** (0.03) | −0.61*** (0.04) |
| CN | −0.29*** (0.11) | −0.47*** (0.12) | −0.43*** (0.16) | −0.59*** (0.20) |
| Constant | −1.39*** (0.04) | −1.56*** (0.05) | −1.88*** (0.05) | −2.07*** (0.06) |
| Year dummy | Yes | Yes | Yes | Yes |
| Subsector dummy | No | No | No | No |
| Observations | 107,723 | 70,273 | 52,065 | 30,894 |
| Number of firms | 49,164 | 37,064 | 26,805 | 18,195 |

Notes: Robust standard errors are in parentheses. All coefficients are rounded off to the nearest thousandth.
*10% level of significance.
**5% level of significance.
***1% level of significance.

In this panel probit model, we implement the analyses for 10 years using all citation information (NPL_D), whereas we conduct the analysis for six years for the case in which the citation information by the examiner is removed or the variable of (NPLapp_D) is used.

Table 9 illustrates that, in the short-cycle sectors presented on the left two columns of the table, the latecomer dummies are all positive and significant at the 1% level in both kinds of dependent variables. This observation implies that latecomer companies rely more on NPL than incumbent firms in the short-cycle sector. Contrarily, in the long-cycle sectors, the latecomer dummy coefficients are not significant at all in both cases. Such a finding argues that firms in the long-cycle sector do not show any different tendencies in citing NPL.

In conclusion, the analysis in this section supports the hypothesis that latecomers use more NPL than the incumbents in the short-cycle sector. This case, however, does not apply in long-cycle sectors, although the results in such a sector are not that perfect. Moreover, this conclusion is safe from any possible bias whether the citations by the examiners are adopted or not.

## 5. Summary and concluding remarks

One of the motivating questions in this study is whether convergence or divergence exists in the knowledge-sourcing behaviour of latecomer and incumbent firms. This study realises that the answer depends on the knowledge regime of the sectors, particularly the cycle time of the technologies of sectors.

The results of the empirical analysis obtained with the patent citation data demonstrate that no significant or consistent difference exists in the knowledge-sourcing behaviour of the incumbents and latecomers in long-cycle time-based sectors, particularly in terms of whether either of them relies more or less on 'recent' and 'scientific' knowledge. By contrast, we detect a significant difference in the short-cycle technology-based sectors such that the latecomer firms tend to rely on 'recent' and 'scientific' knowledge more than the incumbents. This finding conforms to the hypothesised reasoning in the study that the latecomer firms can afford to rely only on recent technologies in short-cycle sectors in which technologies change or rapidly become obsolete, and that they are also keen on their knowledge sourcing to broadly search not only into technological knowledge (patents) but also into scientific knowledge (articles) in short-cycle sectors with rapid change of technologies.

In a sense, this study revisits the interesting relationship identified by Park and Lee (2006) and Lee (2013) between the cycle time of technologies and the advantages or disadvantages of the latecomer firms that try to catch up with the incumbents, but reveals new dimensions. In other words, although the earlier finding suggests that the latecomer firms may enjoy certain advantages in short-cycle sectors because of the quick depreciation of existing knowledge dominated by the incumbents, such studies have not actually confirmed whether this finding is true or not, that is, whether the latecomer firms cite only the recent technologies in short-cycle sectors. One contribution of the current study is providing an evidence for the observation by firm- and patent-level analyses. In particular, this study clarifies that such an indication is valid only in short-cycle sectors but not in long-cycle sectors.

## Acknowledgements

An earlier version of this paper was presented at the 2014 Asialics Conference held in Daegu, South Korea. The authors thank the referees for their comments and the editors for their contributions to the earlier manuscript.

## Funding

The corresponding author acknowledges the support provided by the Korean government through the National Research Foundation of Korea [NRF-2013S1A3A2053312].

## Notes

1. Pat76_06 and Cite76_06 are downloadable at https://sites.google.com/site/patentdataproject/Home/downloads.
2. The cycle time of a class is calculated with the average cycle times of all patents of all countries in a class for 10 years (1997–2006).
3. This implies that the top patent-producing firms, which file numerous patents every year, mostly belong to the group of incumbent firms in our sample (see the standard deviation of the incumbent's patent number, '416.61'; this large variation exemplifies the existence of outliers).
4. If no other patents are referred to, then the implication is that this patent is based on unprecedented knowledge. In other words, the patent is the newest technology by itself at that particular time. Thus, we assign zero values for the cycle times of these patents. Also, 'Nocitation patents' account for only 3% of all the sampled patents. We have tried the same regression excluding such patents to obtain the same results (the results are shown to the referee, and are available upon request).
5. If the numerical value produced by that option is less than 10, then the multicollinearity problem can be considered as not serious. In the results of this study, all values are less than 10.
6. The technological cycle times of 421 sectors are calculated with the sectoral averages of cycle times of worldwide patents registered in the USA between 1997 and 2006.
7. Its significance has been tested.

## References

Alcacer, J., and Gittelman, M. (2006), 'Patent citations as a measure of knowledge flows: the influence of examiner citations', *Review of Economics and Statistics*, 88(4), 774–779.
Fagerberg, J., and Godinho, M. (2005), 'Innovation and catching-up', in *The Oxford Handbook of Innovation*, eds. D.C. Mowery, J. Fagerberg, and R. Nelson, New York: Oxford University Press, pp. 514–543.

Freeman, C., and Soete, L. (1997), 'Development and the diffusion of technology', in *The Economics of Industrial Innovation*, eds. C. Freeman and L. Soete, London: Pinter Publishers, pp. 351–365.

Griliches, Z. (1998), 'Patent statistics as economic indicators: a survey', in *R&D and Productivity: The Econometric Evidence*, ed. Z. Griliches, Chicago: University of Chicago Press, pp. 287–343.

Hall, B.H., Jaffe, A.B., and Trajtenberg, M. (2001), 'The NBER Patent Citation Data File: Lessons, Insights and Methodological Tools', NBER Working Papers, National Bureau of Economic Research.

Hall, B.H., Jaffe, A.B., and Trajtenberg, M. (2005), 'Market value and patent citations', *RAND Journal of Economics*, 36(1), 16–38.

Igami, M., and Subrahmanyam, J. (2013), 'Patent Statistics as Innovation Indicators? Hard Evidence'. *http://ssrn.com/abstract=2263318* or *http://dx.doi.org/10.2139/ssrn.2263318*

Jaffe, A., and Trajtenberg, M. (2002), *Patents, Citations and Innovations: A Window on the Knowledge Economy*, Cambridge: MIT Press.

Jaffe, A., Trajtenberg, M., and Fogarty, M. (2000), 'Knowledge spillovers and patent citations: evidence from a survey of inventors', *American Economic Review*, 90(2), 215–218.

Joo, S.H., and Lee, K. (2010), 'Samsung's catch-up with Sony: analysis with patent data', *Journal of the Asia-Pacific Economy*, 15(3), 271–287.

Lee, K. (2013), *Schumpeterian Analysis of Economic Catch-Up: Knowledge, Path Creation, and the Middle-Income Trap*, Cambridge: Cambridge University Press.

Lee, K., and Lim, C. (2001), 'Technological regimes, catching-up and leapfrogging: findings from the Korean industries', *Research Policy*, 30(3), 459–483.

Lee, K., Lim, C., and Song, W. (2005), 'Emerging digital technology as a window of opportunity and technological leapfrogging: catch-up in digital TV by the Korean firms', *International Journal of Technology Management*, 29, 40–63.

Narin, F. (1994), 'Patent bibliometrics', *Scientometrics*, 30(1), 147–155.

Park, K., and Lee, K. (2006), 'Linking technological regimes and technological catch-up: analysis of Korea and Taiwan using the US patent data', *Industrial and Corporate Change*, 15(4), 715–753.

Perez, C., and Soete, L. (1988), 'Catching-up in technology: entry barriers and windows of opportunity', in *Technical Change and Economic Theory*, eds. G. Dosi, C. Freeman, R. Nelson, G. Silverberg, and L. Soete, London: Pinter Publishers, pp. 458–479.

Trajtenberg, M. (1990), 'A penny for your quotes: patent citations and the value of innovations', *RAND Journal of Economics*, 21(1), 172–187.

**Appendix. Descriptive statistics by the cycle times of the patents**

| | Patents of short-cycle sector | Patents of middle-cycle sector | Patents of long-cycle sector | Total patents |
|---|---|---|---|---|
| Mean cycle time (standard deviation) | 6.33 (3.67) | 8.88 (4.15) | 10.03 (4.11) | 7.27 (4.07) |
| Number of patents with citations to NPL (scientific articles) (share in total) | 368,824 (44.76%) | 84,835 (31.20%) | 32,578 (26.87%) | 486,237 (39.95%) |
| Mean grant year (standard deviation) | 2001.89 (2.8) | 2001.51 (2.76) | 2001.48 (2.78) | 200.176 (2.79) |
| Mean impact factor (standard deviation) | 4.83 (10.37) | 3.41 (6.83) | 2.90 (5.77) | 4.32 (9.33) |
| Share of patents without any citations | 3.4% | 2.5% | 1.7% | 3% |
| Mean of the number of patents held by an assignee (standard deviation) | 251.96 (389.47) | 55.53 (96.84) | 26.53 (52.97) | 185.62 (338.15) |
| Mean of the impact factor of the patents held by an assignee (standard deviation) | 16.76 (256.52) | 7.30 (53.94) | 4.52 (22.85) | 10.75 (178.13) |
| Number of US-held patents (share in total) | 476,022 (57.77%) | 157,922 (58.07%) | 81,862 (67.53%) | 715,806 (58.81%) |
| Number of Japan-held patents (share in total) | 248,134 (30.11%) | 71,218 (26.19%) | 20,855 (17.20%) | 340,207 (27.95%) |
| Number of patents by Germany (share in total) | 43,735 (5.31%) | 31,534 (11.60%) | 15,240 (12.57%) | 90,509 (7.44%) |
| Number of patents by Korea (share in total) | 29,781 (3.61%) | 5847 (2.15%) | 1337 (1.10%) | 36,965 (3.04%) |
| Number of patents by Taiwan (share in total) | 25,549 (3.10%) | 4972 (1.83%) | 1696 (1.40%) | 32,217 (2.65%) |
| Number of patents by China (share in total) | 802 (0.10%) | 440 (0.16%) | 23? (0.19%) | 1474 (0.12%) |
| Number of incumbent firms/number of latecomer firms | 3083/46,081 | 4413/32,814 | 4308/22,497 | 88,489 (no. of the total firms) |
| Average entry year (standard deviation) | 1985.9 (10.35) | 1987.65 (10.57) | 1989.25 (10.61) | 1986.62 (10.48) |
| Total number of patents | 824,023 | 271,933 | 121,222 | 1,217,178 |
| Example sectors | Computer hardware and software/ communications/ semiconductor | Resins/ chemistry/ light industry | Chemistry/ mechanical/ material handling | |

# Index